A PRIMER OF
Social Psychological Theories

A PRIMER OF
Social Psychological
Theories

Stephen G. West / Robert A. Wicklund

Florida State University / University of Texas at Austin

Brooks/Cole Publishing Company
Monterey, California

Consulting Editor: Lawrence S. Wrightsman

Brooks/Cole Publishing Company
A Division of Wadsworth, Inc.

Printed in the United States of America

10 9 8 7 6 5 4 3 2 1

Library of Congress Cataloging in Publication Data
West, Stephen G
    A primer of social psychological theories.
    Bibliography: p.
    Includes index.
    1. Social psychology. I. Wicklund, Robert A., joint author. II. Title.
HM251.W573   302   80-16292
ISBN 0-8185-0395-5

Acquisition Editor: *Claire Verduin*
Manuscript Editor: *Rephah Berg*
Production Editor: *Sally Schuman*
Interior Design: *Cynthia Bassett*
Cover Design: *Stan Rice*
Illustrations: *Lori Heckelman*
Typesetting: *Computer Typesetting Services, Inc., Glendale, Calif.*

PREFACE

SOCIAL psychology is in large part a theory-based enterprise. Much of our accumulated knowledge in social psychology, particularly the knowledge that receives the most attention, can be traced ultimately to a modest number of theories. In recognition of this fact, the present book introduces the reader to theories that have been at the center of research and discussion in social psychology. Rather than being confronted with an encyclopedia of nebulously related findings, readers are introduced to the theoretical frameworks that have been most useful to social psychologists in making sense of those observations. The focus of the book is on a simple explication of these theories; we do not attempt to offer a complete review of the voluminous research generated by the theories. Instead, research is cited only insofar as it helps illustrate an important aspect of the theoretical ideas. It is hoped that this book will result in the reader's gaining a perspective on the nature of theorizing in social psychology, and we would also like to think that the material here will be an incentive to analyze phenomena without the help of an accompanying survey of research observations.

This book differs in salient respects from previous books of theories on social psychology: (1) It uses an informal presentation with the goal of enabling readers to understand the reasoning of each theory and to be able to use the theory to make predictions themselves. (2) No attempt has been made to discuss every theory that has ever been proposed; only those concepts that have proved most useful to social psychologists in understanding "social psychological" phenomena are discussed. (3) We have not undertaken a historical perspective on the ideas. Numerous influential philosophers and psychologists who may be seen as the forefathers of modern-day theoreticians are, perhaps regrettably, not discussed. Rather, the attempt here is to focus intensely on the theoretical statements in their present and most usable form.

The Primer may, therefore, be seen as a definite alternative to traditional social psychology texts. The book is organized according to theoretical concepts, the phenomena taking a subordinate organizational role. This conceptual organization makes it possible to use anywhere between one and all of the chapters and to read them in different orders. The Primer will also be appropriate as an overview of social psychological theory for undergraduate and graduate courses, not just in psychology but also in allied fields that draw on these concepts.

We would like to dedicate the Primer to a number of highly responsive and critical persons whose interest in theory, and expertise in delicate
theoretical matters, greatly reduced our uncertainty about being so bold
as to try to fit seventeen theoretical ideas into so short a space. Among the
commentaries we received, some were from the theorists themselves, doc-
umenting the fact that social psychology is a young science. Chapters
were also read by direct descendants of the schools of thought they discuss, as well as by those whose research was chosen to illustrate the
different theoretical principles.

It is easy to misrepresent a theoretical development, especially because most of the concepts discussed here have evolved beyond their original published form. It is also easy to misrepresent the research, in the
sense of rendering research salient that does not represent the heart of
the theorizing. Although a Primer cannot deal with every significant component of a theory or with each new development, it is hoped that what is
presented here comes close to the intentions of those who have begun and
continued these persuasive theoretical ideas. If the chapters at all approach the proper balance and representativeness, much of this is owing
to the generosity of the following persons, each of whom read at least one
chapter: J. Stacy Adams, Richard L. Archer, John W. Atkinson, Albert
Bandura, Gordon Bear, Daryl J. Bem, Stephen Blumberg, Jack W. Brehm,
Donn Byrne, Joanne R. Cantor, Martin Chemers, Russell D. Clark III,
Gerald L. Clore, Fred E. Fiedler, Michael Flanagan, Dieter Frey, Irene
Hanson Frieze, Toni Giuliano, Robert Glueckauf, George R. Goethals, Peter
M. Gollwitzer, Jerald Greenberg, Charles L. Gruder, John H. Harvey,
Madeline E. Heilman, Jack E. Hokanson, Chester Insko, Edward E. Jones,
Harold H. Kelley, John Lamberth, Melvin J. Lerner, Gerald S. Leventhal,
Lawrence W. Littig, Judson Mills, Volker Möntmann, Richard E. Nisbett,
Michael S. Pallak, Robert Pasahow, Paul B. Paulus, Michael E. Rashotte,
Michael Ross, Susan Roth, Douglas B. Sawin, Lee B. Sechrest, Martin E. P.
Seligman, Phillip Shaver, Melvin L. Snyder, Walter G. Stephan, Jerry Suls,
William B. Swann, Daniel M. Wegner, Bernard Weiner, Midge Wilson,
Camille B. Wortman, and Robert B. Zajonc.

Russell Geen, Robert Kidd, and John Schopler read the entire manuscript and made a number of suggestions that improved the organization and the content. Larry Wrightsman, Brooks/Cole's consulting editor,
gave us the benefit of his many years of writing experience in guiding us
through a number of difficult sections.

The production and organization of this project owe a great deal to
the ingenuity of Bill Hicks and Claire Verduin, whose editorship is to be

commended. The manuscript was masterfully edited by Rephah Berg. And for the many hours of typing and occasional editing we are thankful for the assistance of Amby Peach and Trudy Vincent at Duke University, June Halligan and Claudia Johnson at Florida State University, Ann Gibson at the University of Texas, and especially Faye Gibson at the University of Texas.

Stephan G. West
Robert A. Wicklund

Contents

CHAPTER 1

INTRODUCTION

To ASK a question about human behavior is also to hope that a simple and factual answer exists. Encountering a psychological question or inventing a psychological research problem almost inevitably implies something called the "library search," whereby all books, journal articles, and unpublished papers that appear to relate to the question are tracked down in the hope that they will bear directly on the question. Sometimes the aspiring question asker will find research that answers the question directly. However, all too often students are frustrated in their endeavor to answer the question, since library hunts frequently have one of two consequences: The student encounters a mass of seemingly unrelated literature that cannot be organized in any simple way and hence leads to no satisfactory answer to the problem. Or the myriad of seemingly related literature encroaches on the person's original question, altering it to such a degree that it now becomes answerable because it is identical to a question that has already been researched—but the original question, with all its distinctive aspects, remains unresolved and is eventually forgotten.

We have predicated this book on two assumptions, the first of which may seem somewhat pessimistic: We doubt that psychology currently possesses an encyclopedia of direct answers to most of the questions raised by laypersons, students, and psychologists. Although careful scholarship is important in helping us locate valuable facts and ideas, each question has a number of unique facets that require us to think through the issues carefully in order to put these ideas together in the correct way. Our second—and optimistic—assumption is that such integration can be accomplished and that the original question can be answered by thinking carefully for oneself and by keeping attention focused directly on the original problem. Since few people like to pursue questions without a structure for thought, we have written about a number of theoretical ideas that have proved useful to psychologists in answering hundreds of questions about complex human behavior. We hope that these ideas will prove useful to the student by helping to integrate the literature of accomplished research in many areas, by providing an understanding of some of the basic processes that underlie human social behavior, and by suggesting new approaches to problems that may be verified by research. What we have written is not a book of facts or research findings, but a description of a set of theoretical tools by which one can learn to arrive at the answer sought, going at one's own pace and drawing on concepts as they become relevant.

Enough preamble. At this point the reader may want to take a look at the content chosen for this theories book. An overview of the content is given here in two ways. First we present some examples of general questions that people ask about human behavior, together with some of the theoretical concepts that might be applied to suggest answers. Then we examine some general areas of theorizing in social psychology.

GENERAL QUESTIONS ABOUT HUMAN BEHAVIOR

1. *Why do people compete?* This broad question can be pursued in more than one of the following chapters. For example, in Chapter 14 we discuss a theory about achievement motivation that categorizes people according to the strength of their need to achieve and according to a variable that has to do with fear of failing. The theory also discusses the types

of situations that are most likely to elicit competitive behavior. A related theory presented in Chapter 15 examines the causes that people with varying achievement needs perceive to be responsible for their successes and failures and how these perceived causes relate to future achievement behavior. Chapter 2, on the topic of social facilitation, is also relevant. It suggests that a person who is already highly competitive will become more so when in the presence of spectators, whereas someone who fears competition will become *less* competitive in the presence of an audience. Still another approach to competition can be taken by reading Chapter 11, on social comparison processes. That chapter sets forth the assumption that competition with similar others serves the function of self-evaluation and that we can arrive at a more exact conception of our abilities through competing with others. Many other notions in this book also have some bearing on the question "Why compete?"

2. *Does a crowd of people develop into a single-minded and vicious entity?* This idea was suggested by Le Bon (1896/1960), one of the first people to psychologize about the nature of groups. It is, of course, impossible to prove that a crowd becomes literally single-minded, but some of the chapters here do lend themselves directly to the questions of single-mindedness and viciousness. Certainly Chapter 13, on self-awareness, discusses the undesirable effects produced in crowds when the individual conscience is freed from its normal civilizing influence.

3. *Are people basically rational or irrational in evaluating their actions?* This question, like the preceding one, sounds as if it might be inspired out of philosophy, but there are some definite directions to be taken using two related concepts—to be found in Chapters 6 and 8. One of these chapters, on the topic of cognitive dissonance, proposes that people who have recently made a decision are irrational, self-justifying entities who reorder their cognitive world to appear consistent with their choices. The other approach, self-perception theory, views decision-making people as detached, objective, and analytical commentators on their own actions. Under which conditions each of these positions might be accurate is an interesting question.

4. *How does one arrive at self-knowledge?* This question can be dealt with from a variety of standpoints. One of these, attribution theory (Chapters 8, 9, and 10), proposes that we analyze attitudes, values, and abilities by looking at the conditions under which behaviors are performed. The general guiding principle is that unconstrained, seemingly free behavior provides us the most information about our inner functioning. A related viewpoint is taken in Chapter 12, but with a focus specifically on emo-

tional states. Here it is argued that we infer emotional states in ourselves when we are experiencing physiological excitement and when we are aware of some emotion-laden stimulus.

5. *What percentage of people in the United States are members of the middle class?* This is the type of question that cannot be answered here. A theoretical approach is not appropriate, for a question of pure fact cannot be settled by a self-generated analysis of the question. Better to define *middle class* operationally, in a commonly accepted way, and then consult an encyclopedia.

We should elaborate on question 5. It does not ask about a psychological process or about an explanation, but only for a factual description of some part of the world. The theories described here are highly useful in guiding a person toward an answer as long as the question has something to do with *process*, rather than mere fact. To be interested in process is to be concerned with psychological functioning and with explanation.

GENERAL AREAS OF THEORIZING IN SOCIAL PSYCHOLOGY

The theories in this book fall into six general areas.

1. *Derivations from learning theory.* There is no reason to claim that social psychology discovered the underlying principles used in its theorizing. One can find at least three significant social psychological contributions with roots in classical learning theory. One of these, social facilitation theory, is one of the simplest and most elegant statements about the social behavior of organisms. Reduced to its basics, the idea is that the presence of fellow humans will cause a person to act with greater intensity, especially when the act is simple and well rehearsed. A second model stemming directly out of the learning theory tradition is an explanation for interpersonal attraction, using principles of classical conditioning that one would encounter in experimental psychology. Finally comes a social learning theory that uses a liberalized set of learning principles and is applicable to virtually all forms of human behavior. The focus in this last scheme is on the importance of imitation in our initial learning of a wide variety of social behaviors.

2. *Cognitive consistency.* This section comprises three well-known principles of social psychology—called "cognitive balance," "cognitive

dissonance," and "equity." The idea central to the three approaches is that the human operates so as to create a proper fit among cognitions. It troubles us when our two closest friends dislike each other, and it is upsetting to have purchased a new full-size car only to have one's suspicions confirmed about forthcoming tripled gasoline prices. Finally, in a more interpersonal realm, cognitive turmoil is produced when people are inadequately compensated for their investments or when they are overcompensated. A similar principle runs through all three theoretical approaches: the human strives to bring about harmony among related cognitions.

3. *Attribution.* The three theories falling under this rubric offer a rational view of the human being. The main theme concerns the logical inferences that we make in perceiving people: how do we decide what kinds of traits or attitudes people have, on the basis of watching them behave in different contexts? The first point of view, self-perception theory, addresses the issue of perceiving oneself; it explains how people come to infer attitudes, motives, and traits of themselves. The second view, correspondent inference theory, provides a detailed examination of how one person—an "observer"—analyzes the apparent causes of a single behavior of a second person. Finally, Kelley's attribution theory provides a very general analysis of the inferences that people will make about a series of behaviors, whether performed by themselves or others.

4. *Self-evaluation and self-explanation.* The cornerstone of these three theories is the issue of the human as a self-evaluator and a self-analyzer. The earliest of these is social comparison theory, which began with the assumption that humans have a central need to evaluate their abilities and opinions. The theory then proceeds to show how conformity, as well as persuading others, stems from this evaluative need. The theory of emotion, originally developed out of social comparison theory, builds an entire conception of emotional states out of the assumption that humans try to evaluate, or label, their bodily arousal. Finally, the theory of self-awareness views the condition of evaluating oneself as aversive—and as something that also leads to moral or civilized behavior.

5. *Achievement and leadership.* The kinds of behaviors dealt with here are human strivings, often toward occupational or competitive goals, and always with the prospect of success or failure in view. The first theory, a classic statement on the workings of achievement motivation, addresses the issue of why some people take risks and accept challenges while others do not. The second approach, the attributional model of achievement behavior, focuses on finding specific reasons for achievement behavior. Is a given act of achievement perceived to be the result of

personal qualities, such as skill or hard work, or of external circumstances, such as the ease of the task or luck? Finally, the theory of leadership concerns itself with some of the factors involved in effective leadership, particularly the match between the personality of the leader and the nature of the leadership situation.

6. *Reactions to loss of control.* One of the major statements about human freedom in psychology is the theory of reactance. To be free—that is, to have control—is to expect a free choice among life-styles, automobiles, or any other commodity. Freedom also applies to attitudes and emotional states: freedom of attitude means that we feel that it is up to us which attitude to adopt or defend. When these kinds of freedoms are infringed on, reactance theory proposes, the person resists the infringement and attempts to regain the original free state. The second theory in this section is also about free behaviors and infringements on them, although the loss of control occurs in a very special sense. It is argued in learned-helplessness theory that sharp reductions in control will eventually lead to a condition of passivity called "learned helplessness." In research with animals helplessness takes the form of overt passivity—lying down or not trying to avert danger—and with humans the interesting effects have to do with reduction in cognitive performance.

SOME FINAL COMMENTS

For the reader who begins this book without any special questions in mind, it is our hope that these theoretical ideas will suggest a number of problems worth pursuing. We have intentionally avoided an overload of published research, to allow the reader to focus on the central ideas of the theories, providing room for imagination, argument, and critical thought. The most important contribution psychology can make is the development of guiding theoretical principles, and it is our belief that an uncluttered presentation of these ideas will go a long way toward facilitating an interesting analysis of psychological issues.

Because of our purposes in writing this book, we have given no special attention to the definition of a good theory or to the history of psychological theory. We hope that well before the end of the final chapter readers will begin to form a concept of the common characteristics of good theories; this concept will be far more useful than any formal definition of theory we could set forth. We will also examine a case history of a theory in development, in Chapter 18, to provide a view of the consequences of taking different theoretical approaches to the same phenomenon.

Are these *social* psychological theories? Perhaps yes, and maybe no. It would depend upon how we defined *social psychology*. Certainly not every theory we have included here makes specific reference to groups or to people interacting, and many of the notions discussed here originated in such pursuits as physiological psychology, learning theory, motivation, perception, individual differences, psychophysics, symbolic logic, and sociology. We have included the particular theories that are here for just one reason: Many psychologists, especially those who define themselves as social psychologists, have found these theories to be useful approaches to a number of problems. Each of these theories has a strong enough appeal that it has received considerable research attention, and some measure of favorable evidence, by numerous researchers. We hope that the reader, as well as these many researchers, will be stimulated by these theoretical concepts.

PART ONE

DERIVATIONS FROM LEARNING THEORY

If it can be argued that social psychology borrows its theorizing from the more established or traditional areas of psychology, that contention finds the best support in the case of the three theories of this section. The connection between these extensions of learning theory is the general notion that responses, particularly those important in the social context, can be described in the language of "habits," "drives," "reinforcements," and related learning theory concepts.

The first idea discussed — social facilitation theory (Chapter 2) — is a clever innovation on a traditional learning theory principle about the relation between habits and drives. A central ingredient in social facilitation theory is its assumption that the presence of other humans can increase drive level, with some intriguing implications that include the strengthening of responses that are already highly dominant in the person's behavioral repertoire.

The reinforcement-affect model of attraction (Chapter 3), also beginning with a traditional learning theory basis, discusses how humans become attractive to each other by virtue of being similar. Similarity, for a long time known to be an antecedent of attraction, is cast as a conditioned (learned) source of reinforcement and as a powerful mediator in bringing humans to like each other upon initial contact.

The social learning theory of Bandura (Chapter 4) rounds out this section, perhaps appropriately so, as it has the broadest overall applicability and makes more liberal use of learning principles than the other theoretical frameworks do. A central question for this theory is "How does a pattern of responses come to originate in a social context?" With the use of such concepts as "modeling," "vicarious reinforcement," "attention," and "mental rehearsal," the theory offers the reader a wealth of ideas for characterizing the growth of new, complex behaviors through the process of imitation.

CHAPTER 2

SOCIAL FACILITATION THEORY

HAVING been persuaded that cigarettes are a threat to his health, the former chain smoker can often be found in a state of conflict, torn between the familiar routine of cigarette smoking and the much safer alternative of smoking a pipe. We may imagine that he sits home alone, urging himself to forgo that satisfying first cigarette of the day, and after much deliberation manages to light up a pipe instead. This is the desired state of affairs. The pipe poses little threat of lung cancer and also meets with social approval. Unfortunately, even though there are incentives to quit cigarettes, such as health benefits and social approval, it is also true that people develop what are called habits, and it should not be surprising when the smoker's aspirations to switch away from cigarettes are not fulfilled.

In our hypothetical example we will make some assumptions. First, it is reasonable that the smoker needs to put something into his mouth at more or less regular intervals; the habit of putting something cylindrical in the mouth has probably been in force since early life. Second, the day might be divided up into "choice points." At each choice point, the smoker's behavior can go in either of two directions: cigarettes or pipes. Finally, we may assume that when the person is home alone, his success ratio is 40%. For every six cigarettes smoked, he lights up his pipe only four times.

Now our example will become social psychological, in the most literal sense. We are interested in the impact of a group on the individual's smoking cigarettes and pipes, and a common enough group is the contingent of cronies, over for an evening of poker, drinking, and raucous conversation. As we continue to chart the smoker's cigarette/pipe ratio during the course of the social evening, we find a curious but entirely predictable change—the pipe is laid aside, abandoned in favor of the long-tenured cigarette habit.

Is this simple conformity? If everyone in the group is a cigarette smoker, it could indeed be conformity, but the concepts set forth below imply that this reversion to cigarettes due to the presence of others depends on very little besides their mere presence. If the same man were a passive bystander, watching his nonsmoking children and associates play canasta, he should also increase his cigarette/pipe ratio beyond 60%. Is he embarrassed to bring out his pipe in public, thereby admitting to a weakness or indecisiveness in his personal behavior? Perhaps on some occasions, but even a group of small children, who understand nothing about the fine points of smoking, should cause this same regression to cigarette smoking.

THE THEORY

The principle involved in the example of the smoker is one of the simplest and most elegant notions existing in psychology. The idea is that individual behaviors of almost any sort will be energized if others are physically present but only if those behaviors are highly likely to begin with. Before the introduction of this principle by Zajonc (1965), there had been considerable confusion about the effect of an audience on performance. Sometimes an audience was observed to facilitate motor performance. For example, in an experiment by Meumann (1904) the simple response of pulling a weight tied to one's finger was strengthened by the presence of a spectator. On other occasions an audience had debilitating effects, as in a study by Pessin (1933), in which performance in learning nonsense syllables worsened with the presence of a spectator. As we will soon see, it is possible to explain divergent findings such as these by looking at the *most likely* response in a situation rather than the *correct* response.

Drive versus Direction

As a prelude to Zajonc's notion, it is helpful to draw a distinction between the direction of behavior and the energy level of behavior. To choose cigarettes over pipes is a question of direction, but once cigarettes are chosen, the question of "how intensely" or "how frequently" enters. Analogously, a person might choose to injure or defame an archenemy (direction); the energy component would determine whether the aggression took the form of a gentle tap or a total physical thrashing.

What determines this energy component? For one, deprivation of a particular kind of satisfaction typically produces more intense efforts to be satisfied. The organism that has been deprived of food, sex, or any other vital entity is said to be "motivated," or in a state of "drive." Another source of drive is any condition that should lead to a general state of excitement or increased arousal, such as electric shock or an erotic movie.

The important aspect of the concept of drive is that drive states appear to energize behavior whether or not the behavior has any impact on the conditions that led to drive in the first place. If an organism has learned to go through a sequence of responses to obtain food, it is obvious that food deprivation will heighten the strength of that sequence of responses. Not so obvious is that other sources of drive will have a similar impact on that behavior sequence. This has been shown by Miller (1948), who reported an experiment in which rats first learned to run a T maze (a simple T-shaped maze) for a reward of food. Then the animals were satiated on food but again placed in the maze to see how fast they would run to the original goal area. Some of the rats received a jolt of electricity at the start of each trial, which presumably would raise drive level. The shock increased speed of running the maze even though the drive had nothing to do with the original food-deprivation drive that was basic to running. This result implies that behavior can be strengthened, or energized, by any means available to induce drive, and it is this kind of research that justifies the concept of "general drive" that was set forth in the thinking of Hull (1943) and Spence (1956). Drive states are "general" in the sense that they have the capacity to energize a variety of behaviors, even when those behaviors do not reduce the specific drive state that energizes.

This last consideration allows Zajonc to make a central assumption about a general source of drive level: he proposes that the presence of other organisms, independent of the meaning of their presence to the individual, will increase drive level. Thus Miller (1948) might have done without shock as a stimulus to drive and substituted an audience of rats lined up along the T maze. In fact, this procedure has been followed almost exactly with cockroaches (Zajonc, Heingartner, & Herman, 1969). The individual roach subject, running through a glass tube toward a goal of relative darkness, is found to run faster when in the proximity of a grandstand full of cockroaches.

Dominant versus Subordinate Behaviors

What kinds of behaviors are energized in Zajonc's system? Virtually all behaviors. And on the phylogenetic scale, his ideas seem to apply equally well to humans and cockroaches, plus a number of species in between. But things are not as simple as isolating a behavior and energizing it—first we must know something about the probability that the behavior will be emitted. In any given situation it is possible to talk about a hierarchy of behaviors in that some are more likely to appear than others. At the dinner table eating is most likely to happen, then drinking; perhaps chewing gum is lowest in the hierarchy. The behavior in a hierarchy that is most likely to appear is called "dominant," and others are at various degrees of subordination. For our previously discussed smoker the hierarchy is a simple one: first comes cigarette smoking, then pipe smoking. Note that the hierarchies we discuss here consist of behaviors that are *mutually competitive*. A person does not eat, drink, and chew gum simultaneously, just as the smoker would normally not be found with both a cigarette and a pipe in his mouth.

Returning specifically to Zajonc's theory, exactly what is energized by the presence of other organisms? From the preceding paragraph we know that it is first necessary to isolate a dominant response from among a group of mutually competitive responses, and once this is done, the application of the theory is easy: All responses in the situation will be strengthened by the presence of other organisms, but the responses that are originally strongest (dominant) will be strengthened more. If the total number of responses that can be emitted in a situation is fixed, it then becomes evident that the dominant response is facilitated, while the remaining (subordinate) responses lose strength. If the possible responses in a situation are in competition (that is, only a limited number of them can be made), subordinate responses fall off in intensity because the dominant response crowds them out.

Thinking again about the state of confusion existing before Zajonc's entry, it is instructive to consider Meumann's weight-pulling experiment from the standpoint of what responses were probably dominant. The situation was so simple that we would be justified in saying that the correct response (pulling a weight tied to one's finger) was indeed dominant over competing responses, such as pushing or doing nothing. The presence of others should therefore have facilitated correct behavior. Just the contrary conditions held in Pessin's experiment, in which subjects were trying to learn a complex set of verbal materials. That is, the correct response was likely to be one of several subordinate responses in such a complex situation, which would mean that a spectator would strengthen incorrect responses.

It should now be apparent why we placed special constraints on our example of the cigarette smoker. We assume the necessity of smoking in addition to the incompatibility of the two possible smoking responses. It was also important to know the relative dominance of the incompatible responses when the smoker was not in the presence of others, and we assumed a base rate of 60% cigarettes, 40% pipe smoking. This is a sufficiently clear definition of dominance that there is no ambiguity about Zajonc's prediction when others are introduced: the card party, the presence of children, or any other social contact should increase general drive level, thereby strengthening the dominant response of cigarette smoking and necessarily weakening pipe smoking.

The example may be unnecessarily simple, for this theory is by no means limited to the case of *two* mutually exclusive behaviors. To apply social facilitation theory to the dinner table example, we need assume only that one of the responses, eating, is more likely to be emitted when the person eats alone than drinking or gum chewing. The theory does not say anything specific about which of the subordinate responses is subject to the greatest demise, but it is clear that eating should be strengthened when other people are present.

RESEARCH EXAMPLES

The research on social facilitation provides especially cogent illustrations of how to implement the theory. For the most part, the designs are simple, and probably the most difficult issue is the question of defining the dominant response. Because this can be a tricky issue, we will discuss three ways of defining dominance.

Dominance Defined by Individual Preferences

A simple color preference is a clear expression of a dominant response, since preferences for colors are necessarily mutually exclusive: to the extent that chartreuse is one's favorite color, that automatically prevents other colors from being the favorite. In an experiment by Goldman (1967) subjects were first given 30 color-preference trials, each time being asked to say which of five colors they preferred at the moment. Over the course of these 30 trials it was possible to observe a dominant preference for each subject. Then all subjects proceeded with 30 additional preference-naming trials, half of them in the presence of other subjects who were doing the same thing. Zajonc's theory was upheld, exactly as he would predict: subjects in the presence of others were increasingly likely to choose their originally most-preferred color. Conceptually this experiment is identical with our smoker example, in that dominance was defined in terms of an individual preference (the probability of choosing each possible behavior).

Dominance Defined by Population Norms

Although it is more accurate to know what is dominant for each individual being studied, a rough approximation to that ideal can be had by knowing what characterizes the whole population. For example, in a study by Matlin and Zajonc (1968) subjects were asked to free associate to a number of verbal stimuli. (In the procedure of free association, an experimenter calls out a word, and then the subject is supposed to reply with whatever word comes to mind. When people hear "salt," they are likely to free associate "pepper.") Given no constraints on what could be said, it is obvious that subjects would have generated an impressive variety of free-association responses. At the same time, by looking at the subject sample as a whole, one can isolate certain responses that were common, and it is fair to label these as dominant relative to others.

In the actual procedure half the subjects were alone while free associating, and the others were confronted by one passive observer. Consistent with social facilitation reasoning, subjects who had the small audience were more likely to emit responses that were common in the overall sample of subjects.

Although this type of definition of dominance works, it definitely is disadvantageous for the purpose of predicting directionality for every individual. Some of Matlin and Zajonc's subjects would have possessed dominant responses quite different from those of the population norm, and when given an audience, these same individuals would have been increasingly likely to emit free associates different from those defined as dominant in terms of population norms. Hence this method of defining dominance works best when the population is homogeneous.

Dominance Defined by Special Training

One of the more influential paradigms for training of dominance was developed by Zajonc and Nieuwenhuyse (1964) and was first implemented in a social facilitation context by Zajonc and Sales (1966). Subjects were first asked to learn ten totally unfamiliar "words" (such as *afworbu*), and relative dominance of the words was manipulated through the number of times subjects were asked to pronounce each one. If someone has pronounced *afworbu* 16 times, it is fair to say that it is dominant over *zabulon*, which perhaps was pronounced just once. After a dominance hierarchy was established, subjects were placed in a situation in which they were to guess which of the ten words was appropriate, given an ambiguous stimulus. This test phase consisted of 31 trials. In line with the theory, the better-learned (dominant) words were emitted with increased frequency given an audience. The subordinate words decreased in frequency, as it was possible to give only one response on any trial. This same pattern of results was present when there was no audience but was much less extreme.

SPECIAL TOPICS

Other Effects of Observers

We will see in subsequent chapters that the presence of other people can have a variety of influences. It can raise conformity pressures, thus altering the direction and intensity of behavior; it can generate a feeling of diffusion of responsibility, thereby adversely affecting prosocial behavior; and to the extent that there is communication, the diversity of social types of influences rises beyond the level to which we want to count. The processes examined thus far assume that nothing is conveyed from the audience to the behaving person except general drive, and if we intend to implement Zajonc's scheme without our results being influenced by more complicated and more cognitive psychological processes, we must always be on the lookout for possible additional functions of audiences.

For example, a genuine misuse of Zajonc's notion could have occurred in Goldman's color-preference experiment, in which the others present were also naming colors. Had everyone's trial-by-trial preferences been publicized, the social influence potential of the situation would have been overwhelming. Rather than gravitating toward their own dominant responses, subjects might well have shifted their preferences in the direction of someone present whom they liked or who sounded persuasive.

Another source of influence, this one more subtle, can arise simply because humans often feel evaluated by others. Suppose a typical subject in Zajonc and Sales' experiment had rehearsed the word *zabulon* just once and then, in the presence of an audience, had had the option of calling out that word or the well-practiced *afworbu*. Might subjects possibly be worried about mispronouncing *zabulon* in the presence of attentive observers? If so, their responses would quickly tend toward well-rehearsed words, solely out of fear of implicit evaluation and not for reasons of social facilitation.

We do not suggest that all the research of this area should be explained in more cognitive terms, for the great diversity of effects with humans, rats, chickens, cockroaches, and other species would certainly imply that there is much truth in Zajonc's idea. Our purpose here is to warn against a hastily contrived social facilitation setting that has a potential for the influence of factors other than mere general drive.

The Problem of Defining Dominance

The research we have examined thus far has been explicit on the question of dominance. Competing responses are examined or trained until there is some certainty about their relative likelihood of emission. In each example we have considered, whether concocted situations or research examples, the possible responses that might occur in a given place or time were listed, and the relative likelihood of each behavior was assessed easily. In the smoking example, our hero had only two possible responses. In the experiment on color naming, the possible responses were constrained experimentally, enabling an easy count of the various color choices. But not all applications of this theory have been so self-evident: on occasion the question of dominance becomes difficult, as in the following research on bicycling and running.

The bicycling research is attributable to Triplett (1898), and constitutes perhaps the first experimental social psychology. Triplett observed
that bicycle racers increased their speed when accompanied by a second
cyclist, even if there was no direct competition. In a similar vein, the
study by Zajonc et al. (1969) of running cockroaches found speedier running times due to an audience of fellow cockroaches. But what assumptions must be made by social facilitation theory about dominance in
situations involving speed? We can imagine two alternative assumptions.

First, it might be proposed that moving faster is dominant. But to
say "speed is dominant" seems vague. What, precisely, are the alternative
dominant and subordinate responses when we are considering racing cy-
clists and dashing cockroaches? If we want to think in terms of opposites,
perhaps lethargy is the counterpart of swiftness; hence one could think of
these situations in terms of one dominant and one subordinate response.

But there are other possibilities. The world of running and bicycling
could be divided into three general responses of "present rate," "faster
rate," and "slower rate"—or, to push the analysis further, one could imagine several discrete speeds, any of which might be dominant. In case this
latter suggestion sounds absurd, think of the typical motorist, who shows
a definite repertoire of "school-zone velocity" (15 mph), "inner-city velocity" (35 mph), "radar-trap velocity" (25 mph), and "open-road velocity" (70 mph). If a woman driving in a school zone suddenly
encountered a small audience inside her car, one possible reading of the
theory would lead us to expect her to stick increasingly close to her usual
response in the situation—15 mph. But following the lead of the bicycling
and cockroach cases, we would predict acceleration.

Which assumption is right? First, we might return to the cockroach
runway of Zajonc et al. and think more carefully about how to define
dominance. An approach that would parallel our driver example requires
that we divide the roach's behaviors into discrete, mutually exclusive categories. Why not let the roach run the runway several times, without an
audience, and note the running speed on each occasion? After several observations we find that the times cluster around 41 seconds, enabling us to
say quite reasonably that 41 seconds is the dominant response. If the second assumption is right, introducing an audience should cause running
speeds to hover more closely around 41 seconds. But this did not happen
at all. In fact, the roaches clocked by Zajonc et al. sped up appreciably,
taking only 33 seconds. Does this mean that acceleration is dominant,
rather than the habitual and more common response of 41 seconds?

As it turns out, it is an error in interpretation of the theory to say
that such discrete behaviors as a "41-sec run" are dominant or subordi-

nate. The theory simply talks about whether or not a given habit (such as running) is dominant and proceeds to imply that its *strength* will increase given the presence of an audience. "Strength" can be defined variously—in terms of probability of occurrence, vigor (for example, speed) of response, or a lower starting latency—but the important point here is that the theory is concerned neither with how the organism thinks about the response nor with the usual intensity level. That is, if the human holds a value that 15 mph is the correct speed, the theory in no way implies that responses congruent with the 15-mph value will be strengthened. Rather, the general habit of pressing the accelerator will be strengthened because of the presence of others, and greater speed will result so long as the passengers do not object to speeding. Similarly, just because a cockroach typically runs a maze in 41 seconds does not mean that "41 sec" is dominant. Running *per se* should be viewed as dominant, while responses other than running are subordinate, and the presence of others will serve to intensify the running response.

What Is Mere Presence?

Thus far we have given no attention to the requirements that a group of people, chickens, or roaches must satisfy in order to facilitate an organism's dominant response. One question that has not been touched on in the research has to do with species similarity: no one at this point knows whether a human's responses are facilitated by groups of dogs, cattle, and other species. The answer is potentially quite simple. If those other species can increase general drive in humans, then the mere presence of a herd of cattle would indeed serve the same function as a human audience. The same can be said of variations among human audiences: does the janitor in a funeral home undergo an intensification of dominant responses (perhaps sweeping) when he enters the slumber room? The answer depends on the ability of a corpse to generate arousal. We think that a corpse could probably accomplish this.

Research by Cottrell, Wack, Sekerak, and Rittle (1968), Henchy and Glass (1968), and Paulus and Murdoch (1971) has already shown that the mere physical presence of an audience is sometimes insufficient to create the kinds of effects discussed by Zajonc. This research indicates that the audience must exert an evaluative function. Thus we have at least a beginning into one possible limitation of the notion that mere presence is drive-inducing.

In light of this limitation, we should reconsider our earlier example of the smoker in the presence of children. If the children do indeed not care about smoking and are therefore not in a position to evaluate the smoker, their presence should probably not have much impact on general drive. But if they have been taught to attend to the smoking habits of adults and perhaps to ask a number of soul-searching questions about the merits of smoking, they should then have the capacity to produce the facilitation effects discussed by Zajonc.

It should be kept in mind that this evaluative stipulation has been made in the context of research in which only two kinds of audiences were being considered: those that exerted a definite evaluative role and those that were remarkably passive and in many respects inconspicuous. In the experiment by Cottrell et al. (1968), the passive audience was not expressly interested in the subject's performance, nor could it even see the subject: its members were wearing blindfolds. It seems likely that this passive audience was indeed not a source of drive increments, but it also is likely that the same audience could have been made arousing even though not evaluative. For example, had one member displayed an especially grotesque feature or shown signs of pain or for any reason upset the subject, an increment in general drive should have resulted. This suggests that evaluation may be just one of a number of ways in which the arousal-inducing influence of an audience is enhanced.

SUMMARY

Social facilitation theory is one of the most fundamental social psychological notions we discuss. It applies to animals as well as humans, to almost any behavior, and requires just two conditions for its application: (1) The easier of these is the audience, or mere-presence, variable. The main consideration here has to do with whether general drive results only from certain characteristics of the mere presence of others (for example, the evaluative dimension). At this time very little is known about these characteristics, and so it is reasonable to take Zajonc literally until the drive-increasing potential of an audience is understood more completely. (2) The more difficult of these conditions is the identification of the dominant response. It is a mistake to assume that smoking, eating, driving fast, or any other response is dominant simply because it is salient, habitual, or for some reason interesting to the investigator. The clear applications of the theory deal with classes of behavior that are easily identified, discrete, and nonoverlapping. This means that a person using this theory should map out the possible alternative responses first, then identify the most frequent or strongest one, and finally predict which response will be energized by the presence of others. We think that this is not a terribly difficult task, and further, there is every reason to think that the theory works rather well in situations that allow such analysis.

SUGGESTED READING

Cottrell, N. B. Social facilitation. In C. G. McClintock (Ed.), *Experimental social psychology*. New York: Holt, Rinehart & Winston, 1972.

Paulus, P. B. (Ed.). *Psychology of group influence*. Hillsdale, N.J.: Erlbaum, 1980.

Zajonc, R. B. Social facilitation. *Science*, 1965, 269–274.

CHAPTER 3

A REINFORCEMENT-AFFECT MODEL OF ATTRACTION

ANN AND Bill have just been introduced by friends. Ann tells Bill that she likes to see foreign films and to go to the beach and that Elton John is her favorite musician. Bill replies that he also likes foreign films and beachgoing immensely but that he favors Vivaldi's music. This brief exchange of opinions has now led to mildly favorable feelings between the two. They continue to disclose: Bill explains to Ann his passion for horseback riding, and it happens that she also loves horses. Finally, Bill sheepishly reveals that he enjoys reading the backs of cereal boxes. Ann is charmed: she has never met anyone else who, like herself, was enthusiastic about reading the backs of cereal boxes. Bill also tells Ann that, although he often feels a little insecure and nervous when he first meets women, he feels very comfortable with her. She feels still more attracted to Bill, and they are now eager to go out together.

Why do Ann and Bill feel attracted to each other? One important determinant of initial attraction is similarity. We tend to like people who are similar to us and dislike those who are dissimilar to us. The more things that Ann and Bill discovered they had in common, the more they liked each other.

This example illustrates the most frequent derivation from the reinforcement-affect model of attraction (Byrne, 1971; Byrne & Clore, 1970; Clore & Byrne, 1974). The model is potentially a highly general theory that can be used to analyze determinants of a variety of evaluative responses, such as any kind of value or attitude. Although the theory is indeed general, the research derived from the theory has focused mainly on attitudinal similarity as a determinant of interpersonal attraction. We will begin by considering the theory together with some illustrative research examples; then we will discuss the specific application of the theory to the relation between similarity and attraction.

THE THEORY

The reinforcement-affect model has its origins in the empirical research and theory in the area of learning, particularly classical conditioning. This means we must open with a short review of the basic ideas of classical conditioning.

Classical conditioning begins with what are termed the "unconditioned stimulus" and the "unconditioned response." *Unconditioned stimulus* is a term used to describe a stimulus that can be depended on to evoke some given response, and that response is therefore called the "unconditioned response." For example, the presentation of food (unconditioned stimulus) reliably elicits salivation (unconditioned response) in a hungry dog; blowing a puff of air (unconditioned stimulus) in a person's eye reliably elicits an eyeblink (unconditioned response); and a sudden icy breeze brings forth the shivering response. The main idea behind classical conditioning is that a new stimulus (called the "conditioned stimulus") can be paired with the unconditioned stimulus so that it too will have response-evoking power. We might take the salivating dog as an example.

If we ring a bell in the presence of a young puppy, the bell will have no salivation-eliciting power. This is what we mean by a conditioned stimulus—it is originally unrelated to the response in question, and any relation between it and the response will be brought on only by the procedure called "conditioning." If we now ring the bell each time food is presented to the dog, the dog will eventually begin to salivate when it hears the bell.

The salivation that results from the ringing bell is called the "conditioned response," primarily because it is set off by the conditioned stimulus. Any stimulus that is repeatedly paired with the unconditioned stimulus should eventually elicit a similar response.

How can these ideas be applied to the development of evaluative responses, such as attitudes, values, or liking? Byrne and Clore propose that any reinforcing stimulus (reward) can serve as the unconditioned stimulus, automatically setting off what is called an "implicit affective response." This implicit affective response is approximately the same as a feeling of pleasantness or unpleasantness. For instance, it is clear that an unexpected, sincere compliment is a reinforcer and that it results in a pleasant feeling. In the language of the model, we would say that the reinforcing compliment is an unconditioned stimulus that evokes a positive implicit affective response (the unconditioned response).

Conditioning takes place when a stimulus that is originally neutral is paired with the unconditioned stimulus (the reinforcement). Through repeated pairings the new stimulus (conditioned stimulus) will eventually come to elicit the positive implicit affective response, with the direct result that the subject will have favorable feelings toward the conditioned stimulus. If one repeatedly receives unexpected compliments while standing in the foyer of a friend's house, the foyer (conditioned stimulus) will come to elicit a positive affective response, meaning that one will then like the foyer better.

An experiment by Zanna, Kiesler, and Pilkonis (1970) illustrates the conditioning process quite nicely. Subjects received a series of mild electric shocks of varying duration. During this time an experimenter read a series of words. For some subjects the word *light* was consistently paired with the onset of shock, and the word *dark* was paired with termination of shock. For other subjects, *begin* was paired with the onset of shock and *end* with the termination. In the language of the model, the onset of shock is an unconditioned stimulus that should lead to a negative affective response. The termination of shock is another unconditioned stimulus—one that should lead to a positive affective response. That is, termination of the shock, as a relief from pain, should create a sudden positive feeling. The word (conditioned stimulus) paired with shock onset should come to elicit a negative affective response, and the word (conditioned stimulus) paired with shock termination should come to elicit a positive affective response. This indeed was the case: On a later series of trials in which the words were read without accompanying shocks, subjects showed greater emotional reactivity (as measured by the physiological measure of galvanic skin potential) to the words paired with shock onset or termination than to words that had not been paired with the shock. In addition, when they evaluated a number of words in a different context, the word that had been paired with shock onset (no matter whether *light* or *begin*) was evaluated more negatively than the counterpart word paired with shock termination. Thus, Zanna and his coworkers demonstrated that an affective response and corresponding change in the evaluation of initially neutral words could be achieved through simple conditioning.

The Byrne and Clore analysis, however, may be taken one step further. Affect, regardless of how it is induced, should generalize to other neutral stimuli that are present at the same time. This was illustrated in an experiment by Gouaux (1971), who showed subjects one of two films: a comedy, *Good Old Corn*, or a depressing documentary, *John F. Kennedy, 1917–1963*. These films were selected to induce positive and negative affect, respectively, and, to be sure, subjects who had seen the comedy reported being in a better mood than those who had seen the documentary. All subjects were then asked, just after viewing one of the films, to evaluate a student whom they had never met, knowing only his attitudes. In both cases, the attitudes held by the student were the same. Subjects who had viewed the humorous film were more attracted to the stranger than subjects who had viewed the depressing film. This result suggests that any alteration of subjects' affect will lead to changes in their evaluation of social stimuli (and any other stimuli) that are present in the situation.

In summary, the model proposes that evaluative responses develop through a process resembling classical conditioning. A neutral stimulus (conditioned stimulus) that is repeatedly paired with a reinforcing stimulus will come to elicit an implicit affective response. The strength and direction (positive or negative) of the affective response will, in turn, determine the subject's evaluation of the conditioned stimulus. In addition, other kinds of affect inductions, not based on reinforcement, will influence the subject's evaluation of the new stimulus. The stimulus being evaluated may be a person or an object: the conditioning process does not differentiate between social and nonsocial stimuli.

SIMILARITY AND ATTRACTION

Although Byrne has proposed a rather general theory, the majority of the research conducted by him and his coworkers has focused on the specific application of the theory to similarity as a determinant of interpersonal attraction. Similarity to others is assumed to be an unconditioned stimulus, creating positive affect.* Byrne has insisted that the theory be tested using a standard set of experimental procedures—that is, a "paradigm." As a result of this emphasis, much of the relevant research has used the same context, the same manipulation of similarity to the other person, and the same attraction scale. Note that Byrne does not argue that similarity is the most important determinant of attraction or that it will lead to attraction under all conditions. Rather, he has emphasized the focused study of a specific relation within the context of a standard experimental procedure. Since the similarity-attraction paradigm is so basic to Byrne's research, we will first discuss his methodology, and then we will look at examples of research. Later in the chapter, the advantages and disadvantages of such extensive reliance on a standard methodology will receive some comments.

The Similarity-Attraction Paradigm

Early in the semester, potential subjects—psychology students—fill out a comprehensive attitude questionnaire that assesses their attitudes on various national issues (such as socialized medicine), college issues, and personal preferences (such as music). On arriving at the experiment later in the semester, each subject is shown an attitude questionnaire that supposedly has been completed by another student. The student is described as being of the same sex as the subject but is not in the same psychology class. The subject is then asked to study the student's attitudes and to form an impression. In fact, the student's questionnaire has been filled out by the experimenter in order to create a particular degree of similarity to the attitudes expressed by the subject earlier in the semester. That is, for some subjects, the student's attitudes are very similar to their own, whereas for others, the student's attitudes are rather disparate from their own. Finally, the subject fills out a questionnaire (interpersonal judgment scale) in which two questions that measure attraction are embedded. The two questions are concerned with how much the subject likes the stranger and how much the subject would like to work with the stranger in an experiment. The sum of the subject's scores on these two questions is taken as the measure of attraction (range 2–14).

In an early experiment using this procedure, Byrne (1962) gave subjects an attitude scale on which the hypothetical student's responses were

---

*Similarity to others and other social reinforcers technically are conditioned stimuli that have gained their response-eliciting power through prior learning. Hence, this process is in fact higher order conditioning.

similar to those of the subject on 7, 6, 5, 4, 3, 2, 1, or 0 of the 7 issues and dissimilar on the remainder. He found that the larger the number of issues on which the hypothetical student's responses agreed with those of the subject, the more attracted the subject was to the student. Later research using scales with different numbers of issues have further clarified this result, indicating that it is the *proportion* rather than the *number* of similar attitudes that determines attraction. That is, you will be better liked by people if you share their opinions on 9 out of 10 issues than if you share their opinions on 20 out of 50 issues. In fact, research by Byrne and his coworkers has indicated a linear (straight line) relation between the proportion of similar attitudes and attraction, as shown in Figure 3-1.

Similarity-Attraction and the Theory

The relation between similarity and attraction has been well established empirically, but we have not yet considered the theoretical basis for this relation. In the Byrne and Clore theory, similarity is the uncondi-

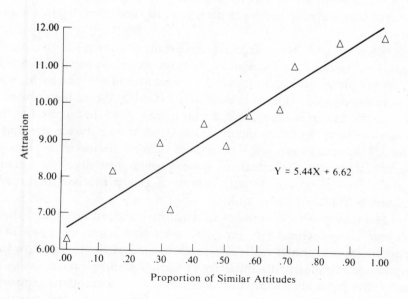

Figure 3-1. Attraction toward a stranger as a linear function of proportion of similar attitudes. From "Attraction As a Linear Function of Proportion of Positive Reinforcements," by D. Byrne and D. Nelson, *Journal of Personality and Social Psychology,* 1965, 1, 661. Copyright 1965 by the American Psychological Association. Reprinted by permission.

tioned stimulus; the implicit affective response is the unconditioned response. After implicit attitudinal pairing of the hypothetical student with a series of similar or dissimilar attitudinal responses, conditioning will occur and the student (conditioned stimulus) will come to elicit the implicit affective response. The implicit affective response will in turn determine the subject's attraction to the student. Note that in this analysis, similarity is assumed to have properties similar to those of other unconditioned reinforcing stimuli, such as the termination of shock or an unexpected compliment. But does similarity really have this reinforcing character?

Golightly and Byrne (1964) investigated this question using a discrimination-learning task. Subjects sat in front of an apparatus that displayed two figures that varied on a number of dimensions (large/small, circle/square, black/white). The subject's task was to pick one of the two figures, and one response was designated as correct. For example, if the subject chose the figure containing the circle, it would be considered correct, whereas the figure containing the square would be considered wrong. Normally, in this type of research the experimenter says "right" after correct responses and "wrong" after incorrect responses, and learning is reflected in an increasing number of correct responses over trials. The fact that learning occurs is presumed to show that "right" is a reinforcer.

Golightly and Byrne exposed one group of subjects to the standard "right" or "wrong" feedback after their responses on each trial. Subjects in another group were given a card with an attitudinal statement printed on it (for example, "There is definitely a God"). When the subject was correct, the experimenter showed him a statement that agreed with his known position, but when incorrect, the subject was shown one that disagreed. If similarity is a reinforcer, these subjects should show significant improvements in performance across trials, just like the standard "right"/"wrong" group. Finally, a control group received only neutral statements of fact on each trial.

The results were as predicted: both the standard group and the attitude similarity-dissimilarity group showed significant increases in performance across trials, while the performance of the control group did not change. Similarity-dissimilarity of attitudes therefore seems to have reinforcing properties comparable to those of other standard reinforcers.

This experiment, however, did not address the related question of whether similarity leads to an implicit affective response. Some evidence on this issue is provided by Byrne and Clore (1970), who found that subjects reading attitude statements similar to their own attitudes reported feeling more positive than subjects reading dissimilar attitude statements. Further, Clore and Gormly (1974) found strong relations between a physiological measure of emotional reactivity and attraction to another student. When the student was described as having dissimilar attitudes, the stronger the subject's measured emotional response, the greater the disliking for the student. In a parallel fashion, when the student was described as being similar to the subject, a strong emotional response was associated with a high degree of liking. These findings suggest that dissimilarity and similarity of attitudes lead to an affective reaction, which in turn mediates the attraction response.

In summary, Byrne and his coworkers have shown that the proportion of similar attitudes is linearly related to attraction for a hypothetical student. They have also shown that similarity and dissimilarity function, respectively, as positive and negative reinforcers and induce positive and negative affects. Finally, the magnitude of subjects' affective responses is related to their attraction to another.

SPECIAL TOPICS

Limits of the Spread of Affect

Byrne's theory proposes that affective reactions can spread from a reinforcing stimulus (unconditioned stimulus) to other stimuli by association. Indeed, Griffitt and Guay (1969) found that subjects receiving a high proportion of reinforcement evaluated the student, the experiment, the experimenter, and even the apparatus more positively than subjects receiving a low proportion of reinforcement. Such results suggest that a simple conditioning process is involved rather than some more complex cognitive process. Still, it seems unlikely that positive and negative feelings will generalize equally to all stimuli that are paired with the reinforcing stimulus. For example, imagine that a young executive woman is greeted with a welcoming kiss by her husband every evening as she returns from work. One might suspect that the positive affect engendered by the kiss might generalize more to the waiting children and perhaps even to the family dog than to nearby inanimate objects, such as her husband's raincoat and galoshes.

A limitation to the spread of affect is suggested by recent research with animals: not all stimuli may be equally susceptible to conditioning (for example, Rescorla & Wagner, 1972). Stimuli that are salient and that predict most reliably the occurrence of the unconditioned stimulus condition most easily. If male subjects were always presented with a picture of an attractive female (conditioned stimulus) just before hearing a female voice agree with their most cherished beliefs (unconditioned stimulus), the presentation of the picture alone should come to elicit strong positive affect, and hence the subjects should be strongly attracted to the picture. However, if the same picture were reduced in size, not consistently paired with the attitude statements, or otherwise made less prominent in the situation, conditioning would not occur so readily. The less salient picture should elicit a weaker affective response, and the males should be less attracted to it.

Long-Term and Short-Term Effects

A major focus of research on conditioning has been on extinction. Conditioned responses do not persist forever. Rather, they gradually lose strength as time passes without further pairing of the conditioned and unconditioned stimuli. This loss of strength is called "extinction." Surprisingly, virtually no research has examined the possibility that the strength of attraction responses may decrease over time. This omission leads to an intriguing question for Byrne's theory: do different sources of positive affect produce the same *long-term* effects on attraction?

This problem can be illustrated by returning to the experiment by Gouaux (1971). To review briefly, subjects who had just seen a humorous movie were more attracted to the student than were subjects who had seen a depressing movie. In addition, the more similar the subject's attitudes were to those of the student, the greater the subject's attraction to the student. Thus, the two sources of affect, the humorous movie and the similar attitudes, had parallel effects. Note, however, that the measure of attraction was taken very shortly after the manipulations. What would happen if the attraction measure were taken considerably later—say, after a week had passed? To answer this question, let's consider the effects of similarity and the humorous movie separately.

When subjects read a series of attitude statements similar to their own, this presumably leads to conditioning of positive affect toward the student. The subjects' attraction to the student should be maximal immediately after reading the statements. As time passes, extinction should occur and the strength of attraction should gradually decrease. Nonetheless, the evaluation should still continue to be positive (though weaker) over a long period of time.

The effect of the humorous movie is more complex. If the movie simply puts the subject in a more positive mood, attraction should be enhanced only as long as the mood lasts. Once the mood passes, the manipulation should no longer have any effect on attraction. However, if the reading of each attitude statement can be considered analogous to a trial in a conditioning experiment, it is also possible that the mood-enhanced affect could become conditioned to the student with whom it is paired repeatedly. If so, then the mood manipulation would have a long-term effect on attraction. Which of these outcomes is actually correct probably depends on the manner in which the mood is associated with the student. If the positive mood is paired repeatedly with the student in discrete trials, then the mood induction may have long-term effects on attraction. However, if the student is simply and continuously present while the subject is in a positive mood, it is likely that the effect of mood on attraction will be more transient. For conditioning to occur, there must be time between successive presentations of the conditioned-stimulus/unconditioned-stimulus pair (see Gibbon, Baldock, Locurto, Gold, & Terrace, 1977).

Problems of External Validity

The reinforcement-affect model has been criticized most extensively on grounds of its external validity (see, for example, Murstein, 1971). Although critics acknowledge that the model provides an accurate account of attraction in the relatively simple context of the similarity-attraction paradigm, they argue that it fails to predict attraction in more complex, realistic situations. We will examine three aspects of this criticism: the interpersonal context, the specification of reinforcing stimuli, and the link between attraction and behavior.

The Interpersonal Context   The similarity-attraction paradigm has a minimal interpersonal context. Subjects never meet the student, and the attitudes and other information subjects receive are not related to their own behavior. This minimal interpersonal context is representative of certain real-world situations, such as hearing a description of a potential blind date or reading the file of a job applicant. However, in many relationships the other person's behavior occurs in response to our own, and this interdependence may have important implications for attraction. For instance, in the example that opened this chapter, Ann and Bill moved slowly toward disclosing more unique attitudes and more intimate facets of their personality as the conversation continued, leading to the development of a strong mutual attraction. In contrast, had Bill disclosed his peculiar reading preferences and his insecurities about women at the outset of their interaction, Ann probably would have been considerably less attracted to him (see Derlaga & Chaikin, 1975). Since much of the research testing the reinforcement-affect model has employed this minimal interpersonal context, critics have questioned whether the model can be applied to more involving situations.

This issue is illustrated by contrasting two research examples investigating the effects of systematic variations in reinforcement magnitude on interpersonal attraction. Using the similarity-attraction paradigm, Byrne and London (1966) exposed subjects to one of four sets of attitude statements. In the first two conditions, the student expressed attitudes similar to the subject's on 56 different issues or else expressed attitudes dissimilar to the subject's on all 56 issues. In the other two conditions, the student expressed similar attitudes on half the issues and dissimilar attitudes on half. In one of the latter conditions, the 28 similar attitudes came first; in the other, the dissimilar attitudes were first.

The order of presentation of the similar/dissimilar attitudes made little difference. Subjects in both these conditions liked the student better than subjects in the 0%-similar-attitudes condition but less than subjects in the 100%-similar-attitudes condition. Thus, in this situation, in which the attitudes expressed by the student did not depend on the subject's behavior, the sequence of agreeing and disagreeing statements had no effect on the subject's evaluation of the student.

A similar experiment was conducted by Aronson and Linder (1965), with one crucial difference: the magnitude of reinforcement appeared to the subject to be contingent on the subject's own behavior. The subject interacted with another student who was in reality a hired accomplice of the experimenter. The subject and the student engaged in a series of brief conversations, and after each of these, the subject overheard the student's evaluation of her via an intercom. Four evaluation conditions were used, similar to those used later by Byrne and London: all negative; negative first, then positive; positive first, then negative; all positive.

In contrast to Byrne and London's results, Aronson and Linder found that the subjects receiving the initially negative, then positive evaluations liked the student more than subjects who received the initially positive, then negative evaluations. Several more recent studies (Hewitt,

1972; Taylor, Altman, & Sorrentino, 1969) have also found that later evaluations have more impact on liking whenever the other's evaluation appears to be contingent on the subject's behavior. That is, whenever evaluators appear to have some basis for changing their minds about the subject, their later evaluations have considerably more impact on subjects' attraction to them than the earlier responses. This type of result has led critics to question whether the findings obtained using the similarity-attraction paradigm can be generalized to more involving situations.*

In fairness to Byrne, he and his associates have found that similarity does lead to attraction in other, more involving situations such as an initial get-acquainted date (Byrne, Ervin, & Lamberth, 1970), and a group of previously unacquainted men living together for ten days in a fallout shelter (Griffitt & Veitch, 1974). Although such studies give us increased confidence in the potential usefulness of the similarity-attraction paradigm, the problem of understanding the many ways in which interdependence influences the attraction process remains a major task for the theory.

Specification of Reinforcing Stimuli In the context of the similarity-attraction paradigm, it has been relatively easy to identify reinforcing stimuli and to demonstrate their effect on attraction. One reason this has been easy is that it has already been shown that similarity of attitudes is reinforcing, in the sense of strengthening behavior. Another reason is that rather straightforward manipulations of positive and negative reinforcement have been used, such as statements of liking versus statements of disliking, and comfortable versus uncomfortably hot room temperature. However, once the researcher leaves the minimal interpersonal context of the similarity-attraction paradigm, it becomes difficult to specify the reinforcing stimulus in advance because changes in the situation may radically shift the reinforcement value of the stimulus. Praising a prima ballerina after a fine performance, for example, may have a different reinforcement value than praising her after she has, to her considerable embarrassment, slipped and fallen on her behind. As a result, the only way to be sure that something is reinforcing is to put it to a test in a context similar to the situation of interest, just as Golightly and Byrne (1964) have tested out attitude similarity.

*One of the most interesting effects of the Aronson and Linder (1965) experiment was that subjects who received the initially negative, then positive evaluations actually liked the student more than subjects who received *all positive* evaluations. Although some investigations have failed to replicate this effect (for example, Hewitt, 1972), it apparently occurs when the change from negative to positive evaluations occurs slowly, the later evaluations update the earlier ones, and the subject is convinced that the evaluator has changed her mind (Mettee & Aronson, 1974).

The Link Between Attraction and Behavior   The reinforcement-affect model describes how people become attracted to objects and to other people. But the reader may have noticed that the theory makes no formal provision for linking affect and behavior. Although attraction researchers have often assumed that behavior will be directly related to verbal reports of liking, this relationship will not always hold. Consequently, it is important for the theory to spell out precisely how attraction and behavior are related if we are to apply the theory to attraction-related behaviors.

As an illustration of this issue, consider the results of studies that have examined the relationship between liking and interpersonal distance. Several studies (for example, Byrne, Baskett, & Hodges, 1971; Byrne, Ervin, & Lamberth, 1970) have found that two highly similar strangers like each other more and sit closer together than strangers who are dissimilar. Note that in these studies the highly similar pairs had a maximum of 80% of their attitudes and/or personality traits in common. A more recent study by Snyder and Endelman (1979), using more extreme degrees of similarity and dissimilarity, replicated these results when the usual self-report measure of attraction (the Interpersonal Judgment Scale) was employed. However, subjects who believed they were highly similar to the student (95% agreement) chose to sit farther away from him than those who were only moderately similar (50% agreement). Thus, when people are too similar to us, we may still express liking for them but want to dissociate ourselves from them in terms of our behavior. The too similar person may threaten our view of ourselves as unique individuals who possess attitudes and personality traits that differentiate us from others, and hence we may be motivated to keep our distance or to perform other behaviors that serve to re-establish our uniqueness (Fromkin & Snyder, 1980). Therefore, an important dual task for the reinforcement-affect model is to specify the mechanism that links attraction to behavior and to identify the situations under which other factors such as needs for uniqueness may modify the relationship.

Advantages of Paradigmatic Research

Note that the previous section on problems of external validity does not criticize the reinforcement-affect model per se. Rather, it indicates difficulties in applying the theory to more involving situations and to behavior. Byrne's response to these criticisms is clear: he has conducted basic research on the reinforcement-affect model, and such research involves "the deliberate and necessary suspension of interest in real life problems"

(Byrne, 1971, p. 9). And from this perspective, Byrne and his coworkers have produced a remarkably coherent body of research.

As we discussed earlier, Byrne has emphasized the testing of the reinforcement-affect model of attraction by using a standard set of procedures, a practice with several advantages. (1) If the methodology is identical across experiments, then the results of different experiments can often be compared. When different procedures are used, it is often difficult to track down the exact difference in the two procedures that is responsible for the result. (2) Use of a standard paradigm facilitates exact specification of the theoretical independent variable. For example, Byrne and his coworkers have been able to specify that the *proportion* of similar attitudes, not the *number* of similar attitudes, specifies the theoretical independent variable of similarity. Specification of the independent variable improves the chances that an exact replication of the experiment will be successful. (3) Finally, the use of a standard paradigm allows development of mathematical equations that indicate precisely the relation between the specific independent variable and specific dependent variable within the paradigm. Figure 3-1 illustrates this advantage: similarity is shown to be related to attraction according to a simple linear equation. Such mathematical formulas allow precise prediction of the results of a new experiment, and the more precise the prediction, the easier it is to detect discrepancies between the predicted and the actual results. A nonlinear relation between similarity and attraction would be detected immediately and investigated by the researcher looking for the predicted relation, whereas the researcher who is unaware of this predicted relation would be unlikely to notice. Note, however, the important qualification stated above: the mathematical relation will hold only within the confines of the specific paradigm. If other procedures or other measures were employed, there is no reason to expect that the same mathematical relation would hold between similarity and attraction.

Some Disadvantages

Although Byrne and his coworkers have pursued admirable scientific goals in conducting paradigm-based research, there are also disadvantages in using this practice in social psychology. As already noted, research that is based on a single methodology is subject to questions of external validity. There may be important variables that are not included in the specific procedures used in the paradigm, and these could modify the relation obtained with Byrne's paradigm. For example, the similarity-attraction relation is modified by the pleasantness of the other person: if the other is obnoxious, a dissimilar other is liked more than a similar other (Taylor & Mettee, 1971). Thus, if the interest of the investigator is in various cognitive and motivational processes not addressed by Byrne, the single-method approach can be inadequate as a basis for research on these interests. Introducing new variables that are not amenable to testing within the confines of the paradigm is also difficult. The investigator may be forced to choose between abandoning a proposed variable or altering the paradigm, and when the former choice is made, the investigator may choose variables not on the basis of what is important to the development and testing of the theory, but on what is easy to implement within the limits of the paradigm. The theory, not the paradigm, should determine the questions addressed by researchers.

SUMMARY AND CONCLUSIONS

The reinforcement-affect model provides a good account of how reinforcements influence evaluations of people and objects. According to the model, reinforcements give rise to affective responses. As a result of repeated pairing of an initially neutral stimulus (either a person or object) and a reinforcer, the initially neutral stimulus will come to elicit the affective response through a process similar to conditioning. This affective response, in turn, mediates the evaluation of the person or object. A great amount of basic research has been conducted that examines the interpersonal-attraction outcomes predicted by the model and the processes postulated by the model. In general, the model has received strong support. With some exceptions (for example, Byrne, Ervin, & Lamberth, 1970; Griffitt & Veitch, 1974), the model has been tested mainly in a minimal social situation. The behaviors of the stimulus person are typically not presented in an interpersonal context, nor are they contingent on the behaviors of the subject. This suggests an important limitation to the application of the theory: to the extent that the subject can interpret or structure the interpersonal situation, other complex cognitive processes may arise that significantly alter the subject's behavior. Consequently, the evaluation of the reinforcement-affect model depends on one's personal domain of interest. If the investigator is interested in the basic problem of how simple reinforcements affect evaluation, Byrne's theory provides an excellent understanding. However, if the investigator is interested in the more applied problem of how attraction develops in naturalistic situations, a more complex model that includes both reinforcements and cognitive variables is necessary.

SUGGESTED READING

Byrne, D. *The attraction paradigm*. New York: Academic Press, 1971.

Clore, G. L. Interpersonal attraction: An overview. In J. W. Thibaut, J. T. Spence, & R. C. Carson (Eds.), *Contemporary topics in social psychology*. Morristown, N.J.: General Learning Press, 1976.

Clore, G. L., & Byrne, D. A reinforcement-affect model of attraction. In T. L. Huston (Ed.), *Foundations of interpersonal attraction*. New York: Academic Press, 1974.

Griffitt, W. Attitude similarity and attraction. In T. L. Huston (Ed.), *Foundations of interpersonal attraction*. New York: Academic Press, 1974.

CHAPTER 4

BANDURA'S SOCIAL LEARNING THEORY

ERICA is a young woman who has what psychologists call "acrophobia." She is terrified at the thought of stepping into an airplane or jumping with a parachute and shuns all forms of flying. These fears have an aversive consequence for Erica. She lives in the Swiss Alps, in the finest skiing vicinity possible, and her brother and sister are both respected ski jumpers. Erica would also like to take to the air on skis, if only her fears would allow it. She knows how to ski but wouldn't dare leave the ground.

Erica's older brother decides that there may be a solution to Erica's problem. He takes Erica to the slopes, equips her with a movie camera, and tells her to take a careful pictorial documentary while he practices his ski jumping. The initial aspects of this little experiment take place on a small hill, as Erica will not set foot in a chairlift.

The brother first demonstrates the most rudimentary components of ski jumping: pointing down the hill, pushing off, crouching correctly, and so on. After demonstrating each component, he proceeds with an actual jump. He points down the hill and executes a perfect approach, only to slip on takeoff, soaring about 30 feet and landing flat on his back. Getting up, he shouts "That doesn't merit any praise," reminds Erica to keep her camera on the action, and continues. After several trials that show an improved form, he succeeds with a perfect flight and says "I deserve something special for that." With this comment, he pats himself on the back and takes a few gulps from a flask of brandy, Erica's favorite winter drink. The jumping trials continue, and each time Erica's brother asks her whether she would like to try. Each time Erica shows increasing interest.

When the brandy is half gone, Erica brushes caution aside, straps on the skis, and heads off the jump. Her first few attempts meet with failure, but upon the first successful flight and landing she immediately compliments herself and reaches for the brandy. Interestingly, she seems to have developed the basic skills just by observing. In like manner, something about observing her brother brought about a reduction in Erica's acrophobia.

THE THEORY

Bandura's (1965a, 1965b, 1971, 1977) social learning theory is an elaborate set of ideas about the ways behaviors are learned and changed. The application of the theory is to nearly all behaviors, with special emphasis on how new ones are acquired through observational learning. The theory applies readily to the development of aggression, dating behaviors, diligence, learning to ski jump, and even the physiological responses basic to emotion.

Bandura's theory takes a decidedly cognitive viewpoint in accounting for learning and behavior. By *cognitive* we mean that Bandura assumes that humans think about and interpret their experiences. For example, Bandura (1977) argues that complex learning can take place only when the person is aware of what is being reinforced. Suppose that a teacher wants to change the behavior of a perpetually tardy pupil, using the pupil's mother as the agent of reinforcement. Every time the pupil shows up at class on time, the teacher makes a secret phone call to the mother, who prepares the child's favorite meal that evening. To be sure, the chain of events here is "desired behavior followed by reinforcement," but Bandura would argue that such reinforcement would have no impact on behavior. Children must first understand the relationship between their correct behaviors and the occurrence of reinforcement.

In contrast to Bandura's position, traditional learning theorists (such as Skinner and Hull) assume nothing about the organism's cognitive processes. Rather, the main problem is to elicit the behavior from the organism so that it can be reinforced. According to the traditional position, the reinforcement "strengthens" the behavior, making it more likely to occur in the future. Using this approach, training Erica to ski jump would be accomplished through the same kind of trial-and-error learning used to train a dog to shake hands. With many complex learning problems (for example, training a teenager to drive a car), this approach would have disastrous consequences.

The crux of the traditional approach is this: for learning to occur, the organism must first perform and then be rewarded. With Bandura's theory neither of these is necessary. A person can learn simply by watching the behavior of another, and reward does nothing to "stamp in" this learning. According to social learning theory, the mere act of watching leads to a cognitive representation of the actions. Erica begins to code her brother's behavior, either verbally or in the form of imagery, and then is able to utilize these representations when she wants to perform the behaviors. The role of reward is primarily to motivate the person to bring the behavior forth, although reward also serves additional functions, as we will soon see. The details of this cognitively based learning process can best be summarized in terms of four stages: attention, retention, motor reproduction, and motivation.

1. Attention

If new responses are to be learned by watching (or listening to) another, then it is evident that the degree of attention given to the other will be of paramount importance. If Erica fails to watch her brother demonstrate the elements of ski jumping, whether as a result of a blinding sun or because her attention is drawn by a handsome lift attendant, there is no chance that her brother's actions will ever reach memory. A person can be prompted to attend carefully by means of rewards and also through qualities of the model (for example, an attractive model should receive more attention).

A more exhaustive list of attention-getting factors, particularly with reference to Erica's situation, would read as follows: (1) accentuation of the important features of the behavior (the model might exaggerate his knee bending), (2) attention-getting remarks, made either by the model or by a bystander, in order to direct attention to the central aspects of the behavior and to the strategies, (3) subdividing the general activity into natural segments so that the component skills can be featured, and (4) allowing Erica to practice intermittently, both before and after exposure to the model, so that she can identify the parts of the skill that give her special problems. In short, the ski instructor or psychological researcher may use a variety of reasonable, common-sense approaches to bring the subject's attention to the relevant behaviors.

2. Retention

Once the behavior is attended to, what happens? A representation of the behavior is either stored in memory or not, and basic to the storage is the method the person uses to encode, or "incorporate," the response. If Erica were too young to have developed verbal abilities, she would store her brother's actions as pictorial images. In other words, she would have a mental picture of her brother aiming for the ski jump, springing forth, and so on. But since Erica is old enough to possess verbal abilities, she no doubt stores what she sees at least partly in the form of verbal symbols. This means that she may remember a verbal sequence such as "point down hill, push off, hold poles back, crouch, spring up, lean forward . . . ." To the extent that the actions are coded in verbal symbols, they are likely to be remembered better at a later time. Coding in verbal symbols is facilitated by having people think actively about or verbally summarize the action while they are observing; coding is inhibited if the person is engaging in a competing cognitive activity, such as counting, reciting poetry, or thinking about something else (Bandura, Grusec, & Menlove, 1966).

Once the observed response is encoded, the retention of visual images or verbal symbols can be furthered by rehearsing them mentally. Accordingly, one should try to think vividly about the action and rethink the verbal coding.

3. Motor Reproduction

Once the particulars of a new act have been coded in memory, they must then be converted back into the appropriate actions. The new action sequence is first symbolically organized and rehearsed, all the time being compared with the memory of the modeled behavior. Adjustments in the new action sequence are then made, and the behavioral sequence is initiated. The actual behavior is monitored by the person and perhaps also by observers who provide feedback on the correctness of the imitative behavior. Adjustments based on the feedback are made in symbolic organization of the new action sequence, and the behavior sequence is initiated again. Through this process the initial approximation to the modeled behavior is refined until it is correct.

Social learning theory has identified three major prerequisites for the successful flow of this process. First, the person must have the component skills. Normally the behavioral sequences modeled in Bandura's research are made up of component behaviors that the person already knows. The teenager learning to shift gears in an automobile, for example, can already execute the movements necessary to depress the clutch pedal and move the gearshift. Second, the person must have the physical capacity to bring the component skills into coordinated movement. Four-year-olds could no doubt perform the individual actions required in shifting gears, but they would be too small to move the gearshift and depress the clutch pedal simultaneously. Finally, the attainment of a coordinated performance requires that one's individual movements be easily observable. Children could rather easily copy an adult model who beats up a doll, for it is a simple matter for children to observe their aggressive impact on the target. But to reproduce the finesse of a violinist would be a different matter. The aggressive movements in beating the doll are available for all to see, whereas playing a violin entails hundreds of subtle and covert movements. Many golf and tennis instructors show students slow-motion films of experts' and their own strokes to enhance the observability of the component movements, just as it is common for ballet dancers to practice before a mirror. Each of these techniques facilitates observation of the components of the behavior.

4. Reinforcement and Motivation

The issues of attention, retention, and motor reproduction have to do mainly with the person's capability to imitate a behavior. Reinforcement becomes relevant when we try to stimulate the person to manifest the learning in actual behavior. Although social learning theory holds that reinforcement does nothing to increase learning in the sense of "stamping the behavior in," it does give reinforcement (reward and punishment) a central role as a motivator. Erica may have learned the principles and particulars of jumping quite well by watching her brother, without being motivated to perform. Within Bandura's system there would be two methods for increasing her motivation. One—the more direct—is to offer incentives for performing. The second, which is more interesting and unique to Bandura's thinking, is through "vicarious reinforcement." Just by observing her brother enjoy the brandy, Erica gains motivation to take her turn at the jump, anticipating the positive consequences. We might add that punishment works just oppositely to reward and thereby functions as an incentive not to perform. Finally, Bandura's system also considers the phenomenon of self-reward, wherein Erica can motivate herself, perhaps by telling herself how fast she is learning or by taking a drink of brandy after a well-executed jump.

Advance knowledge of potential rewards and punishment also affects the first two factors listed above. If Erica becomes aware of possible rewards that could be gained by watching a model, she is more likely to *attend* closely to the model and is also more inclined to *rehearse mentally* whatever has been learned.

In summary, Bandura's social learning theory has two important implications: (1) New responses may be learned without having to perform them (learning by observation). (2) Reward and punishment primarily affect the *performance* of learned behaviors; however, when offered in advance, they do have secondary effects on learning of new behaviors through their influence on attention and rehearsal.

RESEARCH EXAMPLES

Imitation, Reward, and Punishment

According to Bandura's thinking, reward and punishment are far more relevant to the *performance* of a new behavior than to the learning. This principle is illustrated in a classic experiment by Bandura (1965a), in which children learned to aggress toward a doll.

The subjects were young men and women of approximately 4 years of age. They were asked to sit before a television screen and watch a male adult (the model) carry on with a life-size, plastic Bobo doll. The model verbally accosted the Bobo, pulled it down and sat on it, punched it in the nose, pounded it on the head with a mallet, and kicked it around the room. Had the Bobo been a human being, as it was in later research (Savitsky, Rogers, Izard, & Liebert, 1971), it would have been badly bruised and battered.

At the conclusion of this one-sided scene of violence, some of the subjects witnessed a second adult (an authority) running onto the televised scene and either rewarding, punishing, or giving no feedback to the aggressive adult model. The rewards were lavish from a 4-year-old's perspective. The rewarding authority called the model a "strong champion," offered the model some soft drinks and candy, and continued his verbal praise. The punishing authority shouted at the model disapprovingly and issued a harsh spanking.

Theoretically, what is happening here? We might try to examine the procedure from the standpoint of the four stages outlined above. (1) First, it is clear that subjects were attending. The attention-drawing virtues of television are well known, and the children viewed the program in a semi-darkened room with no distractions. (2) What about the manner of coding? Was pictorial imagery or verbal coding used? Probably both were going on, but it is likely that these young children relied more on imaginal coding than would older children with more highly developed verbal skills. An investigation by Gerst (1971) demonstrates that imaginal and symbolic coding are both effective means of coding but that careful verbal labeling that summarizes the action is probably the most effective form of coding. (3) How about the translation of learning into behavior? There were no impediments to motoric reproduction: all the subjects were capable of the necessary component responses, and many had probably performed some of the aggressive responses previously. It therefore should have been easy to translate the learning into the appropriate motor responses. (4) What role did reward play? This is the main question addressed by the Bobo-doll experiment. When they were given the opportunity to "play" with the Bobo doll themselves, the children were much less aggressive when they had witnessed a model who received punishment. The effect of the reward proved to be negligible, although in a later experiment with a stronger reward manipulation (Rosenkrans & Hartup, 1967), rewarding the model was shown to have a definite facilitative effect on imitative aggression. Thus there does seem to be such a process as vicarious reinforcement, whereby an observer can respond to the rewards or punishments incurred by a televised actor.

The question remains—did the observed reward/punishment affect learning, performance, or both? Bandura ran his subjects through a further session in which they were offered some very attractive pictures for each aggressive response they could successfully reproduce. Amazingly, this simple, direct incentive increased aggression in all experimental groups, completely eliminating the earlier effects of reward and punishment of the model—all of which further supports Bandura's claim that reward is more important for performance than for learning.

Self-Control and Modeling

One of the focal points of Bandura's research deals with people's "self-reactive" capacities. The human is not simply a machine that depends on external stimuli, but instead an organism that evaluates its own efforts, rewards and punishes itself, and can regulate its own behavior without outside control. Many of the theories we examine here assume such self-reactive capacities (for example, achievement motivation, self-awareness, social comparison), but they do not address the origins of self-regulation. The development of various self-reward patterns has been studied within the social learning context with some regularity. The kinds of issues dealt with here have considerable applied importance for the social atmosphere conducive to the beginnings of self-control. For instance, does a child come to learn stringent self-reward patterns more by modeling after another child or after an adult? Is modeling the better procedure for instilling patterns of self-reward and self-punishment, or is it more effective to teach the child such values directly—without providing a model for purposes of imitation?

The procedure of these studies comes originally from Gelfand (1962), who created a little bowling game for children. The basic ingredients are a 3-ft bowling lane, a feedback system with signal lights that tells the player how many points have accumulated, and a nearby supply of rewards. The rewards are typically tokens that can later be exchanged for valued prizes.

In an investigation by Bandura, Grusec, and Menlove (1967), subjects aged 7–11 observed an adult model play the bowling game. After each superior performance the model engaged in self-praise and also took some tokens—characteristic behavior for models in the bowling paradigm. Slightly later the subjects also had a chance to play the bowling game, and for the most part, it was found that their self-reward patterns resembled those of the model quite closely.

Some of the subjects were exposed to a peer (child) model as well as the adult. The peer model's performance standards were not nearly as stringent as those of the adult, and as a result, subjects in this condition subsequently showed less demanding standards than subjects who saw just an adult.

Although this experiment shows that a child model with weak standards can interfere with the modeling of strict adult standards, it says nothing about the relative effectiveness of adult and child models. This issue was addressed in an earlier experiment by Bandura and Kupers (1964), who also applied the bowling-game paradigm to youthful subjects. They reasoned that the adult would be the more influential model, since adults are more often associated with rewarded performance.

The children saw only one model, who was either a same-age peer (about 8 years old) or an adult, play the bowling game. The model (whether adult or child) was either quite strict or else more lenient in administering the self-reward of M&M candies. Then subjects had a chance to try the bowling game with the model absent. The strict/lenient variable had a strong effect: children who had watched a lenient model were more lenient in rewarding themselves. And children who had watched an adult model rewarded themselves in much closer accordance with the model's standards than did those who had watched a peer model.

Independent of which sort of model is more effective, one may also ask whether modeling is a more effective procedure than directly rewarding the person. In teaching a child puritanical, nonindulgent behaviors, would it be better to model those behaviors or to reward the child directly according to strict criteria? This issue was explored by Mischel and Liebert (1966), who used fourth-grade children in the familiar bowling paradigm. Once again the model was an adult, and the procedure was oriented around the strict/lenient distinction. The procedure differed from those reported above in that the child played the bowling game together with the model, and the model controlled the reinforcements. In one condition she was strict both with the child and with herself, in a second condition she remained strict with herself but rewarded the child for mediocre performance, and in the third condition she was lenient with self-reward but strict with the child.

Given these differential experiences, how does the child sort out the conflicting information? That is, how are the learning experiences reflected in behavior when the child bowls alone? Not surprisingly, children showed the most "puritanical," or self-denying, behavior when the model had been consistently strict. When she was inconsistent (more generous with the child than with herself or vice versa), then the way she rewarded the child proved to be more influential than the way she rewarded herself.

In summary, these three studies make the point that children can incorporate standards of excellence (or of mediocrity) through observing the self-reward patterns of a model. It also appears than an adult is a more persuasive model than a peer and that direct training by an adult is more potent than simply observing the adult.

SPECIAL TOPICS

Nature and Scope of the Theory

Social learning theory is more general than any other theoretical scheme we will examine. It has been applied to the learning and performance of such diverse behaviors as fear responses, physiological responses, aggression, and self-regulatory behaviors. Indeed, there are few social behaviors than cannot be analyzed using social learning theory. In contrast, the theories reviewed in other chapters focus on a single class of behavior (such as achievement) or on a relatively limited number of situations in which a single process is engaged (for example, reactance theory deals with situations in which a person's freedom is threatened).

As a result of this breadth, social learning theory is more concept-packed than the other theories. Under the umbrella of Bandura's theoretical scheme we find such concepts as direction of attention, learning, motivation to perform, emotion, and social comparison. In any other chapter, almost any one of these would be an adequate basis for building an entire theory. The other theories typically revolve around a single psychological process, and the associated research deals with specifying the conditions that lead to the process and the end result. "Dissonance" is the basic process in dissonance theory, and the main idea of Chapter 6 is to identify circumstances that set dissonance off. In the attribution chapters "rational thinking and conclusion drawing" is the central process, and again the research is designed to detail the directions taken by that process.

There are obviously great advantages in a general theory that can account for nearly all social phenomena with its many and varied concepts. But generality comes at a cost in that it sacrifices predictive ability. There are so many concepts to keep track of that the researcher has a difficult time sorting out the causes and effects of each one. To take an example, an incentive offered to the model for performing a behavior may affect observers in three ways: it may draw their attention to the model's behavior, it may lead them to rehearse mentally their coded representation of the behavior, or it may increase their motivation to perform. In any given instance it is difficult to know which of the three stages is being affected. A similar problem applies with age of the model (Bandura & Kupers, 1964). If adults are more effective models than children, is it because they attract more attention, because they stimulate mental rehearsal and hence better learning, or because they motivate subjects to perform?

This is not to suggest that other theoretical frameworks are free of these kinds of criticisms. Even "mature" theories like cognitive dissonance (Chapter 6), with refinements based on over 20 years of research, do not indicate how one is to manipulate "importance of cognitions" and "number of dissonant cognitions" independently. And in Fiedler's leadership theory (Chapter 16), which shares the applied orientation of Bandura's social learning theory, a manipulation of leader type may also affect group conditions—even though leader type and group conditions are independent factors within the theory.

Even more difficult is the case of a variable's having opposite effects on the different stages of the learning process. Unique or deviant models may well draw the observer's attention but may either interfere with or facilitate coding and rehearsal and may either interfere with or facilitate motivation to perform. If an observer performed fewer imitative behaviors after watching a deviant than a more normal model, it would be difficult to pin down theoretically just why this occurred.

Orientation of Social Learning Theory

These problems have not been of central concern for social learning theory, because its orientation is quite different from that of most other theories we consider. With its research often directed toward clinically related phenomena, it has dealt more heavily with applications than with pinning down the precise theoretical reasons for the phenomena. Indeed, the emphasis has been more on discovering the exact set of conditions that will produce maximal change in behavior.

A second force behind Bandura's research has been his critical reaction to traditional learning theorists. As noted earlier, much of his writing and research has documented the importance of modeling in learning important social behaviors. Bandura has also shown that learning can take place without direct reinforcement of the observer, a position in sharp contrast to that of traditional learning theorists. In response to critics who have argued that mechanistic learning theories do not account for such behaviors as self-denial or creativity, Bandura has amply illustrated that stringent or lenient self-reward and some types of creativity can be transmitted through modeling. Thus a number of phenomena thought by critics to be outside the purview of social learning theory can indeed be produced by modeling.

Results of This Orientation

The preceding discussion implies that social learning theory provides general analyses of a range of important problems, such as identification, aggression, and moral behavior. It is also a fruitful starting point in designing therapeutic interventions involving behavior change. At the same time, it should be recognized that the multiplicity of processes studied sets the theory apart from most other theories, in the sense that the focus of research in this area is not characteristically aimed at establishing the determinants of one given psychological process.

We might examine this latter issue in more detail. Consider how independent variables are selected for inclusion in an experiment. In Bandura's earlier research, variables were often studied that were ecologically valid (that is, having an immediate real-world impact) and either (1) had been found to have an effect in previous research or (2) by common sense seemed likely to affect learning or performance. Some of this early research varied such factors as the age, sex, and nurturance of the model. As noted above, such variables can affect the learning process at several points. In contrast to this approach, investigators interested solely in the theoretical bases of modeling would probably try to identify independent variables that should affect the process at only one point. Such research might, for instance, vary the salience of the model, a variable that should affect only the observer's attentional process.

Perhaps the critical issue for the theory is how the variables affecting each stage of the learning process are integrated. The answer is that they are, in large part, not integrated. The research has commonly identified a number of subprocesses (attention, coding, motoric reproduction, motivation) and specified a number of variables that generally affect each subprocess. This has led to an unusual theoretical scheme in which such subprocesses as attention are defined, followed by a list of variables that may affect this subprocess (model attractiveness, model nurturance, proffered rewards, and televised presentation). This scheme is not very parsimonious, nor is it very predictive. The theory offers few clues as to how the variables should act in combination. For example, what would the effect be of having a nurturant model offer rewards? Would the amount of imitation be higher than when a nonnurturant model offered rewards? Perhaps it would, but we would not be too surprised if there were no difference or even if the nonnurturant model were imitated more under these conditions than the nurturant model.

Major research efforts are still required in order to comprehend fully the theoretical ways in which the stages of the learning process fit together, but Bandura and his colleagues have taken some important first steps toward elucidating the precise determinants of the individual learning stages. For instance, Bandura and Jeffery (1973) have undertaken a careful experimental analysis of the impact of different forms of rehearsal and have found that overt motor rehearsal of an action is less effective for later reproduction than verbal rehearsal of the symbolized actions. Similarly, Bandura, Jeffery, and Bachicha (1974) have investigated the memory codes involved in observational learning. Such research holds the promise of greatly increasing our understanding of the stages of observational learning. However, we might keep in mind that the task of specifying the operation of variables is uniquely complicated within this theory because the scope of phenomena to be analyzed and the number of psychological processes entailed cumulate to the sum of several social psychological theories taken together.

SUMMARY

The social learning theory of Bandura is a novel effort to provide an understanding of the intricate means by which new and complex behavioral repertoires are created. The theory is invaluable as an answer to the more traditional learning theory approaches to similar problems, for Bandura's theory is unique in giving the human credit for learning new actions through the process of observation and mental rehearsal. The responsibility that the theory gives to the individual learner is great: In Bandura's scheme the person can develop behaviors through self-administered reward, the new behavioral repertoire can develop largely through thinking about the individual actions, and perhaps most important, reward is not assigned the simple function of "stamping in" new behaviors. Rather, rewards motivate one to act, call attention to acts to be performed, and stimulate the person to rethink a behavioral sequence.

Although such a theoretical scheme is important for its recognition of the role of cognitive work in the learning process, the number of psychological processes it postulates is rather great. In this respect the theory stands out as unique in this book, for research surrounding the theory has not had the simple task of examining one specific psychological process. The subject of social learning theory remains a multiplicity of interrelated psychological processes, and the correct application of the theory must recognize the complex series of psychological events that underlies the acquisition of new behaviors.

SUGGESTED READING

Bandura, A. Vicarious processes: A case of no-trial learning. In L. Berkowitz (Ed.), *Advances in experimental social psychology* (Vol. 2). New York: Academic Press, 1965.

Bandura, A. *Social learning theory.* Englewood Cliffs, N.J.: Prentice-Hall, 1977.

Rosenthal, T. L., & Zimmerman, B. J. *Social learning and cognition.* New York: Academic Press, 1978.

Staub, E. *Positive social behavior and morality* (Vol. 2). New York: Academic Press, 1979.

PART TWO

COGNITIVE CONSISTENCY

The ideas discussed here may be said to stem out of the Gestalt psychology tradition of the 1920s and '30s. The three chapters illustrate the human propensity toward finding balance, or consistency, among our thoughts and perceptions. Originally this Gestalt-based thinking had primarily to do with the psychology of perception, but as transformed by the three notions here, the issue of cognitive balance or consistency now has largely to do with the immediate social situation and the way it is viewed or ordered by the individual participant.

The focus of balance theory (Chapter 5) is on the two-person relationship. The balance principle tells us when someone will feel uncomfortable in a relationship, particularly as a function of the way each of the two persons thinks about some third object or person. The theory then spells out the forms of cognitive restructuring undergone in the interest of participants trying to bring a sense of cognitive "fit" to a relationship.

Cognitive dissonance theory (Chapter 6) concerns itself mainly with the psychology of the person who has just made a decision and who must live with its consequences. The theory discusses the ways in which we come to bias our perceptions in the interest of placing the outcome of the decision in a more positive light.

Equity theory (Chapter 7) — originally an elaboration on the cognitive dissonance principle — brings our focus to the investments and outcomes of people in interactions. In the context of the workplace, equity theory describes the satisfactions and dissatisfactions experienced as a result of individuals' comparing their amount of work and compensation against that of other relevant people. Away from the workplace, the theory addresses the same kinds of issues; here investments and compensations are viewed broadly and include love, kindness, and compliments. The central theme running through the applications of equity is simple: when people calculate the investments they make in a relationship and compare those against the benefits received, the benefit-to-investment ratio should be similar in magnitude to the benefit-to-investment ratio of other participants in the relationship.

CHAPTER 5

BALANCE THEORY

FOR SOME reason we are fraught with discomfort when we witness two friends or lovers who do not share reciprocal feelings for each other. One member of the pair exhibits devoted affection, while the other remains aloof. Why do we think there is something wrong with the dynamics of such a relationship? Is there something inside us that is disturbed at the thought of a relationship that is unequal, nonreciprocal, or unbalanced? The universality of the discomfort created in us by such a pair of persons suggests that reactions to "nonfitting" relationships are deeply rooted in our makeup.

Suppose we try to change our perception of such a relationship in the interest of reducing our discomfort. One approach is to try to imagine the aloof member as an affectionate and devoted companion, and if this could be accomplished, we would then view the situation as "reciprocal," "equal," "balanced," and "correct." There is another tack: Why not try to view the relationship as nonexisting? Now the situation can be pictured as one person who is aloof, another who still is affectionate, and a nonrelationship. Yet, since one member continues to be affectionate, a relationship is still implied. We continue to experience discomfort; we still know something is amiss or unbalanced. The final resolution is to distort our perception of the situation, trying to view the perpetually affectionate member as a ruggedly independent individual. If we are successful in altering our perception, everything fits and we experience a degree of comfort.

GESTALT PSYCHOLOGY: THE FOUNDING IDEAS

The theoretical thinking basic to our understanding of unbalanced situations like the one described above has its roots in what is known as Gestalt psychology. *Gestalt* may be translated from the German as "configuration." Gestalt psychology deals with the manner in which different objects and events are perceived as configurations. More specifically, the Gestalt approach has focused on the way humans, through processes of perception, build isolated events into meaningful forms. Most of the research and theoretical thinking associated with the Gestalt tradition has dealt with perception of inanimate objects (Koffka, 1935; Köhler, 1940; Wertheimer, 1923). It is Heider (1946, 1958) who has applied the principles of Gestalt psychology to interaction between humans and who has caused us to think about our discomfort on witnessing a nonreciprocal intimate relationship.

Our understanding of the psychological imbalance created in observers of the above example of nonreciprocated affection can be traced directly to a discussion of perception by Wertheimer (1923), who has described two important factors in perception. One is the *proximity* factor, which means that two elements (of any kind) that are perceived will be seen as belonging together to the extent that they are near one another. The other factor has to do with *equality:* two elements are perceived as belonging together if they resemble each other in form. These laws, or factors, were originally illustrated with examples pertaining to perception of inanimate objects. For instance, take the following row of boring little asterisks to be your "visual field":

** ** ** ** **

What is perceived here is probably not a line of ten discrete asterisks, but instead five small groups. Let us now change the example slightly and group ten different symbols in a similar manner:

$$@ \ \# \ \$\% \ ¢\& \ ^* + \ ? =$$

The tendency to perceive the symbols as five small groups is weakened because the symbols have a lower degree of equality than the identical asterisks. Thus, your perception of the situation (field) follows Wertheimer's ideas precisely in that the "equal" asterisks that are in close proximity have an "attraction" to each other that sets each pair off from the next, whereas the "unequal" symbols do not show a similar "attraction."

    This kind of reasoning may be extended from asterisks to humans, a possibility recognized by Koffka (1935, p. 654) and elaborated by Heider. When two persons are seen to be in close proximity, and when they have some basis for equality with each other, the perceiver tends to view them as attracted to each other. Hence, our discomfort in viewing a nonreciprocal relationship is understandable using a 1923 law of Gestalt psychology.

    To summarize, the Gestalt psychologists assume simple laws of "good form" or "good figure" as their basic unit of analysis. These laws are then used as the basic structure for analyzing the attractions between objects or people.

    In applying this approach to humans, Heider has based much of his social psychological thinking on a very general Gestalt law, known as Prägnanz. The general idea behind Prägnanz is that the perception of any situation will tend to be coherent. In other words, in perceiving the elements of any "field," we will attempt to impose a meaningful structure, balance, and completeness. Heider's reasoning is quite global, yet it has led to a number of highly specific applications in social psychology.

    Before turning to a more complete description of Heider's theory, we would like to offer one further illustration of his field of interest. Not long before this writing, Senator Sam Ervin of North Carolina visited the University of Texas. Senator Ervin had recently completed his work as chairman of the Senate "Watergate Committee," in which he played a pivotal role in uncovering Nixon administration scandals. His presence created intense interest, and predictably the auditorium was packed with members of the university community.

    Senator Ervin chose to begin his remarks with a few ingratiating words for the Austin audience. Among his friendly overtures he expressed some highly complimentary thoughts about the former First Lady, Lady

Bird Johnson, who at the time was a highly regarded member of the University of Texas board of regents.

What is the impact of Senator Ervin's forming an association between himself and Lady Bird Johnson? Does the audience like him better—or worse? Before moving on to Heider's analysis, we might try to arrive at an answer by common sense. If we assume that the audience was generally favorable toward Mrs. Johnson, the senator seemingly would have nothing to lose by associating himself with her. It would be discomforting—and unbalanced—to feel a strong liking toward Mrs. Johnson while feeling an aversion toward her close associates. In short, if the audience began with uncertain or ambivalent attitudes toward Ervin, his remarks should have worked in his favor. If they began with an intense affection for him, his remarks would have been unnecessary, because there would have been no further affection to gain from the audience.

THE THEORY

How would Heider analyze the examples we have discussed? First, he would identify the way the social (or physical) entities are connected to each other. Heider distinguishes two types of associations, which he terms *unit relations* and *sentiment (liking) relations*. We will discuss these two relations separately.

Unit Relations

One means of connection between two entities is through their being perceived as a unit. A married couple is a unit, a father and his offspring form a unit, Erica Jong and her book *Fear of Flying* are a unit, and with respect to the preceding example Senator Ervin and Mrs. Johnson form a unit. More generally, two entities are perceived as forming a unit when they are similar, when they are close in space, when they have a common goal, when they constitute a larger whole, or for a variety of other reasons. The opposite of unity is, of course, disunity. Finally, and most important, Heider says that there is a *positive relation* between two elements characterized by unity, and a *negative relation* exists when two elements are not unified. The relation between a shoemaker and his product is positive, whereas the relation between an atheist and religion is negative.

Liking Relations

The second way two entities can be connected is in terms of liking or disliking. Not surprisingly, Heider calls a liking relation *positive* and a disliking relation *negative*.

Analysis of Dyads

Much of Heider's analysis deals with the case of two entities, such as a dyad (pair) of persons or a person and some object. The central idea is that we tend to view a unity relation as a liking relation and, moreover, a liking relation also tends to be viewed as a unit relation. Returning to our example, if the audience accepts the Ervin-proclaimed unity between himself and Mrs. Johnson, it should then tend to perceive Ervin and Lady Bird as liking each other. Consequently, a dyad is viewed as *cognitively balanced* when the unit and the liking relations are both positive or both negative. It is cognitively upsetting to hear that a couple in love (liking relation) is obtaining a divorce (disunity) or that two enemies are about to marry.

Another source of imbalance within a dyad is nonreciprocity, as in our first example. Heider's analysis of this situation is very simple: there is a tendency to perceive all parts of a unit as homogeneous, meaning it is cognitively unbalanced to find that person A hates B but B likes A.

Analysis of Triads

Heider's analysis also extends to the triad. The question here has to do with the nature of the various unit and liking relations that can exist among the three entities involved. In applying this analysis to triads, we must first decide how to characterize the three possible relations *from the viewpoint of the perceiver.* Analyzing our example from the audience's perspective, Senator Ervin has already established a unit relation (that is, a positive relation) between himself and Mrs. Johnson, Second, the audience already liked Mrs. Johnson, meaning that the audience/Johnson relation is also positive. All that remains is the audience/Ervin relation and according to Heider's rules (which we will discuss below), there will be a tendency for the audience to perceive this final relation as positive. In other words, it will like Senator Ervin.

Heider's rules regarding triadic relations are derived from the Gestalt law of Prägnanz, discussed above. This Gestalt influence can be seen in Heider's definition of a balanced state: "By a balanced state is meant a situation in which the relations among the entities fit together harmoniously; there is no stress towards change" (1958, p. 201). Let us now consider the possible relations among three entities and whether the triad would be perceived as balanced in each case.

1. If all three relations are positive, the triad is balanced. This seems eminently reasonable. If everybody likes everybody else, there is little room for tension.

2. Balance also exists when two of the three relations are negative. We might suppose that some member of the Ervin audience had entered the auditorium with a negative attitude toward Mrs. Johnson. He may, for example, have been at odds with her earlier highway-beautification program, or perhaps he blamed her for the escalation of the Viet Nam war. No matter how this antipathy arose, we now have a situation with one negative relation and one positive, the latter being the unity between Senator Ervin and Mrs. Johnson. Balance can be attained here through adopting an anti-Ervin sentiment, thereby reaching the state of one positive and two negative relations.

3. Imbalance results when one relation is negative and the other two are positive. The characteristic example of this kind of imbalance occurs when two people who like each other disagree over an object or over a third person. A woman might be quite attached to her mother (relation #1) as well as to her husband (relation #2), but the husband/mother-in-law relation (#3) may very well be marred by antagonism.

4. Heider indicates that the case of three negative relations is ambiguous, and for this reason we will not refer to this case in our subsequent discussion.

How is imbalance dealt with? Conceptually the answer is easy. People will try to arrange their cognitions so that all three relations are positive or else so that two of them are negative. (Note that it is always the *cognitions* of a single perceiver that are rearranged; the actual relations are not necessarily physically readjusted.) Any other solution is unsatisfactory according to Heider's theory. But more specifically, how do we know which relation(s) will be altered in order to achieve balance? Although this question cannot be answered in any exact form, it is instructive to examine the primary methods of attaining balance within the context of our Ervin/Johnson example.

Although the majority of the audience arrived with positive feelings toward the senator, there was an important development during the question-and-answer session following the speech. During this session, the audience members were reminded of some of Ervin's positions that they had probably forgotten. Ervin had been a definite "hawk" during the Viet Nam conflict, he had voted against a number of civil-rights bills, and he was unfavorable toward women's liberation. On leaving the auditorium, many members of the university community were now confronted with a strong case of imbalance: They liked Lady Bird Johnson, they had witnessed a positive (unit) relation between her and the senator, but they had come to feel mildly disgruntled with Ervin. From the audience's perspective, there existed a triad of entities connected by one negative and two positive relations. How could the audience have resolved this imbalance? (1) One solution would have been for the audience to deemphasize the senator's stand on the war, civil rights, and women's liberation, focusing instead on his brilliant work during the Watergate hearings. This solution would lead to three positive relations. (2) The audience could have also come to dislike Mrs. Johnson, the result being two negative relations and one positive relation. (3) Finally, the unity relation between Ervin and Johnson could have been altered in the audience's minds. They could have forgotten that Ervin made the complimentary statement about Lady Bird, or they could have attributed the statement to common political motives, thereby undermining its authenticity. Destroying the unit relation would have produced two negative relations and one positive relation, just as in solution 2.

These are the elements of Heider's reasoning. It is a broad framework that has led to a large amount of research, controversies, and the further development of cognitive consistency theories. At this point, we will take a brief look at some of the kinds of research that Heider's balance theory has generated.

BALANCE AND INTERPERSONAL LIKING: RESEARCH EXAMPLES

When a Disliked Defendant Is Found Guilty

One of Heider's more important ideas is that people want to see the parts of a unit as homogeneous. Taking a person as our unit, the implication of Heider's idea is rather clear: If we have a generally positive opinion of someone, we then tend to view all of that person's particular traits and behaviors in a positive light. In contrast, if we are negatively disposed toward some person, we are likely to vilify other features of the person that are brought to our attention. This principle has some ominous implications for jury trials. Should a defendant be obtrusively ugly, disreputable, or disliked for any reason, a jury would be prone to associate that person with the crime in question. It is cognitively balanced to associate undesirable behaviors with an undesirable person.

Landy and Aronson (1969) tested this idea by asking students to play the role of jurors. They were asked to determine the number of years in prison that should be served by a defendant who had been charged with negligent homicide. The homicide was quite definitely a reprehensible act, in that the defendant first became inebriated at a party, rejected an offer of a ride home, and finally killed an innocent pedestrian.

In order to vary the personal attractiveness of the defendant, Landy and Aronson gave the jurors one of three descriptions of the defendant: attractive, unattractive, or neutral. The attractive defendant was said to be friendly and a good worker. The unattractive defendant was described as a janitor who, in spite of having been divorced twice, was currently married and was still engaging in flagrant adultery. The neutral defendant was given no special positive or negative traits.

Given the above description, the jury members now had to recommend a prison sentence for the defendant. Applying Heider's analysis, how should the jurors perceive the defendant in order to attain a state of cognitive balance? If the defendant is liked, there should be a tendency to view all aspects of the person as positive, meaning that the jury should lean toward excusing him for the homicide. When the defendant is disliked, however, balance would be achieved by perceiving the defendant as a blameworthy, wicked person. The results were consistent with this analysis: the personally attractive defendant was given a 5.5-year sentence, on the average; the neutral defendant was given 6.0 years; and the janitor/adulterer was given the longest sentence, 7.1 years.

This type of effect is by no means limited to the domain of attractive versus reprehensible personalities. It should also be possible to vary simple physical attractiveness with similar results. In fact, Sigall and Ostrove (1975) have done exactly this, once again in the context of subjects making decisions about a defendant's sentence. When subjects were told that a physically attractive female defendant had been accused of burglary (a crime unrelated to her physical attractiveness), the mean sentence handed down to her was 2.8 years. In contrast, a physically unattractive defendant accused of the same crime was given a judgment of 5.2 years.

The results of these experiments, then, suggest that observers tend to perceive others as having consistently positive or consistently negative traits and behaviors.

The Just World

Research by Lerner and his associates illustrates a potentially cruel element in human nature that appears to stem from balance-theory principles. A typical example is an experiment by Lerner and Simmons (1966) in which subjects watched a peer receive electric shocks and then indicated how personally attractive they found the suffering person. If they expected the victim to continue to receive shocks, they showed considerable derogation of her (giving low attractiveness ratings). This derogation was greater than in a condition in which the victim had suffered in the past but would not suffer any longer.

Why should people perceive a helpless victim to be personally unattractive? Lerner proposes that people generally believe in a just world, in the sense that punishments and rewards are usually seen as merited. In balance-theory terms, the fact that an attractive and likable woman was being shocked and would continue to be shocked would create imbalance. A balanced state could be restored by coming to regard her as unattractive, thus rendering her deserving of her suffering. However, when the woman would no longer be shocked, the unit relation between the woman and suffering had already changed to disunity, and so there should be little motivation to alter one's perception of the woman's attractiveness.

This finding complements Landy and Aronson's experiment quite well. In Landy and Aronson's experiment, an unattractive defendant was given a stiff penalty; in Lerner and Simmons', a person who received a stiff penalty was viewed as unattractive. The conceptual point is simple: feelings about people and their particular traits or actions tend to be brought into cognitive alignment—either consistently positive or consistently negative.

Our Enemy's Enemy Is Our Friend

Much of the interest surrounding Heider's balance theory has involved the triangular situation exemplified by our Ervin/Johnson/audience example. An experiment by Aronson and Cope (1968) illustrates

Heider's analysis. The experimenter gave the subject feedback on his performance on a series of tasks in either a pleasant or a harsh manner. The purpose of this first stage of the experiment was to create either a positive or a negative liking bond between the subject and the experimenter. Then the experimenter's supervisor entered and gave the experimenter an evaluation of a report that the experimenter had previously written. In one condition, the supervisor totally belittled the experimenter's report, claiming it was "virtually worthless." In another condition, the experimenter's report received high praise. Note that the supervisor's evaluation was unrelated to the experimenter's treatment of the subject.

From the subject's viewpoint there are three relations in this interpersonal situation: the relation between himself and the experimenter (which is either positive or negative), the relation between the supervisor and the experimenter (which also is either positive or negative), and finally the relation between himself and the supervisor. This last relation is the one that was measured. Aronson and Cope assumed that the subject's willingness to help the supervisor in a further research project would be an index of the subject/supervisor relation. At this point we can return to our Heiderian analysis:

1. What should happen when the subject has been insulted by the experimenter, but the experimenter has been complimented by the supervisor? To complete the triad of relations in a balanced way, the subject should try to make the relation between himself and the supervisor negative, which means that he would be unlikely to offer much help to the supervisor. This is exactly what happened. In short, our enemy's friend is our enemy.

2. Changing the above situation just slightly, what happens when the supervisor derogates the experimenter? Now we have two negative relations in the triad, which means that balance is attained if the third one is made positive. And indeed, subjects offered a great deal of help to the supervisor in this case, revealing a positive subject/supervisor relation. This condition was the essence of the experiment: our enemy's enemy is our friend.

3. Suppose the experimenter is friendly toward the subject, and the supervisor gives the experimenter harsh treatment. Again, we have one positive and one negative relation, so that the subject should try to create a further negative relation by not offering much help to the supervisor. As it happened, the amount of help was indeed quite low in this condition.

4. Given a friendly experimenter followed by a complimenting supervisor, the simplest route to balance is to create a third positive relation. Predictably, subjects in this condition offered a great deal of assistance.

This experiment is a classic example of the kind of dissociation from others that is predicted by balance theory. Given a triadic set of relations, the individual will try to cognize them in such a way that either they are all positive or two out of three are negative. Subjects might conceivably have chosen another route to cognitive balance. For example, subjects in Condition 2 could have distorted all the negative input, perceiving all relations as positive, and this would have short-circuited the enemy's-enemy outcome. In some instances that kind of distortion might be preferred, but in the present situation the reality of the feedback was quite imposing: it would have been difficult to deny either of the negative relations and therefore the only remaining method of attaining cognitive balance was to create an appropriate positive (or negative) bond between oneself and the supervisor. Later in this chapter we will have more to say on the subject of different routes to balance.

SPECIAL TOPICS

Unpleasantness of Balanced States

Our attention thus far has been given to the variety of ways in which people go about restoring or creating balanced sets of cognitions, but there remains an aspect of Heider's theorizing that we have not yet addressed. This is the question of the unbalanced state itself. Is it uncomfortable? Does it make people feel tense or nervous? The reader's common sense will probably answer yes. It is often uncomfortable or tension-provoking to discover that a supposed friend dislikes us or that Senator Ervin is both liberal and conservative.

Although there is some reason to think of a balanced state as pleasant, it also makes sense that certain kinds of imbalanced states might be even more pleasant. Suppose that a child perceives a strong positive relation between his mother and father, but at the same time he despises each of them, and they feel the same way toward him. From the child's viewpoint this is a balanced situation: there are two negative relations and one positive. But it is unlikely that the child will consider this situation very pleasant. Now, suppose one of the parent/child relations were changed to positive. In particular, we might suppose that the mother loves the child and loves her husband but that the husband still dislikes the child. In this situation we have two positive relations and one negative relation. This is an unbalanced state of affairs, but it certainly seems more pleasant than the previous one.

A number of studies have now shown that positive relations between people might be at least as strong a source of pleasantness as a balanced relationship. To take one example, Gutman and Knox (1972) asked college students to rate a number of situations on the dimensions of pleasantness and consistency. The situations given to the subjects were similar to the following:

> You have an associate whom you like, and the associate likes you. Your associate dislikes something that you like.

In our example there is mutual liking between the two persons, but imbalance is created in that they disagree about the "something." This means that the subject should perceive one negative relation and two positive relations and should therefore find the situation unbalanced. By comparison, the following example would be balanced:

> You have an associate whom you dislike, and the associate dislikes you. Your associate dislikes something that you like.

The results were striking. On ratings of unpleasantness, the unbalanced situation that was characterized by mutual liking was seen as much more pleasant than the balanced, mutual-dislike situation. In contrast, when subjects were asked how consistent they thought each situation was, they rated the balanced situations as more consistent than the unbalanced situations.

The results of Gutman and Knox's experiment and other experiments that have addressed the same issue lead to a simple conclusion. A balanced situation is characterized by good form, or good Gestalt, but is not necessarily pleasant. That is, balanced states are perceived as being consistent, and they are easy to learn and easy to remember, but they will not necessarily be perceived as pleasant unless all three relations are positive.

Methods of Attaining Balance

We have already discussed the multiplicity of methods of attaining balance in the context of the Ervin/Johnson/audience example, but unfortunately Heider does not provide a method by which we can decide which route should be preferred. Following Heider, several psychologists have offered possible solutions to this problem. Abelson (1959) indicates that the easiest method of attaining balance will be preferred, and Feather (1967) suggests that the weakest relation(s) will be the first to change. Some of these suggestions have been followed, at least implicitly, in the research we have considered. For instance, it would have been difficult for the subjects in Aronson and Cope's experimenter/supervisor study to change the two relations that were induced in the situation. They were left with no alternative except to change the third and last relation. Thus, Aronson and Cope created the relations in such a way that the suggestions of Abelson and Feather were implicitly followed.

Exceptions to Balance

We have seen that some kinds of imbalanced situations are more pleasant to perceive than certain kinds of balanced situations. Evidently, mutual liking is often preferred to a balanced situation; a negative relation between two persons is apparently too high a price to pay for a balanced situation. But there are also some other curious circumstances in which balance does not seem quite "right," as the following example illustrates.

Two intense young gentlemen are in love with the same woman. This means that there exist two positive relations—one between suitor A and the woman and the other between suitor B and the woman. How about the third relation in this triad, which is the relation between the two young men? We would commonly expect them to despise each other (out of jealousy), yet this would not be a stable situation according to Heider's analysis. Balance theory would require that all (or just one) of the relations be positive, but common sense tells us that a good Gestalt in this setting is attained by the existence of exactly one negative (jealous) relation.

This particular case is more complicated than the other examples we have considered, because there is a hidden element. *From suitor A's point of view,* B is inhibiting A's progress toward the attractive woman. A's perception is that the woman will be unhappy in her relation with B, which means a perceived *negative* relation between B and the woman. If A does indeed focus on that negative relation, the triad is then balanced, since the only positive relation left is the one between himself and the woman. Needless to say, B's perception of A and the rest of the situation is parallel to that of A. An interesting implication of this analysis is that the two suitors will each find the situation quite balanced, while the woman will simply perceive two positive relations (the attraction of A and B for her) and one negative relation (between A and B). She should find the situation imbalanced and therefore should show more concern with making it balanced than either of her suitors. The solution outlined here to the jealousy problem is quite akin to one proposed by Spinoza (1677/1936), which Heider (1958) discusses.

SUMMARY

Heider's theory of cognitive balance is an important beginning point. By borrowing principles from Gestalt psychology, and through his insightful elaborations, he has provided social psychology with a flexible system that says a great deal about how the individual perceives dyadic and triadic relations. His ideas have led to a great deal of research on interpersonal attraction, on dissociation from others, and, more generally, on the question of how the individuals structure their perceptions of social relations so that they "fit harmoniously."

SUGGESTED READING

Abelson, R. P., Aronson, E., McGuire, W. J., Newcomb, T. M., Rosenberg, M. J., & Tannenbaum, P. H. (Eds.). *Theories of cognitive consistency: A sourcebook.* Chicago: Rand McNally, 1968.

Harvey, J. H., Ickes, W. J., & Kidd, R. F. (Eds.). *New directions in attribution research* (Vol. 1). Hillsdale, N.J.: Erlbaum, 1976.

Harvey, J. H., Ickes, W. J., & Kidd, R. F. (Eds.). *New directions in attribution research* (Vol. 2). Hillsdale, N.J.: Erlbaum, 1978.

Heider, F. *The psychology of interpersonal relations.* New York: Wiley, 1958.

CHAPTER 6

COGNITIVE DISSONANCE THEORY

BRENDA Moon is a creative, energetic Phi Beta Kappa at a university renowned for its journalism department. For years she has planned on a life career in some aspect of journalism, and now, in the last semester of her senior year, she must decide on her professional directions. Representatives from the *New York Times*, *Paris Match*, the *Midnight Star*, and the *London Times*, among others, begin contacting her with offers of a position as beginning reporter. She begins to think about the relative merits of these offers and also contemplates such issues as salary.

In the midst of these interviews her wealthiest uncle arrives in town. For years he has been expanding his real-estate business and has been specializing in homes in new, lower-middle-class subdivisions. The uncle is known to be unscrupulous in his real-estate dealings, and so Brenda was never very attracted to him.

Out of nowhere he makes her an exciting job offer: he will start her in his local office at $35,000 a year, with a strong probability of clearing over $100,000 a year after she gains two or three years' selling experience. Brenda knows the offer is realistic, as his son has done at least this well in the short time he has sold real estate.

In no time she is in deep conflict. By accepting the real-estate position, she stands to make four times as much as she would as a reporter. Further, there would be some advantages to staying close to home in case she wanted to raise a family. However, the reporter's job would be more exciting, she would get to meet international personalities, and besides, she was trained to do that kind of work. But finally she succumbs to her uncle's appealing offer and signs on at the real-estate office, going to work immediately.

Some curious changes take place in Brenda's thinking shortly after her decision. For one, she starts to derogate journalism as a way of life and also curtails her associations with former friends who followed the journalism route. Further, she begins to view real estate as a highly involving profession and listens attentively to her uncle's monologues about her potential in real estate. She also takes extreme pride in the first house she sells. These "postdecisional" effects stemming out of Brenda's decision are illustrations of the workings of cognitive dissonance.

THE THEORY

Festinger's (1957) theory of cognitive dissonance has been the most influential cognitive consistency theory to grow out of Gestalt psychology. Just as in Heider's thinking (Chapter 5), the fundamental psychological processes described by Festinger are ultimately traceable to a simple law of Prägnanz, which means that perceptions of events are structured into meaningful patterns. However, there is only scant similarity between Heider's and Festinger's formulations once we move from the law of Prägnanz to the detailed elaboration of the theory.

Dissonance theory has evolved in several directions since its original statement. In a current interpretation that is quite similar to the original (Brehm & Cohen, 1962; Wicklund & Brehm, 1976), it is a consistency theory about the person who has recently made a decision. The person's awareness of having made a decision is our starting point, and we will trace the psychological processes from that point forward.

Just as with all theories of cognitive consistency, the central concepts of dissonance theory are "cognitions"—that is, elements of knowledge, or individual instances of opinions, beliefs, or values. It has come to be an axiom that cognitions about decisions already made are highly resistant to change. Brenda's decision to sell real estate was central to the dissonance analysis, as the decision was highly resistant to change. Given this starting point, it is then assumed that the amount of cognitive dissonance produced in the context of a decision is a function of the number (and importance) of cognitions that are "dissonant" with (contrary to) the direction taken in the decision. The knowledge that she was already trained to be a journalist, as well as the excitement of working abroad for a big newspaper or magazine, was dissonant with the decision to stay home in the real-estate business.

Next, we may assume that all cognitions implying that the decision should have been made are "consonant." *Consonant* means that a cognition is in alignment with the direction of a decision. Two such cognitions in the example were the expectation of a fabulous income and the uncle's compelling arguments for the advantages of a career in real estate.

Finally, the theory postulates that cognitive dissonance is created to the degree that there are many dissonant cognitions but only few consonant cognitions. Dissonance is said to be a tension state, and the person experiencing cognitive dissonance is thereby motivated to reduce that state. There are two general ways in which this can be accomplished: by reducing dissonant cognitions or by adding consonant cognitions.

It will be useful to elaborate on our example in order to illustrate how the theory works. The starting point is a decision, and in our example this is the decision to go to work in the real-estate office. The cognition (knowledge) of having decided is firm and is highly resistant to change. Now, in the situation, what cognitions are dissonant with and what cognitions are consonant with the initial decision? Any cognitions implying that the decision for a career in real estate should have been made are consonant—for example, monetary advantages, the thrill of making a sale, and the uncle's convincing arguments. Also consonant are any unattractive features of the career in journalism, such as unpredictable working conditions and physical dangers encountered by reporters. Dissonant cognitions would exist in the form of anything unappealing about real estate (the uncle's sleazy selling tactics; repetitious job), as well as anything appealing about the rejected alternative (the excitement of reporting for a newspaper; performing a job for which one is trained).

If any dissonant cognitions are present, dissonance is aroused and the person is motivated to reduce that tension state. How is dissonance reduced? By adding more consonant cognitions, subtracting dissonant ones, or both. The most common type of dissonance reduction, at least in research, is the distortion of attractiveness of the decision alternatives. A person who finds something good in the chosen alternative and who can also derogate the unchosen alternative is thereby increasing consonant elements and reducing dissonant elements.

Not only did the heroine above demonstrate these kinds of cognitive changes, but she also engaged in something called "selective exposure," meaning that she exposed herself to information that was consonant with her choice and avoided discrepant information. By listening to her uncle revel in the delights of the real-estate business, she was selectively exposing herself to consonant cognitions, and by refusing to associate with former journalism majors, she avoided contact with discrepant information.

This is a good place to reemphasize a crucial point: the decision serves as a starting point for the dissonance analysis because the cognition of having chosen is highly resistant to change. This is crucial because dissonance theory assumes that the cognitive work involved in dissonance reduction will be performed on whatever cognitions are not too resistant to change. This means, for instance, that attitudes about the enjoyment of selling are easily changed, since they are not firmly anchored in physical reality. In contrast, there is no good way to tell oneself that a decision has not been made; hence, people generally have to live with their decisions, and dissonance between the nature of the decision and other cognitions will normally be reduced by changes in those other cognitions.

Responsibility

Dissonance theory is not simply a theory about inconsistent cognitions. It is a notion about the cognitive work of the person who has recently made a decision and who is *responsible* for the outcomes of that action. By "responsible" we mean that people who decide feel that there is some clear connection between themselves and the outcome of their decisions. But before we can conclude anything about responsibility, we must first know how to define it in detail.

The accumulated research on dissonance theory has indicated that the outcome of a decision must be *freely chosen* and *foreseen* before that outcome can arouse dissonance. The combination of these two elements defines responsibility. Both elements were present in our example. Brenda was completely free to choose either occupation, and she knew the qualities of the jobs before deciding. In other words, she was aware at the time of choosing of the effects of her decision. If either choice or fore-seeability of consequences had been missing from the situation, the result would have been an absence of dissonance. Had her family insisted on her staying in the community under threat of being disinherited, or had she known nothing about her uncle or his business before committing herself, there should have been no dissonance. Under this latter condition her uncle's sleazy operations would have been an unforeseen conse-quence and should not have contributed to dissonance arousal.

There is one special exception to this foreseeability rule. If some cen-tral aspect of the person, such as a personality trait or ability, leads to the unforeseen and undesired consequence, dissonance reduction can then be observed (Sogin & Pallak, 1976). What this means is that central aspects of the self, such as important abilities, are sources of responsibility in the same way as free choice and foreseeability of consequences. Brenda might have taken a reporter's job with a prestigious newspaper, expecting to perform well in light of her college training. If she had then been fired a month later because of inadequate writing skills, dissonance should have been generated because a central aspect of herself—writing abil-ity—led to the consequence. And this would be so even if the firing were unforeseen.

Dissonance as a Tension State

Festinger's theory bears a certain parallel to other notions discussed in this volume, particularly Zajonc's treatment of social facilitation (Chap-ter 2) and Schachter's treatment of emotion (Chapter 12), in that cognitive dissonance is characterized by drive, or arousal. There is one convincing kind of evidence supporting the idea that the state of dissonance leads to physiological arousal (Kiesler & Pallak, 1976). This evidence is ex-emplified by the research of Waterman (1969), in which dissonance was created by inducing subjects to write an essay supporting a position they did not believe in. Subjects then engaged in a verbal task in which there were clear dominant and subordinate responses. (The notion of dominant and subordinate responses is explained in Chapter 2.) As would be ex-pected from the Hull/Spence drive × habit model (see Chapter 2), high-dissonance subjects evidenced a stronger emission of dominant responses than low-dissonance subjects. It can be seen that manipulations of arousal through inducing dissonance are substitutable for audience presence, test anxiety, or other sources of arousal.

In summary, the elaborated theory of cognitive dissonance must take into account two central prerequisites for its successful application: (1) there must be a decision around which the dissonance processes are defined and organized, and (2) the decision must be a responsible one, normally in the sense of the person's having free choice and having foreseen the potentially dissonance-arousing consequences. As we have seen, the foreseeability factor may be replaced by involvement of the person's central traits or abilities.

RESEARCH EXAMPLES

Simple Decisions

Brehm (1956) conducted the first experiment on dissonance following simple decisions and set it up as a consumer-preference study. Undergraduate women were given a choice between two distinct consumer items, such as a toaster and a coffeepot, with the understanding that they could keep the chosen one. Subjects were asked both before and after the decision for ratings of the two items. In each case, the chosen item increased in attractiveness, while the unchosen item decreased.

This effect is not hard to analyze using the theory. Suppose the subject decides to choose a toaster. Her cognition corresponding to this decision is highly resistant to change and serves as the focal point for all subsequent dissonance reduction. What are the sources of dissonance? There are two: any undesirable features of the chosen alternative will create dissonance, and so will desirable features of the unchosen alternative. To reduce dissonance the person can try to minimize both of these elements, with the result that the chosen alternative comes to be perceived as more attractive, while the unchosen item falls in attractiveness.

It seems ironic that a person would wait until after a decision to alter ratings of decision alternatives. The rational view of humans would portray them as contemplating carefully the various virtues and deficits of the alternatives and then going into the decision with a degree of confidence and stability. Evidently this is not so. Festinger (1964) has accumulated some evidence indicating that systematic changes in ratings of choice alternatives are not observed during the predecision period and that the postdecision period is indeed characterized by the kinds of biased changes in evaluation noted by Brehm (1956).

The Paradoxical Effect of External Justification

One of the oldest dissonance-arousing techniques is to ask people to argue for positions in which they do not believe. A Protestant might be asked to argue in favor of Catholicism, a member of the Young Socialists could be asked to come out in favor of the Ku Klux Klan, or more generally, someone supporting a simple political belief would be asked to take a public stand in opposition to that belief. This technique works only so long as the request gives the person some feeling of having made a free choice to carry out the discrepant act. If too much force is applied in coercing people to perform the discrepant behavior, they will then not feel responsible for the act, and dissonance effects will not become manifest.

Within this paradigm, which is called the "forced compliance" paradigm, investigators have found it interesting to vary the extent of external justification provided for performing the act. For instance, Linder, Cooper, and Jones (1967) located subjects who favored permitting controversial speakers to speak on campus. These subjects were asked to take an overt, attitude-discrepant stand: they wrote an essay arguing that controversial speakers should be banned from campus. Some of the subjects were given no choice, meaning that they were under a strong obligation to carry out the attitude-discrepant act. These "no choice" subjects should not have felt responsible for their actions, and so dissonance should not have been aroused. Other subjects were given a somewhat free choice: the experimenter indicated that he would like them to argue against controversial speakers, but at the same time he insisted that they were under no obligation to do so.

Now comes the external justification. Each of the two groups described above was divided in half, such that some of the subjects were offered 50¢ and others were offered $2.50 for their attitude-discrepant be-behavior. In dissonance theory this variable has a very clear meaning: Any payment received for an act directly implies that the act should be carried out. In other words, the payment acts as a consonant cognition. Further, the more money offered, the more consonant cognitions, and hence the less dissonance aroused. Therefore, within the free-choice condition, in which subjects are in a position to experience dissonance, there should be more dissonance arousal among those paid less.

How is dissonance measured? In most research of this nature it is argued that subjects can eliminate dissonant cognitions (and simultaneously add consonant ones) by shifting their attitudes in a direction consistent with the attitude-discrepant behavior. More specifically, the subjects of Linder et al. shifted their attitudes in the direction of being opposed to controversial speakers, but only to the extent that they had been given a choice *and* were underpaid.

This finding is called *paradoxical* because of the common-sense idea that people will comply, work, strive, change attitudes, and so on to the degree that they are paid to do so. This common-sense idea has a certain grain of truth to it and is likely to be correct as long as dissonance is not operating. In fact, a similar process is assumed in Byrne's reinforcement/affect model of attraction (Chapter 3), as well as in Bandura's social learning model (Chapter 4). In the Linder et al. no-choice condition, in which dissonance should have been completely absent, subjects did indeed change their attitudes more when they were paid more. However, when dissonance was introduced (that is, in the free-choice condition), that effect was completely reversed, as we have just seen.

This external-justification effect was first noted by Festinger and Carlsmith (1959) and has been replicated since using a great variety of issues and justifications. It works not only with monetary justification but also with such entities as "scientific merit" (Rabbie, Brehm, & Cohen, 1959). The more general point is that as long as a person has chosen to perform some dissonance-arousing act and is responsible for that act and its negative consequences, dissonance reduction will be observed only to the extent that good external justifications do not exist for performing the act.

Some Applications

Whether we focus on the forced compliance or the simple decision paradigm, cognitive dissonance theory has been put to a fruitful use by those wishing to extend the dissonance principle to phenomena observed in a wide array of psychological settings, including interpersonal attraction, consumer behavior, personality processes, and individual motivation. Indeed, Irle and Möntmann (1978), in a recent review, list 856 titles that bear directly on the theory.

One appealing application of the theory is to the area of interpersonal attraction: Kiesler and Corbin (1965) have shown that subjects will come to like a group to the degree that the group indicates a *dislike* for the subject. This result may seem rather astonishing, especially in light of equity theory (Chapter 7), but perhaps it is not so surprising when we analyze Kiesler and Corbin's study according to dissonance theory. In some conditions of the study, the subject was committed to remain in the group and could not readily change this cognition. Accordingly, other cognitions had to be changed, and one readily available means of dissonance reduction was to come to like the group. And as the dissonance stemming from rejection rose to a maximum, subjects tended more and more to try to find something attractive about the other group members.

Another application of dissonance theory has been in the area of "motivational" phenomena, including hunger, thirst, and pain. As an example, an early study by Brehm (1962) investigated the effects of dissonance on thirst. Subjects chose to go without water for several hours, and it was predicted that the dissonance aroused by the commitment would be reduced by subjects' convincing themselves that they were not thirsty. This happened, but only to the extent that an external justification ($5) was *not* provided as an incentive for not drinking. When the subjects had a good external justification (the consonant cognition of $5) for their commitment, little dissonance should be aroused, and consequently the subjects should experience little need to change their feelings of thirst. A number of studies have also shown that hunger and pain are modifiable by dissonance techniques (reviewed in Zimbardo, 1969).

There has also been a sizable research effort to show how the motivational state of dissonance is related to some of the processes discussed in earlier chapters. The research reviewed by Kiesler and Pallak (1976) shows that dissonance-arousal acts as a general drive, thereby enhancing dominant verbal responses. Studies by Drachman and Worchel (1976), Pittman (1975), and Zanna and Cooper (1974) have shown that dissonance is related to the cognitive labeling process described by Schachter's theory of emotion (Chapter 12). These experiments suggest that dissonance may be characterized as a state of arousal plus the explanation that the arousal is due to cognitive inconsistency. If another explanation of the arousal is provided (such as that the arousal is due to a pill or a picture of a female nude), dissonance reduction ceases.

SPECIAL TOPICS

Multiplicity of Effects

A common criticism of dissonance theory (see Brown, 1965) is that subjects in dissonance-arousing situations have a variety of dissonance-reduction methods from which to choose. To cite an example, subjects in an experiment by Brock and Buss (1962) were induced, through a forced-compliance procedure, to administer shocks to an innocent victim. Sometimes the victim was a male and sometimes a female. One of the strongest manifestations of dissonance reduction in that experiment was subjects' coming to feel that they were "obligated" to participate when the victim was female. By telling themselves that their shocking the female victim was not voluntary, they were evidently trying to minimize their feeling of responsibility. When the victim was a male, there was no effect on perceived obligation. Instead, subjects reduced their estimate of the amount of pain experienced by the victim.

But what else might subjects have done? More typically measured would be attitude change toward the victim. Glass (1964) showed that subjects who elect to shock others, under high-choice conditions, come to derogate the victims.

How does the investigator know in advance which of these means of dissonance reduction subjects might implement? And in applying the theory, how would we know where to channel our efforts in trying to measure the person's coping with dissonance? There are at least two general answers to this issue.

One solution comes directly out of the original theory. Some cognitions are more resistant to change than others, and the method used to reduce dissonance will use the least resistant cognitions. For instance, Götz-Marchand, Götz, and Irle (1974) found that subjects would not use a dissonance reduction tactic that affected self-esteem adversely, as long as other tactics were available. This makes perfect sense if we assume that a person's self-esteem is highly resistant to change. Taking this same line of reasoning back to Brock and Buss' (1962) experiment, it can be argued that it is easier for subjects to tell themselves that they were forced to give the shock than to use an alternative, which would be to claim that the shocks did not hurt the female victim.

Although the resistance-to-change concept is an elegant solution, in that it is an integral part of the original theory, the reader may find difficulties in some cases in ascertaining that certain cognitions are more resistant than others. Hence, the solution is a remedy mainly in the more extreme cases.

A second solution is that a means of dissonance reduction may or may not be salient. Sometimes people just do not think of effective ways of rationalizing decisions, and if a certain one can be made especially clear to subjects, their use of it should increase. For example, Götz-Marchand et al. (1974) generated dissonance by giving subjects unfavorable test feed-

back, and when it was suggested to some subjects that the test might possibly be invalid, those subjects relied exclusively on test invalidity as a
route to dissonance reduction. More generally, certain manipulations induce people to think primarily in terms of one method of dissonance reduction, such that the prediction becomes completely clear.

The Role of Attention

It might be implicit in cognitive theories that people must think
about the cognitions, but the issue of the direction of attention has never
received formal treatment within dissonance theory. Other cognitive consistency approaches (see Abelson & Rosenberg, 1958) have proposed that
"not thinking about the inconsistency" is one way of dealing with the lack
of cognitive fit. The implication is that the process of dissonance reduction could be hastened or curtailed by focusing subjects' attention toward
or away from the relevant cognitions. This implication is well supported
in research. When subjects' attention is taken away from the dissonance-
arousing issue and toward irrelevant communications or technical tasks,
dissonance reduction is not at all in evidence (Allen, 1965; Pallak, Brock,
& Kiesler, 1967). Turning the procedure around, the course of dissonance
reduction can be accelerated if subjects' noses are rubbed in the dissonant
cognitions by such attention-focusing devices as shining a light over the
unchosen alternative (Brehm & Wicklund, 1970; Carlsmith, Ebbesen, Lepper, Zanna, Joncas, & Abelson, 1969).

Resistance to Change or Recency?

Of the central theoretical issues, just one remains as a theoretical
mystery. This is Festinger's original idea that the cognition most resistant
to change will serve as the point around which dissonance reduction will
be oriented. The issue here is what, in an empirical sense, does resistance
to change mean? An experiment by Brock (1962) illustrates the problem.
Non-Catholic students were asked to write an essay that favored Catholicism, and consistent with the other examples we have given here, subjects
who chose to write the essay changed their opinions in a pro-Catholic direction. The commitment to the essay apparently served as the source of a

cognition that was highly resistant to change. But what about all the times the Protestant or Jewish subjects had made prior commitments to their own religious institutions? A priori, 18 years of church/synagogue attendance and countless financial and spiritual pledges would be expected to produce a more resistant set of cognitions than would half an hour of essay writing—yet subjects reduced their dissonance by shifting opinions in the direction of the essay, not by bolstering prior attitudes.

This issue seems especially dramatic in Brock's experiment, but it is present in various degrees in virtually all forced-compliance experiments. What can we conclude from this apparent paradox? It is evident that the total number of opinion-relevant actions has very little to do with resistance to change, but instead *recency* begins to take on a central importance (Wicklund & Brehm, 1976). In fact, Bem (see Chapter 8) has made this statement in the context of his own reasoning about self-perception, though he has not extended the argument directly to dissonance theory. It is as though the most recent commitment guided the person's current thinking, at least in the context of cognitive consistency processes, and that the person's history is of little importance. This issue, which has received no direct examination in research, remains probably the most central aspect of dissonance theory yet to be explored.

SUMMARY

Dissonance theory addresses the psychology of the person who has made a decision. In applying the theory, it is useful to keep in mind that dissonance is aroused only when the person is responsible for the decision. Dissonance-arousing consequences of the decision must have been chosen freely and either have been foreseen or be attributable to a central aspect of oneself. Many of the misuses of the theory and failures to find dissonance-reduction effects have been traceable to the absence of these components of responsibility or to the presence of too much justification for the person's actions. Many of the predictions drawn from dissonance theory have seemed contrary to common sense, and it is this quality that has led to the remarkable proliferation of experimental tests and applications of the theory.

SUGGESTED READING

Aronson, E. The theory of cognitive dissonance: A current perspective. In L. Berkowitz (Ed.), *Advances in experimental social psychology* (Vol. 4). New York: Academic Press, 1969.

Brehm, J. W., & Cohen, A. R. *Explorations in cognitive dissonance*. New York: Wiley, 1962.

Festinger, L. *A theory of cognitive dissonance*. Stanford, Calif.: Stanford University Press, 1957.

Festinger, L. *Conflict, decision, and dissonance*. Stanford, Calif.: Stanford University Press, 1964.

Frey, D. (Ed.). *Kognitive Theorien der Sozialpsychologie*. Bern: Huber, 1978.

Irle, M., & Möntmann, V. (Eds.). *Theorie der kognitiven Dissonanz* (by L. Festinger, originally published 1957). Bern: Huber, 1978.

Wicklund, R. A., & Brehm, J. W. *Perspectives on cognitive dissonance*. Hillsdale, N.J.: Erlbaum, 1976.

CHAPTER 7

EQUITY THEORY

SQUIRREL Heights is a settled, quiet American residential community, having slowly developed its traditions over a 50-year period. The neighbors are friendly with one another, share a life-style, and never have to cope with the unusual. One day one of the original Squirrel Heights residents, George Poe, finds that the next-door neighbor has moved out and impatiently awaits the fate of the vacant house.

After a couple of weeks Poe is visited by a Mrs. Trebelocinni, who introduces herself as the new neighbor. She asks to borrow a cup of sugar, inquires about the local school system, and then disappears. The next morning Poe is awakened at 6:00 by the piercing resonance of a mezzo-soprano belting out passages from a famous opera. Even after closing his windows, Poe finds there is no escape: the impact of Verdi and Wagner resounds throughout his entire house. The source of all this is obvious—the new neighbor, Mrs. Trebelocinni, must be a professional opera singer.

Poe is outraged. Not only has he generously given away a cup of sugar to the new family, but now his peace and quiet seem permanently endangered. The whole situation for him is unfair—he suffers because of the neighbors and gains nothing in return. He finds no solution, other than beginning to deprecate the new neighbors.

Just at the height of the crisis Mrs. Trebelocinni reappears and issues a formal dinner invitation. Accepting out of curiosity, Mr. Poe finds himself at a five-course Italian-style banquet, with the finest selection of wines, desserts, and cappuccino. As a hostess, Mrs. Trebelocinni is indeed charming, and she goes out of her way to ascertain from Mr. Poe that her singing is not a source of disturbance. Given the elegance of the meal, Poe begins to think that it might be all right to be awakened to opera: after all, it would be a fair trade. He awakens the next morning at 6:00, once more to the droning solos of Mrs. Trebelocinni but this time with a full stomach plus knowledge that he will be invited back weekly for dinner as long as the Trebelocinnis are his neighbors.

"Is this equitable?" Mr. Poe asks himself. "Is my suffering adequately compensated by the dinner invitation?" His conclusion is positive; it seems to him that the weekly cost-free banquet is appropriate payment for three hours of early-morning disturbance. And at this point the relationship between neighbors stabilizes.

Several weeks later there is a new development. Mr. Trebelocinni arrives at the door, armed with hammer and saw, and explains that he noticed some weather damage to Poe's roof. He asks whether he might scramble up on the roof and spend a few hours replacing shingles. Not wanting to upset anyone's feelings, Poe gives his carpenter neighbor the go-ahead, and as it turns out, the needed roof repairs are extensive, requiring a four-week investment of Mr. Trebelocinni's time. Mr. Poe now senses that the relationship between him and the new neighbors has grown inequitable, and he is not at all sure how to handle the situation. He offers to pay for the carpentry, but they will not take any money. He thinks of backing out of the free-dinner arrangement, but given his commitment, this is unfeasible. He cannot think of any other appropriate means to compensate them.

Curiously, over the next several weeks, Poe develops a disaffection for his new neighbors. He becomes critical of the classy Italian meals, he thinks he notices the roof leaking, and he seems to be finding the singing louder and more dissonant. It is the theory central to this chapter that gives us insight into the workings of Mr. Poe and the neighbors, as well as a sweeping array of interpersonal relationships in general.

THE THEORY

Equity theory was formulated much earlier than the other theories we have discussed, and it has hardly changed in form. The best-known early postulation of an equity theory comes from Thomas Hobbes, writing in the mid-17th century. Hobbes views human nature as a greedy, totally thoughtless commodity, whereby people in a state of nature would do very little except war with one another in the interest of gaining the best and most immediate rewards. In such a condition no one would have any measure of security, and for this reason Hobbes lays down a law of human conduct, noting that individuals should be willing, to the degree others are also willing, to put aside their claims to obtaining everything at will. By this law we should be content to take advantage of others only to the extent that we would allow them to take advantage of us.

It was a long time after the 17th century before social psychologists became interested in equity, but the principle remains approximately the same. For instance, Homans (1961) formulated an idea of "distributive justice," whereby justice prevails when the profit of each person in a relationship is proportional to that person's investment in the relationship. This definition of distributive justice is hardly different from the law set forth by Hobbes: we cannot demand everything from another person; instead, demands can be placed on others only to the degree that they can place demands on us in turn. The early-morning singing of Mrs. Trebelocinni placed a definite demand on Mr. Poe, but distributive justice was reached once Poe could demand free dinners.

After Homans' analysis of distributive justice, a major theoretical and empirical development was stimulated by Adams (Adams, 1963, 1965; Adams & Freedman, 1976), falling under the label of "equity." Equity theory applies most readily to a two-person or two-party relationship, at least so far as our comments here are concerned. The formula for an equitable relationship is simple and has scarcely changed in 300 years:

$$\frac{\text{outcomes of A}}{\text{inputs of A}} = \frac{\text{outcomes of B}}{\text{inputs of B}}$$

The building blocks of equity theory are the concepts "input" and "outcome." An input is something a person invests in a relationship, usually entailing a cost. An outcome is whatever the person receives from the relationship—which may be good or bad. Poe's input into the neighbor/neighbor relationship was his tolerance of singing; the Trebelocinnis' first input was the weekly Italian gourmet dinner. Poe's main outcome, positive in this case, was the free dinner, and Mrs. Trebelocinni's outcome, also positive, was the license to continue her operatic wailing each morning. Inequity, conceived of as an unpleasant psychological state, develops when either of the people in the relationship finds that one's input-to-outcome ratio is not the same as that of the other participant. This concept might be easiest to understand in a work context. Suppose that one person earns \$2 per unit of work and a colleague earns \$3 for the same work. Translating this notion back to our example, the ratios would look like this: DINNERS RECEIVED/SINGING TOLERATED should equal LICENSE TO SING/DINNERS GIVEN. In slightly more common terminology, the benefits Poe receives from the relationship, in proportion to his costs, should equal the benefit/cost ratio of the Trebelocinni family.

It is important to realize that equity in a relationship does not necessarily exist in any objective sense, independent of the minds of the people involved. A relationship might seem totally equitable to one participant and completely inequitable to the other—and, for that matter, an independent observer might also find the relationship variously equitable or inequitable.

Further, Adams makes an important stipulation about the use of the terms *input* and *outcome:* Inputs and outcomes must be *recognized* by the participant before they play any part in equity/inequity. An objective analysis of a relationship by a scientist may reveal certain inputs and outcomes, but these are of importance only insofar as their presence is known by the person we are studying. Adams also notes that the inputs and outcomes must be *relevant* to the relationship we are considering. For instance, although Mr. Poe regularly pays his rent, this input should not be considered an input into the relationship between him and his neighbors. Only if the rent were paid directly to the Trebelocinnis would that input be calculated into the overall equity/inequity nature of their relationship.

REACTIONS TO INEQUITY

Inequity as a Tension State

According to Adams' formulation, as well as the most recent account of equity (Walster, Walster, & Berscheid, 1978), a person experiencing inequity encounters a tension state, which then moves the person toward trying to deal with the inequity. This tension-state notion has been examined closely by Austin and Walster (1974), whose subjects experienced inequity while performing a proofreading task. For proofreading a standard set of material the subject was rewarded either equitably or else inequitably, compared with a second subject who ostensibly had performed an identical amount of work. *Inequitably* here meant two things— some subjects were underpaid compared with the other subject, and others were overpaid. Subjects' mood states were then assessed, on the assumption that inequity would make for a less positive feeling state. It turned out that underpaid subjects showed a definite drop in mood state. The more ironic finding, and something we might expect only with equity theory as a basis of prediction, is that *overpayment* also led to decrement in mood relative to equitable payment. Thus the tension-state idea is well supported, in that no matter what form inequity takes, the subject undergoes a shift in tension, as reflected in a decrement in mood.

Altering Actual Inputs and Outcomes

Stemming from the tension state are a great variety of possible reactions aimed either at reestablishing equity or at avoiding the inequitable situation (Adams, 1965). Some of these seem entirely straightforward, given the formula for equity described above. For instance, people experiencing inequity can try to alter their own inputs (or outcomes) or else alter any of these entities for the other person involved. How would this fit the dilemmas of Mr. Poe? The source of Mr. Poe's problems, at one stage, was the overpayment he received relative to his inputs into the relationship. His outcomes from the neighbors were too high, and this created the tension state called inequity. One direct strategy for reestablishing equity would have been to alter his own outcomes. For instance, he could have refused to come any longer to dinner. Alternatively, his inputs into the relationship might have been increased, perhaps by paying for the carpentry or by inviting the neighbors for dinner once a week.

An equally good solution is to adjust the outcomes or inputs of the *other* party. The primary outcome, or benefit received, for Mrs. Trebelocinni was her freedom to sing opera at 6 A.M., and if her total outcome level could have been increased, equity might have been restored in Poe's eyes. For instance, if she had been given the green light to begin singing at 5 A.M., and perhaps also with electronic amplification, her outcomes (as perceived by Poe) would have jumped dramatically. Finally, another logical solution is to lower the costly inputs of the Trebelocinnis, which means persuading them to cut out the free dinners or perhaps to serve just frozen meat pies.

Before proceeding further, we might note something a bit redundant about these calculations. Quite often the costs for one party (for example, giving a free dinner) constitute the second party's positive outcomes. Adjusting one of these entities (party A's input) will automatically adjust the other (party B's outcome). The redundancy is not always this conspicuous, but in this case one can see that going through all four logical possibilities is partly a repetitious effort. This ceases to be an issue as the examples increase in complexity.

Altering Inputs and Outcomes Subjectively

To change the elements of the equity equation in an objective way is not at all necessary. Equity theory is an idea about the way people *perceive* relationships, and if the perception, or subjective estimate, of the relationship can be altered, that is sufficient for restoring the equitable situation. Mr. Poe's final reaction to developments with his new neighbors is a case in point. He wound up derogating the Trebelocinnis' contributions: he began to find the food tasteless and criticized the carpentry. To the extent that he could convince himself of the inferiority of the neighbors' inputs, equity would have been restored.

Leaving the Field or Changing Comparison Object

There is no reason in equity theory that the person necessarily must remain in the inequitable relationship and try to patch it up. Another alternative is to enter a new relationship, which has better prospects for equitable dealings, or else avoid relationships in general. The latter alternative, known as "leaving the field," was demonstrated by Schmitt and Marwell (1972). The subject found himself together with a coworker, and the level of inequity between the subject and his partner grew over time. Inequity in this case was defined as being deprived compared with the partner. Subjects were given an alternative to working with the partner that carried less payment. The interesting result was the high frequency of subjects who preferred to take this pay cut in order to remove themselves from an inequitable but higher-paying setting.

RESEARCH EXAMPLES

Inequity and Worker Productivity

It is useful to begin with an instance in which the elements of equity theory are quantifiable, for it is here that the application of the theory is most direct. This brings us immediately to the world of business and labor, in which the important questions revolve around such dimensions as gross amount of work, amount of work per hour, and rate of payment. The issue as applied to the worker setting is normally whether workers see themselves as overqualified or overworking relative to the amount of payment, or else the opposite—underqualified and lazy or inefficient.

A classic study by Adams and Rosenbaum (1962) dealt with people who were hired to perform a simple task of conducting interviews. The interview itself took a short time, and payment was geared so that subjects would perceive the rewards as fair provided that they viewed themselves as qualified and sufficiently dedicated. However, some subjects were given the unequivocal message that they were not qualified—in other words, that they were being overpaid relative to their skills (inputs). They were told such things as "As long as you're here and we don't have anyone else, I guess we can use you."

A further variable was whether subjects were to work at an hourly rate or a piece rate, and a bit of explanation is necessary to show how that variable is germane to equity principles. From the standpoint of subjects who feel they deserve the pay (high-equity condition), there is no problem. They will proceed at what seems a reasonable pace, whether under piece or hourly rate. In fact, to try to capitalize on the situation, subjects might perform better under piece rate than hourly rate. The situation for overpaid subjects (inequitable condition) is much different. If paid by the hour, they should feel an obligation to produce a great quantity of interviews, in an effort to try to raise their productivity to a level that would match the pay rate. It is as though they were trying to compensate for personal incompetence or lack of training by producing more. The ironic prediction is for the piece-rate condition. If the unqualified subjects work harder here, they will earn more money, thus raising their total outcome level. Unfortunately, that would just increase the inequity. In some sense it is more inequitable for an unqualified worker to earn $100 for 100 units than $1 for one unit, for production of each unit is an inequitable act. The results followed this reasoning precisely: with hourly-rate payment, the "underqualified" subjects turned in considerably more work, but with piece-rate reward they produced much less than their "qualified" counterparts.

Greed versus Equity: Adjusting Estimate of Self-Worth

In Adams and Rosenbaum's experiment subjects had just one 1-hour opportunity to gather interviews. Lawler, Koplin, Young, and Fadem (1968) reran the piece-rate conditions of Adams and Rosenbaum but conducted the study over three separate sessions. Their results add a new wrinkle to our understanding of equity processes.

Subjects were again sent out, for about 1 hour, to conduct as many interviews as they desired. For this first session the results resembled those of Adams and Rosenbaum: the "competent" group, who felt the pay was equitable, turned in many more interviews than the "incompetent," or overpaid, group. Beginning with the second session, approximately a week later, and then continuing through a third session, this difference between conditions vanished. In other words, the overpaid subjects suddenly accelerated their production rate, thereby increasing their outcomes. On a measure of perceived self-worth, administered to all subjects, Lawler et al. discovered that the overpaid group had shifted its perception of its own qualifications upward. What does this mean in terms of equity processes?

Given payment by piece rate, there is really no good way for "poorly qualified" subjects to bring about total equity. When they compare themselves against a hypothetical other who is qualified, they cannot escape the conclusion that they are being paid too much relative to their inputs—the inputs being the competence they bring to the task. Given this dilemma, the perfect solution is to alter one's *perceptions* of inputs/outcomes, and this is what subjects did. By subjectively upgrading their level of competence, they could convince themselves that they were not overpaid.

Paying Someone Back: Only If Equity Can Be Reestablished

The final dilemma in which we found Mr. Poe was that of overpayment—his outcomes were too great, and he would have been much happier had the preexisting inequity been redressed only with the free dinner. Among the types of compensation he might have arranged to repay the Trebelocinnis, many would not have been fair. For instance, simply paying Mrs. Trebelocinni a compliment would have been inadequate to restore equity, and paying her mortgage would have been too much. In equity theory, compensations are made only to the extent that they are appropriate for bringing about an equitable condition. Berscheid and Walster (1967) looked at this issue by studying dyadic relationships between church-club members who collected Green Stamps.

Each subject, a female member of a church auxiliary group, was assigned a partner to work with in a game of skills concerning facts about the Minneapolis–St. Paul area. The subject was the leader of the duo and therefore was responsible for deciding on a strategy to be followed. As it happened, the subject was systematically convinced that through an error in her strategic thinking, her partner was deprived of a nice prize (two books of S&H Green Stamps). The source of inequity is clear. The subject was responsible for seeing that she, as well as her partner, would win lots of Green Stamps, but owing to the subject's own error the partner was deprived.

How might equity be restored? Certainly all the ways listed above in our theoretical section are possible, including convincing oneself that the partner was undeserving or perhaps leaving the field (running out of the church-laboratory). But in this experiment the means of equity restoration was fixed and was defined through the experimental procedure. The subject was given the opportunity to award a number of Green Stamps to her unfortunate partner; the size of this potential contribution was constrained by the experimenter. Some subjects could make an award of two books—exactly the amount by which the partner was originally deprived. In a second instance *over*compensation was the only possibility—the subject had to award either five books or nothing. Finally, in an *under*compensation condition, the subject could award three *stamps* (not books) to the partner or else nothing.

The results were quite clear. If the compensation could only be three stamps, 58% of the subjects made no award at all. If five *books*, more subjects were generous, and if the compensation was the appropriate two books, the number of people compensating the partner was still higher.

Why didn't subjects who had three stamps to give at least try to compensate? And why were subjects in the five-book condition so stingy? Although these actions violate common sense, they are all understandable within equity theory. The use of a means of restoring equity should be related to the possibility of restoring equity adequately, and if the person's compensatory efforts are inappropriate, the person might look in another direction.

Whether another direction was taken here is not known, but a comparable study by Gergen (1969) makes one of these possibilities explicit. Gergen placed a number of subjects in a state of deprivation, in the sense of rarely winning in a game. Given the structure of the game, subjects probably did not view it as inequitable that they were losing. Later the subject received a number of chips from the winning player, together with a note explaining the contingencies surrounding the chips. In one condition the subject was expected to pay the loan back later, but in another the chips were simply given to the subject. Then the subject's liking for the winner was measured. It was argued that inequity would prevail in the "no debt" case, in that subjects received something free, without having made any inputs into the lender's stockpile of riches. Hence, it was these subjects who should have tried to restore equity by giving higher ratings of liking. Interestingly, the outcome was *decreased* liking for the generous partner. Why? If the subject can conclude that his benefactor is somehow not meritorious, then it is not so inequitable that the benefactor receives no payment in return.

The Gergen study has a clear parallel in international relations, whereby we are always surprised to hear that small nations dependent on the United States seem to resent accepting our aid (Fulbright, 1966). From equity theory this should be no surprise: if the United States can be perceived as wrong, immoral, or corrupt, then it deserves its fate of not gaining anything by bestowing gifts on other nations.

Commitment: Determining the Direction of Equity Restoration

Modern equity theory (Adams, 1963; Patchen, 1961) began as a derivation from cognitive dissonance theory, and because equity theory has not changed radically since that formulation, we can still find obvious parallels between dissonance and equity. One of these has to do with the variable of commitment. In order to test propositions in cognitive-dissonance theory, it is necessary to wait until the person has decided, for only then does dissonance reduction begin. Similarly, it is likely that a person's commitment to (or against) another is a determining factor in predicting the direction of equity restoration—whether decreasing own outcomes, raising other's inputs, or other devices.

Walster and Prestholdt (1966) dealt with the variable of commitment in the following way. Female subjects were asked to play the role of a kind of social worker and were given a lengthy case history to read, about the way a 13-year-old girl treated her poor, sick mother. (Note that the subject in this instance is a bystander to the inequitable relationship, rather than an actual participant. For the theory, this is all right, as observers should also be disturbed by inequity.) The case history led subjects to the conclusion that the daughter had been extremely self-centered and uncaring, going out on a date just when the mother was about to pass into a coma.

After reading the case history, subjects were asked to make an initial written evaluation of the daughter, and here Walster and Prestholdt carried out the commitment variation. Some of the subjects were asked to write their names on their evaluations, and the evaluations were also read at that point by the experimenter. This should have solidified their evaluations, making it difficult for them to reverse their judgments at a later time. The other subjects had no commitment and were asked to tear up their evaluations and throw them away. Thus they were in a highly flexible position with respect to being able to alter their judgments later.

Then came the inequity-generating information. Subjects were informed that the daughter had *not* acted uncaringly toward her mother, as this negative aspect of the initial report had been inaccurate. Since subjects had not known this before evaluating the daughter, the information should have generated feelings of inequity. They had written a negative evaluation of the daughter, which now turned out to be unwarranted. How were these subjects to handle the inequitable judgment? The appropriate measure was a second evaluation, which showed the following results.

Subjects who were uncommitted to their earlier negative evaluation adjusted their sentiments toward the 13-year-old in a positive direction, in a sense compensating for the earlier negative (and discarded) premature judgment. In fact, their positive judgments exceeded those of the subjects in another condition, who had never made a prematurely negative judgment. In the language of equity theory, subjects had initially mistreated the girl, through making a less-than-favorable evaluation based on faulty evidence, and they set out to restore equity by increasing the girl's positive outcomes (that is, raising their evaluation of her).

Just the opposite was observed for committed subjects: their earlier behavior, "fixed" in the sense of the experimenter's having read it, steered their final evaluation in the negative direction, as if they were restoring equity by convincing themselves that the daughter was essentially contributing nothing to the mother/daughter relationship and therefore deserved nothing in return.

This latter effect needs a bit more explanation. If inequity is created, and there is no possibility of eliminating inequity by increasing the outcomes of whoever has suffered, an alternative is to convince oneself that the person deserves to suffer (Lerner & Simmons, 1966). This was the case with the highly committed subjects. It was too late for them to compensate for their misjudgment by reevaluating the daughter as positive, and so the only remaining strategy was to tell themselves that the girl merited no praise.

Independent of the commitment variable, this experiment is also important in that it shows that the person experiencing inequity does not have to be actively involved in the relationship. The subject had never met the girl and was in this sense detached emotionally from her. Going a step further, it can even be shown that an independent observer of an inequitable dyad will take action to restore equity within the dyad (Baker, 1974), meaning that the workings of the theory extend well beyond the individual's personal involvement in relationships.

SPECIAL TOPICS

How Is Equity Attained?

Unusual Restorations of Inequity   Among the most intriguing equity-restoring devices are increasing one's own outcomes by cheating and decreasing one's own outcomes by inflicting self-punishment. In the first category, Stephenson and White (1968) gave young boys the opportunity to play an auto-racing game, whereby the subject would be either the actual player, controlling the course of the race car, or else a kind of lackey, whose job was to pick up cars that departed from the track. Inequity, obviously enough, was defined as having to spend too much of one's time picking up derailed cars. After the racing session all subjects took a test on the nature of auto racing, in which high scores merited prizes. Interestingly, the boys who had spent an unfair amount of time in the inferior position were more likely to cheat on the test. In equity theory, this means that they received inferior outcomes during the playing period and therefore felt entitled to higher outcomes (winning prizes by cheating) when taking the test.

An even more unlikely but intriguing route to reduction of inequity comes out of a study by Wallington (1973). Subjects who had cheated an experimenter administered more electric shock to themselves than subjects who had not. In other words, they were lowering the level of their outcomes within the experimental situation. What is interesting about this seemingly masochistic equity-restoration maneuver is that the other participant in the relationship, the experimenter, is not compensated for losses. Rather, the subjects merely lower their own outcomes.

Which Mode When? Adams (1965) lists a number of determinants of which route is taken under what circumstances. We will not go into this in great detail here, since the whole issue has not received adequate experimental treatment. However, one of the most general themes running through such discussions is that equity restoration methods are used that do not upset one's normal habits, interfere with valued rewards or self-esteem, or run counter to commitments. The role of commitment, closely tied up with dissonance theory, has already been spelled out above in the context of the Walster and Prestholdt investigation.

In considering the accomplished research, the reader might keep two points in mind: First, many of the experiments have made the use of certain modes extremely salient, so that it would be obvious to subjects that a given route to equity would be appropriate. For example, the subjects of Adams and Rosenbaum, who were receiving too much *hourly* payment for their interview work, could most readily increase their pace of working. Second, it is conceivable that subjects were using simultaneous modes of equity restoration. Even though an experiment focused on only one of these, alternative subtle measures might have revealed others. For instance, the church ladies of Berscheid and Walster might have derogated their partners, who lost out on two books of Green Stamps, in addition to compensating them through awarding more stamps. Or the subjects of Wallington who deceived their experimenter might well have been derogating her in addition to inflicting pain on themselves.

If the reader notes a certain ambiguity in our discussion of "which route to inequity reduction," this reflects a genuine difficulty with equity theory—one that could be solved only by putting severe constraints on the theory. To take one instance: Since equity theory grew directly out of dissonance theory, we might want to carry the dissonance language over entirely and say that equity-theory predictions are unambiguous only when subjects have first engaged in a free decision. At the very least, we would then know that equity restoration would go in the same direction as the commitment. However, the present area of application of equity theory is sufficiently broad that this is not about to be done, and it remains to be decided in each individual instance whether one's own outcomes, derogation of the other, changing of comparison person, or some other tactic is the most prominent or accessible potential route to establishing equity.

Noncomparable Entities

Is $2 worth one compliment? Is self-administered shock equivalent
to deceiving an experimenter? One of the complicating problems in applying the theory to complex social situations is the difficulty of assessing the
equivalence of outcomes that are in noncomparable modalities. Mr. Poe
seemed adequately compensated for suffering through the early-morning
singing by receiving a weekly Italian feast, but how could we have known
that beforehand? Wouldn't the case for equity have been clearer if he had
set up his quadraphonic sound system on the front porch at 6 A.M. and
played selections from his collection of heavy-metal rock groups?

One of the realities of social exchanges is that people often do not
have comparable entities to exchange, meaning that there is no general
solution to this problem. Solutions in individual cases depend on one's
ingenuity in viewing the situation from the subject's standpoint and in
trying to ascertain the possible fit between noncomparable outcomes. This
means that the application of equity theory to complex social situations—
those in which one person's praise is traded for the other's prestige or
ingratiation is traded for sexual performance—is a delicate business, in
which the investigator must be sensitive to the equivalence/nonequi-
valence of different modalities from the actors' viewpoints.

Other Principles: When Equity Fails

Beginning with the observations of Hobbes, we have assumed rather
blindly that humans in relationships worry mainly about whether their
outcomes in relation to their investments match those of the other person.
This may not invariably be the primary concern, and for all we know, it
might be a negligible concern. For instance, Leventhal (1976) informs us
that the issue of how much is *contributed* to a relationship is only one of at
least three ways of defining whether things are fair. A second viewpoint
on relationships is that everyone should be equally rewarded, independent of input. This is called the *equality* definition of justice or fairness. It
is common enough that workers are paid by the hour, and even though
one worker might be three times as productive as another, there are no
charges that the system is unfair. Similarly, in socialist countries, the
wealthy often lose almost all their income through taxation, a device that
works in the direction of equality of income. By our definition of equity
this would not be tolerated; yet it is tolerated and approved on a wide
scale. Leventhal suggests that the equality criterion is especially likely to

displace the equity criterion when a person's inputs are difficult to ascertain. It is as though we threw up our hands and admitted that we could not evaluate the outcome/input ratio, thereby leaving nothing but the simpler principle of equality.

Another exception to equity is the idea of *need*. In this case there is neither a calculation of input nor of specific outcomes, but instead just a response to people who have been acutely deprived. The bystander who witnesses a purse snatching and is about to intervene does not worry about whether the victim would return his favor of intervention, and once the deed is accomplished, there is no necessary concern about having intervened and gaining nothing material in return. Similarly, when we contribute to the March of Dimes or the Muscular Dystrophy Fund, we are concerned neither about being repaid (in any specific sense) nor about whether everyone's outcomes are equal.

It is Leventhal's thesis that the needs rule overrides other rules, such as equity, when we like the other and when we feel an individual responsibility for redressing the other's problem. However, at this point in the development of his thinking it is difficult to know precisely when each of the three rules (equity, equality, need) will come to function.

Equity can fail for still a further reason. If the distribution of rewards serves some special function from the standpoint of the individual allocating rewards, that function may have nothing to do with considerations of equity. For instance, a child may be depressed for no obvious reason, and its mother then decides to implement "present" therapy. She buys the child some new playthings or a new set of clothes to try to drive away the depression. Note that the mother's reasoning here has nothing to do with the child's having merited the presents by some equity principle, with equality with other children, or with need for the presents. The important element here is the reasoning of the allocator; that is, the presents are a tool for dealing with depression, not a tool of justice in social relations.

One can find similar reasoning among employers who give bonuses. A bonus is not always compensation for good work, but can also be handed out as an incentive to stimulate work in the future. In a study by Greenberg and Leventhal (1976) subjects were asked to role-play an industrial consultant, whose job was to disperse bonus pay of up to $100 to punch-press operators in a factory. One of the variables in the study was whether or not individual teams of workers were likely to meet a deadline. Greenberg and Leventhal described one team of punch-press operators as headed toward success (that is, making the deadline) and another team as bound to fail. One might see this as a manipulation of deserving-ness. When subjects were requested to distribute the bonuses according to productivity, bonuses were handed out exactly as the equity principle would imply. The successful workers received an average of $47; the failing workers were given an equitable $32.

Now comes the crucial condition: in some cases subjects were instructed to "pay each worker the amount of bonus that will motivate him to meet the deadline" (Greenberg & Leventhal, 1976, p. 181). With this simple instructional set the equity effect just described turned completely around. Members of the successful teams received $46, about the same as before, but the failing teams were given a surprisingly high $53. The principle behind this effect is clear. If money is to be used for purposes other than establishing justice in the social situation, then allocations can often appear highly inequitable.

Of course, there is still a further question, which could be settled only with additional information: do extra-high bonuses *actually* motivate workers? If so, then giving the less efficient teams more money may not be inequitable at all. The difference would then be that their extra payment precedes their hard work, whereas the people who have already been functioning at a high level are being paid C.O.D.

SUMMARY

Equity theory is an impressively broad scheme by which relationships are enacted and evaluated according to rules about what is fair or just. The dominant principle of equity has to do with the ratio between our outcomes from the relationship and the amount we invest (inputs), compared with those same entities for other participants. Adjustments are made in inequitable situations in a variety of ways, including altering one's own outcomes or inputs, adjusting the other's outcomes or inputs, and subjectively distorting the inputs or outcomes of either party. One of the greatest problems confronting the theory is the issue of when these alternative means of inequity reduction come into play, and although we can see some basis for calculating the direction of equity-seeking efforts in advance, this remains an issue for the investigator to solve without explicit theoretical guidance.

A further difficult but intriguing issue is whether we always concern ourselves with *relative* contributions. Sometimes the simple need of another person, or a rule of straight equality of outcomes, suffices to define a relationship as fair. These latter two criteria of fairness in relationships have not been fully developed, but they are important exceptions to recognize, given that we do not know which of the three rules typically characterizes relationships.

SUGGESTED READING

Adams, J. S. Inequity in social exchange. In L. Berkowitz (Ed.), *Advances in experimental social psychology* (Vol. 2). New York: Academic Press, 1965.

Homans, G. C. *Social behavior: Its elementary forms*. New York: Harcourt, Brace, 1961.

Lerner, M. J., Miller, D. T., & Holmes, J. G. Deserving and the emergence of forms of justice. In L. Berkowitz & E. Walster (Eds.), *Advances in experimental social psychology* (Vol. 9). New York: Academic Press, 1976.

Leventhal, G. S. Fairness in social relationships. In J. Thibaut, J. T. Spence, & R. C. Carson (Eds.), *Contemporary topics in social psychology*. Morristown, N.J.: General Learning Press, 1976.

Walster, E., Walster, G. W., & Berscheid, E. (Eds.). *Equity: Theory and research*. Boston: Allyn & Bacon, 1978.

PART THREE

ATTRIBUTION

The three notions discussed here owe a great deal of credit to Heider (1944, 1958), who first stimulated psychologists to think systematically about the human propensity to explain others' behavior. These three chapters have in common a *rational* picture of the human—a human who gathers information about others (and about the self), processes it in seemingly logical ways, and then draws conclusions in the form of explanations for behavior. The conclusions often consist of personality traits, attitudes, or abilities that are imputed to the person whose behavior is being explained.

The first of these approaches, self-perception theory (Chapter 8), is not presented first because of chronological reasons. Rather, it is in most ways the simplest of the three, and its purpose is somewhat more focal: the central idea is to account for the phenomenon of humans' figuring themselves out on the basis of their own decisions. The parentage of this theory is different from that of the other two approaches, as it was inspired by Skinner's (1957) radical behavioral analysis of private events. However, as the theory developed, its underlying logic came to resemble the attributional logic spelled out by Heider (1958).

The second, the theory of correspondent inferences (Chapter 9), is an explicit elaboration on the ideas of Heider (1958). Correspondent-inference theory is a set of ideas that allows an observer to calculate a person's attitudes, traits, or other dispositions on the basis of knowing something about what the person was trying to achieve in a certain sequence of behaviors.

The third attribution theory, formulated by Kelley (Chapter 10), is often described as the "three-dimensional cube" attribution theory. In the same vein as correspondent-inference theory, Kelley's system takes up where Heider's attribution theorizing left off and, using diagrams in the form of a cube, gives us some specific rules for arriving at an analysis of the reasons behind a person's behavior.

CHAPTER 8

SELF-PERCEPTION THEORY

O NE DAY as Karl is walking across campus, he is approached by a young woman carrying a petition. She stops him and asks "Would you please sign this petition favoring increased U.S. economic aid to the Sudetenland?" Although he does not know much about the issue, Karl is in an agreeable mood and decides to sign the petition.

Suppose that a passer-by has observed this series of behaviors and we ask the person what he thinks Karl's attitude is on this issue. Having observed that Karl chose to sign the petition, the passer-by would likely infer that Karl has a favorable attitude toward increased U.S. economic aid to Sudetenland.

Suppose that we also ask Karl the parallel question "What is your attitude toward increased U.S. economic aid to the Sudetenland?" Even though Karl probably had not considered this issue before being confronted with the petition (indeed, he may have had no attitude at all on this issue), he will now be prone to say that he is in favor of increased economic aid. The behavior of choosing to sign the petition seems to have "changed" Karl's attitude on this issue.

This chapter presents a theory of self-perception (Bem, 1967, 1972) that provides a means of analyzing situations like that presented above. The theory deals with the problem of how people infer their own attitudes and feelings from their behavior and its situational context. As we will see, the theory makes the assumption that in many cases the observer and the person engaging in the behavior will infer the person's attitudes in exactly the same manner.

THE THEORY

The Perception of Others

On what basis did the passer-by make the inference about Karl's attitude? According to the theory, the observer considers two elements in forming an inference. (1) First is the *direction* of the person's behavior. In our example, Karl engaged in the clearly pro-increased-aid behavior of signing the petition. (2) Once the observer has identified the direction of the behavior, the particular circumstances under which the behavior has occurred are examined. In our example, the observer would not perceive that there were any special pressures on Karl to sign the petition. Any possible constraining forces on Karl are rather subtle and are not detected by the observer. Rather, it appears to the observer that the petition is eliciting Karl's "true" feelings about the issue. The opposite case is found when the observer perceives that pressures are operating on the person to engage in the behavior. If two members of the wrestling team threatened to stomp Karl unless he signed the petition, or if the young woman offered Karl a sum of money for signing it, the observer would see Karl as responding to explicit constraints or reinforcers in the environment. The behavior is considered to be under the control of the environment whenever the observer perceives that the person has behaved in a particular manner in order to gain reward or to avoid punishment. Note that in applying this analysis, the viewpoint of the observer is taken. If, unknown to the observer, Karl had signed the petition in an attempt to get the young woman to like him, his behavior would still be free from reinforcement control from the perspective of the observer. Thus, self-perception theory defines two types of extreme circumstances: (1) situations in which the behavior is free of explicit reinforcement control and (2) situations in which the behavior is perceived to be under the control of particular constraints or reinforcers.

Now that the observer has identified the direction of the behavior and the circumstances surrounding it, how does he infer the person's attitude? If the performance can be characterized as free from explicit reinforcement control, the observer will infer an attitude that is consistent with the behavior. In our initial example there were no special pressures on Karl to sign the petition; hence the observer should have inferred that Karl had a pro-increased-aid attitude. However, if Karl had ostensibly signed the petition in order to get a big hug from the interviewer, the behavior would be perceived as under the control of a reinforcer. The observer would therefore be uncertain about the reason Karl signed the petition, and so he would infer a rather weak pro-aid attitude or perhaps even a neutral attitude. Given the occurrence of some behavior, the observer will infer that the person has a much less extreme attitude in the direction of that behavior to the degree that the behavior is viewed as controlled by reinforcement contingencies.

Self-Perception

Thus far we have outlined the process by which an observer infers the attitudes of another. How does this differ from the way people infer their own attitudes from their own behavior? Bem's somewhat surprising answer is "Not at all." For self-perception theory, the person engaging in the behavior and the observer are equivalent: they both identify the direction of the behavior and its accompanying circumstances and then infer an attitude according to the rules outlined above. The person performing the behavior and the observer should normally infer the same attitude.

Bem's position seems surprising because it is based on a unique view of the nature of attitudes. For instance, dissonance theory (Chapter 6) conceives of attitudes as relatively enduring dispositions that lead to consistent behavior, at least under some conditions. According to this conception, changes in people's attitudes are likely to lead to changes in their related behaviors. In contrast, self-perception theory takes the view that many attitudes are simply self-descriptive statements that the person makes when asked by a social psychologist or peer. The person does not generally have salient and enduring attitudes; they are inferred only when the person is asked "How do you feel about X?"

Self-perception theory further contends that at best attitudes only weakly determine behavior. Such factors as inducements and social pressure are normally far more important in determining behavior than the person's self-descriptive statements, such as attitudes. For example, if Karl received a telephone call two weeks later, asking him to write a letter to the State Department supporting increased U.S. economic aid to the Sudetenland, his decision to write or not to write would be mainly a function of subtle factors in the situation, such as the communicator's tone of voice and the manner of the request. His previously stated attitude on this issue would play little role in the decision (Bem, 1968).

But self-perception theory does not stop with the assumption that attitudes are relatively unimportant determinants of behavior. The theory also proposes that previous attitudes have only minimal input into the attitude-inference process itself. Once Karl signs the petition, he will infer that he has an attitude consistent with his behavior to the degree that his behavior is free from apparent reinforcement control. His previously expressed attitude on this issue, whether pro or anti, hardly enters into the inference process. Rather, the previous attitude is simply replaced by the newly inferred attitude.

RESEARCH EXAMPLES

Why Is That Cartoon Funny?

One consequence of Bem's definition of *attitude* is that a number of self-descriptions that would not traditionally be considered attitudes fall under the purview of the theory. Any self-description of one's feelings can be analyzed using the theory. Thus, self-reports of pain, emotion, and other internal states should be subject to self-perception processes, just like attitudes. An illustrative example is Bem's (1965) experiment on the ratings of funniness of cartoons.

In this experiment Bem took the unusual approach of attempting to create an environmental stimulus that would signal the subject as to the reinforcement properties of the situation. The reason was to be certain that the self-observers correctly perceived the particular circumstances in which their behavior occurred. Subjects participated in a pretraining session in which they were asked simple questions about themselves (for example, "What is your home town?"). They were instructed by the experimenter to contrive a false answer (lie) whenever an amber light came on during the question. Whenever a green light appeared, they were to respond truthfully.

What is the effect of this pretraining session on subjects' perception of the lights? According to Bem, the amber "lie" light should lead them to perceive the situation as under environmental control. Subjects are responding in an abnormal manner—complying with the experimenter's request to lie. However, when the green "truth" light is on, subjects are responding to the questions in the way they normally would, even if the experimenter were not present. They should infer that when this light is on, the behavior is free from reinforcement control. This pretraining session, then, established the lights as indicating that the situation was free from reinforcement control (green) or else under reinforcement control (amber).

In the second part of the experiment subjects were shown a number of cartoons that they had previously rated as neutral (neither funny or unfunny). They were then requested to say "This cartoon is very funny" or "This cartoon is very unfunny," the statement being determined by the experimenter. This statement established the direction of the behavior. Just before the subject made the statement, either the green or the amber light appeared, establishing the apparent reinforcement circumstances. The subject had been told that the lights would continue to come on during this part of the experiment but that they could be ignored. Once the statement about the cartoon had been made and the light extinguished, the subject was asked to rate the cartoon.

To summarize, the subject stated "This cartoon is very funny" or "This cartoon is very unfunny" in the presence of a light indicating that the behavior was free from or under reinforcement control.

When subjects made their statements in the presence of the green light, their ratings were consistent with their statements. That is, if subjects made a positive statement, they rated the cartoons as being funny, whereas if they made a negative statement, they rated the cartoons as unfunny. But when the statements occurred in the presence of the light indicating that their behavior was under reinforcement control, their statements did not affect their ratings, which continued to be near the neutral point. Thus, subjects took both the nature of the situation and the direction of their statements into account in inferring the funniness of the cartoons.

When Avoidance Leads to Pain

Many internal states have external manifestations that can be perceived by the person as well as by others. Suppose, for instance, that a young boy falls off his bicycle and scrapes himself. A preliminary look indicates that no harm was done, but the boy later notices blood trickling down his arm. He breaks into tears and runs to tell Mommy that he has a "bad hurt." An observer of this sequence, on seeing the blood and the crying, would also infer that the fall was more painful than it had previously appeared.

Bandler, Madaras, and Bem (1968) investigated whether one's own external behavior would serve as a source of information in the perception of pain. Once again lights were used to signal the apparent level of external control over the subject's behavior in the situation. In the first two conditions, the experimenter emphasized that the subject had a choice in deciding whether to terminate the shock but suggested a preferred direction for behavior—either to escape or to tolerate the shock. For example, in the escape condition, the experimenter's instructions were as follows: "In this condition, the red [light] condition, you *should* press the button and turn off the shock. However, if the shock is not uncomfortable, you may elect to not depress the button. The choice is up to you" (Bandler et al., 1968, p. 206). The instructions in the no escape condition were parallel, except that the suggested direction of behavior was to tolerate the shock. In both conditions, this emphasis on subjects' choice should have led them to perceive that their behavior was free from external control.

In a final condition, subjects were instructed to press the button as fast as they could (reaction time condition). On some trials pressing the button terminated the shock, and on other trials pressing the button had no effect on the shock. Since the subjects should have perceived no choice in responding, they presumably perceived their behavior as under external control.

To summarize, the subject either terminated or did not terminate an electric shock under conditions that indicated that the behavior was free from or under external control.

After each trial the subject rated the discomfort produced by the shock. Of critical importance was that all the shocks were equally intense. The shock terminated automatically after 2 seconds if it was not terminated by the subject.

Applying the self-perception analysis, behavior in both the escape and the no escape conditions would be perceived as free from external control, and so subjects should have inferred the discomfort of the shock from the direction of their behavior. In other words, when they terminated the shock in the escape condition, they should have inferred that the shock was uncomfortable, whereas in the no escape condition, when they did not terminate the shock, they should have perceived the shock as less uncomfortable. This is just what happened. However, in the reaction time condition—in which the behavior was viewed as under external control—subjects did not find any difference in the discomfort of the shock as a function of whether or not the shock terminated. In fact, these subjects actually rated the nonterminated shocks in this condition as more painful, simply because they lasted longer. Once again, for people to use behavior as a source of information about their internal state, the behavior must be free from strong external control.

Cognitive Dissonance and the New Haven Police

One of the classic studies derived from cognitive dissonance theory (Cohen, 1962) dealt with students' attitudes toward the New Haven police. The experiment was one of the first investigations of the paradoxical effects of external justification. We will first summarize the original study and then provide a reinterpretation in accordance with self-perception theory.

Following a student riot at Yale, the New Haven police entered the campus and engaged in a variety of repressive actions. This led immediately to hostile attitudes toward the police on the part of most students. Taking advantage of this animosity, students were then approached by an experimenter and asked to write an essay supporting the actions of the police. The situation was structured in such a way that the students perceived that they had a degree of choice in deciding whether to write the essay. According to the dissonance analysis presented in Chapter 6, writing the essay should have been dissonant with the students' negative attitudes. As in other dissonance experiments, varying amounts of external justification were offered for writing the essay: four experimental conditions were created by offering students different amounts of money ranging between 50¢ and $10. The more external justification, the larger the number of consonant cognitions, and consequently the less need to reduce dissonance by altering the central attitude toward the police. The results were entirely consistent with this analysis: the more money offered for writing the essay, the less subjects' attitudes changed in a pro-police direction.

How would self-perception theory interpret these results? If subjects had not been offered any money, they would be perceived as free from reinforcement control. In that case the subjects would infer that their attitudes were consistent with the pro-police position expressed in the essay. However, as the amount of monetary inducement increased, the more likely it is that subjects would have perceived their behavior as governed by reinforcement control, thereby decreasing the tendency to infer a propolice attitude from behavior. If the offer were as high as $10, subjects would not have inferred much of an attitude at all. Bem's position, then, leads us to exactly the same predictions as dissonance theory does. We will have more to say, later in this chapter, about the relative merits of the two theories as explanations for findings in classic "dissonance" contexts as well as in other areas.

Arguing for Air Pollution Controls

One of the unique assumptions of self-perception theory is that initial attitudes do not enter into the attitude-inference process. Rather, people simply observe the direction of their behavior and the context in which it occurs, inferring their attitudes only from these two elements. An interesting implication of this analysis is that behaving in a manner consistent with one's previously expressed attitudes should lead to attitudinal inferences that are parallel to those inferred when the behavior is inconsistent with the initial attitude. We have already seen experiments involving behaviors inconsistent with prior attitudes; the following experiment illustrates what happens when behaviors are consistent with initial attitudes.

Kiesler, Nisbett, and Zanna (1969) asked students to commit themselves to deliver arguments against air pollution, a position with which they had earlier agreed, to a passer-by on the street. For some of the subjects an accomplice of the experimenter, posing as another subject, indicated that he perceived his behavior to be under external control, emphasizing that he was giving his communication (on another topic) because of the potential scientific value of the experiment. For other subjects the accomplice said he was giving the communication because this was an issue he really believed in, implying that his behavior was free from external control. In line with the self-perception analysis, subjects who committed themselves to deliver the communication and who perceived their behavior as free from external control—owing to the subtle social influence of the model—were definitely opposed to air pollution when their attitudes were measured after the model's statement. However, subjects who witnessed the "external control" model imputed to themselves a less extreme attitude toward air pollution.

Undermining Intrinsic Motivation

Giving people rewards for doing something they already enjoy may actually cause them to enjoy the behavior less. The principle is really no different from that guiding the research we have just discussed. If a behavior is under reinforcement control, the person performing the behavior will not be sure whether to ascribe performing it to the internal factor of liking for the behavior or to the external constraint.

Deci (1971) asked subjects to play a puzzle game called "Soma," which consists of putting various pieces together to form a wide variety of three dimensional objects. This game is quite intriguing, and most subjects spent most of an initial warm-up period playing with the puzzle. Now comes the manipulation of reinforcement control: some of the subjects (reward condition) were told that they would receive $1 for each puzzle they solved during the next part of the experiment; control subjects did not expect to receive any money for solving the puzzles. At the end of this portion of the experiment, subjects in the reward condition were paid, clearly implying that their behavior was under reinforcement control. The consequence of this perceived constraint should be a decrease in interest in the task per se, for reward subjects cannot be sure that they are working because of an innate desire or personal enjoyment. And, to be sure, when subjects were then left alone in the room with a totally unconstrained opportunity to resume playing with the puzzle, control subjects spent more time playing with the puzzle than reward subjects. This suggests that intrinsic interest stays at a higher level if there is no obvious external reason for performing a task. Note, however, that actual behavior rather than a reported inference was the dependent measure in this study, a point that we will return to later in this chapter.

SPECIAL TOPICS

Strength of Internal States

In a recent statement of the theory, Bem (1972) has qualified his proposal that people infer their attitudes (and other internal states) from their behavior and its external context. He now points out that this process occurs only "to the extent that internal cues are weak, ambiguous, or uninterpretable" (p. 2). Returning to our opening example, if Karl had signed a petition concerning an issue about which he held strong feelings, the simple self-perception process described by Bem would less readily apply. In this case, Karl's initial attitude would be an important determinant of his final attitude after signing the petition.

The Attitude-Behavior Relation

The theory has it that the behavior and its environmental context determine subjects' attitudes. Subjects' attitudes, however, do not typically determine their behavior: the link goes mainly in the direction of behavior to attitude. It is not correct to use self-perception theory to analyze experiments that do not employ a self-report of an attitude or other internal state as the dependent measure. For example, in Deci's (1971) research the dependent measure was the amount of time that the subject played with the Soma cubes during the final period of the experiment, obviously a measure of the subject's behavior. But Bem's theory does not make any assumption that the subject's attitude toward the Soma cubes will influence actual game-playing behavior. Strictly speaking, then, the results of that experiment do not fall under the purview of the theory. The theory would apply more readily to a measure of liking for the game, and as a matter of fact, a similar study by Amabile, DeJong, and Lepper (1976) did find parallel effects on a liking measure and a behavioral measure. But, since the *behavioral* measure was effective, one cannot help questioning the assumption that behaviors are uninfluenced by attitudes.

What Is Overt Behavior?

The behavior that serves as the basis for both the observer's and the person's inferences is the person's overt, publicly observable behavior. In all the research examples discussed, a single episode of an overt behavior was the focus of the self-perception analysis. For instance, Karl's act of signing the petition served as this element in our opening example. The only case in which there was no central overt behavior was Kiesler, Nisbett, and Zanna's (1969) experiment, wherein subjects believed that they would be delivering arguments against air pollution to a passer-by. In this experiment subjects did not deliver the arguments; the overt behavior never actually occurred. However, the subjects did make a public commitment to deliver the arguments, and this act can easily be construed as the overt behavior. Thus, either overt behavior or public commitments to engage in behavior can serve as the basis for the application of the theory. In contrast, private, internal cognitions and private decisions are not subject to a self perception analysis. Someone who freely decides to donate a large sum of money to charity cannot, by the theory, use that internal decision as a basis for inferring a trait of generosity. Only if one engages in an overt behavior, such as writing a check, telling someone about one's decision, or writing a note on the calendar to have the bank send the money in the morning, can the self-perception analysis be applied clearly and the inference of generosity drawn.

Complex Situations

The examples in this chapter have all involved a single behavior with a well-defined beginning and ending point. Only one action, rather than a series of related behaviors, was the focus of each self-perception analysis. In these simple cases, the overt behavior and external circumstances can be easily identified, so that the self-perception analysis is straightforward. However, there is at least one kind of complex situation in which the application is more difficult.

Consider a woman who buys a loaf of the same brand of bread every time she goes to the store. It is clear that she should report liking for the bread. But what behavior is the basis for this inference? Is it the most recent bread-purchase decision? Or is it her history of bread-purchase decisions, which may span years? Bem does not explicitly address this point, although he does indicate that the most recent behavior is critical in the attitude-inference process. Consequently, no clear-cut inference can be made if the woman chooses not to buy the customary bread on her most recent shopping trip after a long history of purchasing that brand.

A related problem is how inferences are drawn from a series of similar behaviors. Suppose that in our opening example, Karl freely signed four petitions on unrelated issues during his walk across campus. What would the observer (and Karl) infer about Karl's attitude? If the observer uses Karl's behavior only on the relevant petition (Sudetenland), it would be inferred that Karl is favorable to this position. But if the observer used Karl's behavior of signing four different petitions as the unit of analysis, the resulting inference might be that Karl is the type of person who signs petitions and that he probably does not have strong attitudes on this (or any other) issue. Either of these outcomes is possible, and which outcome occurs is probably a function of the relation between the positions expressed in the petitions and the time span over which Karl signed them. If Karl signed four petitions advocating inconsistent positions in a short period of time, an observer would not infer that Karl held strong attitudes on these issues. But if the petitions advocated consistent positions, or if Karl signed the four petitions over a period of several years, it is likely that the observer would use the most recent behavior as the unit of analysis and infer that Karl's attitudes about the issues were consistent with his behavior. Presumably, Karl would make inferences paralleling the outside observer's.

This problem illustrates a definite difficulty in applying Bem's analysis. In complex situations, observers apparently form inferences using a more complex inference process than that proposed by the theory. The next two chapters will address this problem: Chapter 9 focuses on a more complete analysis of the inferences made from a single behavior, and Chapter 10 examines the process by which inferences are made from a series of behaviors. In those two chapters, we will also look at some criticisms of Bem's position that the actor and observer manifest identical inference processes.

Self-Perception versus Cognitive Dissonance

Occasionally two social psychological theories will contend as explanations of the same phenomenon. One classic example is the conflict between self-perception and dissonance theories in accounting for some of the research discussed in Chapter 6—namely, the consequences for attitudes of the free choice and forced compliance procedures. When two theories collide, researchers sometimes undertake so-called critical studies that identify the exact conditions under which each theory best applies. This has been done in the confrontation between dissonance and self-perception theories; the course of this confrontation has been detailed in Wicklund and Brehm (1976), and we will illustrate with one experiment how research has been brought to bear on the controversy.

Green (1974) conducted a study involving external justification for engaging in an unpleasant behavior. Subjects were made either very thirsty by eating crackers laced with Tabasco and horseradish or else less thirsty by eating crackers covered with conventional peanut butter. The purpose of this manipulation was to vary the extremity of subjects' feelings of thirst. The subjects were then asked to make a commitment to go without water for 24 hours following the experiment. Some of them were offered high external justification ($20) for their commitment to further

thirst, others only $5. After this commitment to water deprivation, sub-
jects were asked to rate how thirsty they were and were allowed to drink
as much water as they pleased.

What do the two theories say about this experiment? For dissonance
theory, the more extreme the person's initial thirst, the more dissonance
will be aroused upon a commitment to go without water for a long time.
Subjects who are thirsty from the hot sauce should have more dissonance
over making this commitment than subjects who have eaten the neutral
peanut butter. For self-perception theory it is just the opposite: subjects
should use their behavior to infer their attitudes more when their internal
state of thirst is weak (that is, they are not thirsty) than when it is strong.

The justification variable works in the same direction for the two
theories. In dissonance theory, increasing monetary incentive adds cognitions consistent with the commitment and thereby reduces dissonance. In
self perception theory, the money manipulation varies subjects' perception of the degree to which their behavioral commitment is under reinforcement control: they will infer that they want to go without water
more when the payment is low.

Now, when both variables are taken together, we find the two theoretical frameworks making opposing predictions. For dissonance theory
the payment variable should have the strongest impact in the high-thirst
condition, for in the case of low thirst the decision is less dissonance-
provoking, so that the $20 payment will have less of a dissonance-reduc-
ing effect. In other words, the decision must be highly dissonance-arousing before a justification variable ($5 versus $20) will have any impact on
the dissonance process. In sharp contrast, the payment variable should
have a greater impact in the *low* thirst condition when the experiment is
viewed from a self-perception theory angle. This is because the self-inference process is said to occur primarily when internal cues are lacking
(that is, low thirst); thus variables relevant to that process can operate
primarily under those circumstances.

The results of Green's experiment were in the pattern prescribed by
dissonance theory. The largest difference between the $5 and $20 conditions, both in terms of reported thirst and amount of water drunk, was
obtained when subjects had been made highly thirsty. Taken together with
results of several other relevant experiments (for example, Fazio, Zanna,
& Cooper, 1977; Ross & Shulman, 1973), the domain in which each of the
theories best applies can be better specified. Dissonance theory applies
readily when the person holds an extreme attitude or is in an extreme
state such as thirst and then carries out a behavior that is contrary to that
attitude or state. Self-perception theory generally provides the best ac-

count of attitude effects and other self-description effects when the person does not have a strong attitude. Further, when the behavior is consistent with the attitude, as in the oversufficient justification studies described above, self-perception theory clearly provides the best account of what is going on. Note again, however, that self perception theory applies mainly to the inference of internal states such as attitudes and reports of thirst but does not address itself explicitly to consequent behaviors.

New Theoretical Directions

Bem has noted that self-descriptions are often learned under the guidance of others. People learn to label their internal states on the basis of descriptions by others. The young girl who spends hours cooking with her Suzy Homemaker baking and cooking set is told by her parents that she has strong culinary interests. Or the parents of a young boy who spends hours each day reading gun catalogues and attending kung fu movies may tell him about the inferences they make about him. They may say that they can find no external reason for his behavior, and so he must be very aggressively inclined. In short, the complicated self-inference process described by Bem may originally develop as a carbon copy of the cognitive operations of those around us.

This developmental view raises a number of interesting questions concerning how we learn to infer important and enduring traits, as contrasted with the more temporary traits and attitudes that appear in the examples in this chapter. When will people infer that a trait such as aggressiveness is more than just a description of their behavior in a particular situation, but rather characterizes their behavior across a wide variety of situations and at different times? And how do people learn to include information about their enduring attitudes and personality traits as an important factor to be considered in the inference process, along with their behavior and its external context? Some beginnings to an answer to these questions will be explored in the next two chapters.

Another interesting issue for the theory concerns the degree of attention to one's own behavior. Many successful business executives, for example, are so narrowly focused on meeting the demands of their jobs that they rarely give attention to their behavior. Often, as middle age approaches, they begin to focus more on their own behavior with the result that they discover new insights about themselves: Perhaps they notice for the first time the considerable external pressure that is placed on them to work long hours, and hence they begin to like their jobs less than before.

Or they may observe that they spend little time with their children, leading to the inference that they are poor parents. Thus, the degree of attention toward our own behavior may have a strong bearing on the accuracy of our inferences about ourselves and the method by which we make those inferences. To be sure, there is already evidence that the inference processes described by Bem are set into motion by bringing people to focus attention on themselves (Chapter 13).

Finally, self-perception theory has emphasized the importance of recent behaviors in determining our current attitudes. Although important attitudes can show remarkable persistence under normal conditions (Newcomb, Koenig, Flacks, & Warwick, 1967; Sears, 1975), performing a counterattitudinal behavior under free-choice conditions seems to have profound effects on attitudes. A recent counterattitudinal behavior seems to swamp preexisting attitudes and behaviors, even those that have been repeatedly performed. For example, Brock (1962) found that non-Catholic students who wrote essays favoring Catholicism under free-choice conditions became more favorable toward Catholicism. Before the advent of self-perception theory, the import of such research was not fully recognized, because the dominant theoretical perspectives conceived of attitudes as highly stable. With the insight provided by self-perception theory, we can now better conceptualize the influence of the person's most recent behaviors on attitudes. Further, we can ask whether these changes in attitude are then integrated into the person's attitudinal structure and behaviors or whether these changes are only temporary, the person reverting to the long term structure with the passage of time. These are important questions raised in part by self-perception theory that have received little attention thus far.

SUMMARY

Self-perception theory provides a parsimonious explanation of the inferences that a person and an observer make from the person's behavior. The observer, as well as the person, considers the direction of the behavior and the circumstances in which the behavior takes place. If the situation constrains behavior, so that the person is perceived to be engaging in the behavior in order to gain reinforcement or avoid punishment, then the observer will infer a very weak or neutral attitude. If there are no special pressures on the person to engage in the behavior, an observer will infer that the person's attitude is consistent with the direction of the behavior. To the extent that internal cues are weak, the person will infer an attitude using a process identical to that of the observer. Self-perception theory may also be applied to analyze the self-reports of other internal states, such as pain and amusement. Finally, the theory assumes that the causal direction between behavior and attitudes is behavior-to-attitude; the question whether behaviors can stem out of preexisting attitudes receives little theoretical attention.

SUGGESTED READING

Bem, D. J. An experimental analysis of self-persuasion. *Journal of Experimental Social Psychology,* 1965, *1,* 199–218.

Bem D. J. Self-perception theory. In L. Berkowitz (Ed.), *Advances in experimental social psychology* (Vol. 6). New York: Academic Press, 1972.

Bem, D. J. Self-perception theory. In L. Berkowitz (Ed.) *Cognitive theories in social psychology.* New York: Academic Press, 1978.

Wicklund, R. A., & Brehm, J. W. *Perspectives on cognitive dissonance.* Hillsdale, N.J.: Erlbaum, 1976.

CHAPTER 9

A THEORY OF CORRESPONDENT INFERENCES

AS TOM enters an elegant Manhattan restaurant, a drunk reels out of the restaurant bar and staggers into him. The drunk proceeds to berate and insult Tom, and in response, Tom punches the drunk, ending the confrontation.

Suppose, at this point, we asked an observer who had witnessed the entire confrontation to describe Tom's personality. It is likely that the observer would say "Tom is very aggressive." From his observation of the one behavioral episode described above, the observer has inferred that Tom is the type of person who would act in a similarly aggressive manner in a number of situations.

But what if the confrontation took place in a somewhat different cultural setting—say, a barroom in West Texas or the Philippines? What would an observer infer in this situation? In such a context it is much less likely that the observer would infer that Tom is aggressive. Rather, punching the obnoxious drunk would be considered the normal and expected response to provocation. Indeed, should Tom fail to punch the drunk, it is likely that the observer would infer that Tom was cowardly or perhaps "not a real man."

THE THEORY

This chapter presents one theoretical approach to the problem exemplified above: how do people make inferences about the dispositions (attitudes, personality traits) of others? This approach is the theory of correspondent inferences proposed by Jones and Davis (1965). The central concept of this theory is *correspondence*, a term that refers to the clarity or directness of the relation between the disposition and the behavior. If the observer believes that an action could be the result of any number of dispositions, then the action is low in correspondence. However, if the observer believes that the action could be due only to one disposition, then the behavior is high in correspondence (that is, the behavior corresponds to the inferred disposition).

Correspondence is normally reflected in two related ways: (1) the person will be perceived as being extreme, compared with the average person, on the disposition, and (2) the observer will make a highly certain judgment of the person's standing (extremity) on the disposition. In our example above, if Tom's behavior is high in correspondence, then the observer will infer that Tom is aggressive, compared with the average person, and this inference will be made with a high degree of certainty.

The theory of correspondent inferences has a restricted focus. First, the theory focuses on inferences that are made about a person's dispositions from observing a *single* behavioral episode. There is no attempt to consider inferences that are grounded in a *series* of interactions. (Such inferences are discussed in Chapter 10.) Second, the theory considers only two persons—the actor and the observer. The actor is the person engaging in some behavior; the observer views the behavior and the situation in which it occurs. The observer is normally assumed to be uninvolved in the situation, perhaps as a passive bystander, and in fact the observer might not even be present in the situation. The observer may read about the actor's behavior in the newspaper, be told about the behavior by friends, or view it on television.

A further assumption is that the observer will attempt to infer a simple, plausible explanation for the actor's behavior. Unlike the scientific observer, who may be seeking a very complex explanation of behavior, the observer will usually find that one of two types of explanation is sufficient to explain the actor's behavior: (1) *An enduring disposition of the actor, an attitude or a personality trait, caused the behavior.* In our example of Tom punching the drunk, inferring that Tom is aggressive and that he would respond similarly in a wide variety of situations provides a sufficient explanation of the behavior for the observer. (2) *Strong pressure from the environment or another person caused the behavior.* For example, it may be that the drunk's provocation of Tom was so extreme that anyone would have acted aggressively under the circumstances. With these basic ideas in mind, the principles of the theory and its supporting research can now be discussed.

Social Desirability

The first factor the observer considers in making an inference is the social desirability of the actor's behavior. *Social desirability* may be defined as how likely the observer thinks the average person would be to carry out this action under the same circumstances. The higher the social desirability of the action, the less likely the observer is to make an inference about dispositions of the actor. Socially desirable actions are simply not informative for the observer.

For instance, one socially desirable action that many adults perform is paying taxes. Suppose we observe that John pays his income tax. What can we infer about John's dispositions? Virtually nothing, since we know that the average person is also very likely to pay taxes under the same circumstances. John could pay his taxes for any number of reasons, ranging from patriotism to fear of imprisonment. However, should John refuse to pay his taxes, his actions then become very informative. In this case, when the action is socially undesirable, it is likely that we would infer that John is an activist protester. Thus, unusual behaviors, those that are not consistent with role requirements, and those that are contrary to social norms provide the observer with a clear basis for making a dispositional inference about the actor.

This idea was first tested in an experiment by Jones, Davis, and Gergen (1961). Observer subjects listened to a tape of a simulated job interview between a psychologist and a student (the actor). (Note that the psychologist is neither actor nor observer in this case. Rather, the psychologist is simply an additional person who presents the requirements of the situation to the actor and observer.) Before the interview, the observers heard the psychologist instruct the student to present himself as if he were ideally suited for a job. The psychologist then gave the student a description of the ideal candidate for the job. For some of the observers, the job was that of submariner, a role described as requiring an other-directed person who was friendly, relaxed, and nonirritable. Other observers heard the job described as being that of astronaut, a job requiring a very inner-directed person. The observers then heard the student answer a series of questions in either a highly inner-directed or a highly other-directed manner.

Observers who heard the student answer the questions in a manner consistent with the role expectations (presenting himself as other-directed for the submariner position or inner-directed for the astronaut position) did not form a strong impression of the student. They described the student as moderately affiliative and moderately independent and had little confidence in their judgments. But when the student answered the questions in a manner inconsistent with the role expectations, observers made stronger inferences about his personality. The student who presented himself as inner-directed for the submariner position was confidently rated as independent and nonaffiliative, and the student who presented himself as other-directed for the astronaut position was confidently rated as very conforming and affiliative. Thus, only the out-of-role behavior provided a basis for making strong inferences about the dispositions of the actor.

Choice

A second factor the observer considers in making inferences is the actor's degree of choice in performing the behavior. The more choice the actor is perceived to have in engaging in an action, the more confident the observer will be that the action does indeed reflect an underlying disposition. If environmental pressures to perform the behavior are present, it will be unclear to the observer whether the behavior was due to situational or dispositional factors. Consequently, the observer should make a less extreme and less confident dispositional attribution.

Jones and Harris (1967) investigated this idea in a simple experiment. Observer subjects were given an essay on Castro's Cuba—supposedly written by another student. Some of the observers (choice condition) were told that the student had been given complete freedom by his instructor to take a pro- or anti-Castro position on this issue. Other observers (no-choice condition) were told that the student's instructor had required that the student support the position taken in the essay. All observers then read an essay of moderate (C +) quality, ostensibly written by the student. Some observers read a pro-Castro essay; others read an anti-

Castro essay. The observers were then asked to estimate the student's true attitude toward Castro.

Observers who read the anti-Castro essay inferred that the student had more extreme anti-Castro attitudes when he had freely chosen to support that position than when it had been assigned. Similarly, observers who read the pro-Castro essay inferred that the student had a more favorable attitude toward Castro when he chose rather than was assigned that position. We see that freely chosen behaviors are more informative for the observer than behaviors that are required by an environmental contingency.

There was also one unexpected finding in this experiment. Jones and Harris initially expected that when the position taken in the essay was assigned by the instructor, the direction of the essay would make little difference: Observers reading a required pro-Castro essay and observers reading a required anti-Castro essay should have made the same inference concerning the student's true attitude toward Castro. Since the position taken in the essay was required in both cases, the essay should have been uninformative about the student's true attitude. However, the student writing the pro-Castro essay was perceived to have a more favorable attitude toward Castro than the student writing the anti-Castro essay, even though the position had been assigned in both cases. Apparently the observers tended to underestimate the influence of situational factors in determining the behavior. This is a topic to which we will return later in this chapter.

Analysis of Effects

The influence of choice, discussed at a general level in the preceding section, can be specified at a more detailed level. This more fine-grained analysis requires us to note that behaviors often have multiple consequences, or effects. If a student goes to a dance, he may be going for one or more reasons. He could be going as a break from homework, to listen to the music, to meet members of the opposite sex, or to socialize with friends. We should also note that at any given time, the actor has a number of different behaviors in which he can choose to participate. Continuing with our example, suppose that the student can also go to the coffee shop or to a Bergman movie. If he goes to the coffee shop, he will have his break from homework, he may meet members of the opposite sex, and he can eat his fill of culinary delights. If he goes to the movie, he will have a break from homework and be intellectually stimulated. Each choice, with its effects, is shown in Figure 9-1.

Dance	Coffee Shop	Movie
break from homework	break from homework	break from homework
listen to music	food	intellectual stimulation
meet women	meet women	
socialize with friends		

Figure 9-1. The Friday night choice dilemma.

Given that the student selects one of the alternatives, how does the observer analyze the reason for the choice? Jones and Davis suggest three steps in this process. First, the observer identifies the choices and their associated effects that are available to the actor. This is what was done in Figure 9-1. Second, any effect that is common to both the chosen and non-chosen alternatives is eliminated, since such effects provide no useful information about a possible cause for the choice. In our example, the effect "break from homework" is present in all three alternatives. Regardless of which alternative is chosen, this effect will be common to both the chosen and nonchosen alternatives, and it can therefore be eliminated as a cause of choosing one activity over another. Third, effects associated with only the chosen alternative are assumed to be desired by the actor. Further, the actor is assumed to be avoiding any effects that are associated with all the nonchosen alternatives. Finally, those effects associated with only one of the nonchosen alternatives are assumed to be unimportant.

Back to the example. If the student chooses to attend the dance, the observer will infer that he enjoys listening to music and socializing with friends and that food and intellectual stimulation are relatively unimportant. The observer can infer nothing about meeting women or taking a break from homework, since they are common to both the chosen and nonchosen alternatives. If the student chooses to go to the coffee shop, the observer will infer that he enjoys culinary delights and that socializing, music, and intellectual stimulation are not important to him. Last, if the student chooses to go to the movie, the observer will infer that the student desires intellectual stimulation, wants to *avoid* meeting women, and feels that music and food are unimportant. What dispositions would the observer, using this analysis, attribute to the student in each case? Should the student go to the movie, he would be perceived to be an intellectual; if he went to the coffee shop, he would be perceived to be a gourmet or gourmand (depending on the quality of food in the coffee shop); and if he went to the dance, he would be perceived as a social type.

This rather elaborate inference process postulated by Jones and Davis has not been investigated extensively. In the only experiment to examine the process directly, Newtson (1974) independently varied two factors: the number of effects eliminated by a choice and the number of effects remaining after a choice made by the actor. To illustrate, in our example, imagine that the student had only a choice between the dance and the coffee shop. If he chose the dance, one effect (food) would be eliminated by the choice, and two effects (listening to music, meeting women) would remain after the choice. Newtson found, consistent with the theory, that the smaller the number of positive effects remaining after the choice, the more correspondent the inference that was made by observer subjects about the actor's disposition. That is, the observers would with greater confidence attribute to the actor a personality trait that was consistent with his behavior. In addition, Newtson found that the more positive effects eliminated by the choice, the higher the correspondence.

Finally, when the observers could use either the number of effects remaining after the choice or the number of effects eliminated by the choice to make their inference, they generally preferred to use the number of effects remaining. Evidently, then, observers use both the number of effects remaining after a choice and the number of effects eliminated by the choice to form inferences about the actor's disposition, but the former factor is weighted more heavily.

Motivational Influences on Attribution

Up to this point we have assumed that the observer is a passive bystander who is not involved in the situation. However, there are many situations in which the behavior of the actor directly affects the observer. We will look at two of these.

Hedonic Relevance   Many of the actor's behaviors directly affect the outcomes of the observer. Some actions are gratifying to the observer, and others are punishing. To the extent that the actor's behavior affects the observer's outcomes (either positively or negatively), the action is said to be "hedonically relevant" to the observer. The more hedonically relevant the action is to the observer, the more correspondent the inference that the observer will form about the actor's dispositions. Returning to the case of Tom punching the drunk, if I am an observer of the action who is also involved in the situation (for example, if I am the drunk or the drunk's brother), I am much more likely to infer that Tom is aggressive than if I am not involved in the situation. To the extent that Tom's actions affect my outcomes, the action is hedonically relevant and will lead to a more extreme dispositional inference.

By what process does hedonic relevance affect inferences? Hedonic relevance seems to simplify the inference process. The actor may ignore certain effects of the action, may treat similar effects of the action as being identical, or may perceive originally neutral effects as now being positive or negative. The result of this simplification of the inference process is to decrease the number of environmental factors as well as the number of dispositions that may be perceived as being possible causes of the action, thereby increasing correspondence.

Some empirical evidence for the operation of hedonic relevance is found in an experiment by Jones and de Charms (1957). In this experiment an accomplice of the experimenter always failed at a task. In some groups the failure prevented the other group members from winning a monetary reward (high hedonic relevance). In other groups the failure had no effect on the outcomes for the other group members (low hedonic relevance). The accomplice was rated as being less competent and less dependable when his failure affected the other group members than when it did not. Thus the increase in hedonic relevance led to increased correspondence between the observed failure behavior and the attributed disposition of incompetence.

Personalism When the actor's behavior is high in hedonic relevance, an additional factor becomes important in the inference process. The observer attempts to determine whether the actor chose to behave in a given manner because of the observer or for some other reason. If an action is directed specifically toward the observer, it is high in personalism. However, if the action is directed toward people in general or if it affects the observer but only as the by-product of behavior directed toward another goal, it is low in personalism. Actions high in personalism lead to more extreme inferences than actions low in personalism.

Our original example may again be helpful. Suppose that in an attempt to punch the drunk, Tom inadvertently strikes the observer instead. This action would be high in hedonic relevance (being hit has an adverse effect on the observer's outcomes) but would be low in personalism, since the action was not directed specifically toward the observer. Only when the observer believes that the actor had knowledge of him prior to the action and that the action was directed specifically toward him is the action high in personalism.

In summary, Jones and Davis consider two motivational biases related to the observer's personal involvement in the situation. Actions that positively or negatively affect the observer's outcomes are high in hedonic relevance. Actions directed specifically toward the observer are high in personalism. To the extent that each of these factors is high, the observer should make a more extreme dispositional inference about the cause of the actor's behavior.

SPECIAL TOPICS

Nonmotivational Biases

In our discussion of Jones and Harris' experiment an anomaly in the results was noted: observers who read a pro- or anti-Castro essay inferred that the writer's attitude was consistent with the position presented in the essay even when the writer was required to take the position expressed in the essay. This result, that observers underestimate the importance of situational factors in determining the actor's behavior, has now been obtained in a number of experiments. Indeed, Snyder and Jones (1974) found that even when the observers themselves had previously been required to write an essay supporting a given position, they still inferred that the attitude of a student who wrote an assigned essay was consistent with the expressed position. Only when extreme measures were taken to make the importance of the environmental constraints salient to the observer was this bias eliminated. For example, when the actor was described as having been required to copy a prepared essay, observers did not infer that the actor's attitudes were consistent with the position expressed. Thus, observers seem to underestimate the influence of environmental constraints in making inferences about the causes of the actor's behavior.

What is responsible for this bias in the inference process? In an earlier paper, Jones and Nisbett (1971) pointed out that at any given time, the observer can focus on only a few elements in the situation. Those elements will be salient to the observer and will be weighted heavily in the inference process. The nonsalient components of the background of the observer's attention will receive less consideration. For example, when observers read an essay supporting Castro's Cuba, their attention is focused on the essay and its content; the conditions under which it was written exist only as background. In general, the actor's behavior is the most dynamic and potentially informative element in the situation, and it will therefore elicit the observer's attention. The actor's behavior will be more salient to the observer than the situational background in which it occurs. Thus observers will tend to look for the cause of the behavior in the actor's dispositions rather than in the environment. This seems to be a very pervasive bias, although it can be eliminated or even reversed through the use of special techniques that increase the salience of environmental causes of behavior (Jones, 1979).

Comparing the Inferences of Actors and Observers

Thus far in our discussion of the inference process we have considered only the observer of the action. But what about the actor? As we saw in Chapter 8 on self-perception theory, actors do make inferences about their own attitudes from their behavior. According to Bem's self-perception theory, actors and observers follow identical processes in inferring the attitudes of the actor. However, we have just noted that observers tend to be biased in that they underestimate the influence of environmental conditions in determining the actor's behavior. For self-perception theory to be correct, then, actors must show the same bias as observers in inferring the causes of their own behavior. However, actors seem to have a bias different from observers' in their perception of the causes of their own behavior.

To understand this, reconsider the roles of the actor and observer. The observer is conceived of as a passive bystander whose attention is focused on the actor's behavior. The actor, in contrast, is actively engaging in behavior in response to the demands of the situation. The actor will focus attention on important aspects of the environment in order to make decisions about the future course of the interaction. The important elements of the *situation* will be salient to the actor, and these will weigh heavily in the inference process. The actor's own behavior, from the actor's perspective, is just background. This means that actors will weigh situational constraints more heavily in the inference process than observers will. Actors will usually perceive situational factors as the cause of their behavior, while observers will typically perceive the actor's dispositions as the cause of the behavior.

The importance of this difference between actor's and observer's focus of attention is graphically illustrated in an experiment by Storms (1973). The actor engaged in a brief conversation with another person and then observed a videotape recording of the conversation in which the picture was from the actor's viewpoint (the camera was pointed at the other person) or the observer's viewpoint (the camera was pointed at the actor).

Subjects who viewed the video replay of the conversation from the actor's point of view accounted for the actor's behavior in terms of situational factors. However, subjects who viewed the replay from the observer's standpoint accounted for the actor's behavior in terms of the actor's dispositions. Thus, the attributions a person (either the actor or the observer) makes concerning the causes of an actor's behavior tend to follow the person's focus of attention.

The Problem of Accuracy

We have not mentioned the accuracy of the inferences that observers make about the dispositions of the actor. Many instances come to mind in which the observer seems to follow the principles of correspondent-inference theory yet makes a serious error in judging the personality or the attitudes of another. Why, then, should one be concerned about the observer's inference process, when the inferences are often "incorrect"? The answer is that it is the observer's impression of a person, not the person's "true" personality and attitudes, that will be a determinant of the observer's behavior toward that person. Returning once again to our original example, we will probably act very differently toward Tom if we infer that he is highly aggressive rather than average in aggressiveness. Whether Tom is in fact aggressive or not makes little difference in our initial behavior toward him.

SUMMARY

The theory of correspondent inferences presents a number of principles that detail how an observer makes inferences about the dispositions of an actor. To the extent that the actor's behavior is socially undesirable (deviant or unusual) and is freely chosen, it is informative to the observer, and the observer will infer that the actor possesses dispositions consistent with the behavior. The fewer effects remaining after a choice, and the more effects eliminated by the choice, the more certain the observer will be in inferring a disposition that is consistent with the actor's choice. To the extent that the observer is involved in the situation, two additional factors are important: (1) behaviors affecting the observer's outcomes are hedonically relevant and lead to a more extreme dispositional inference, and (2) behaviors perceived to be directed specifically toward the observer are high in personalism and lead to a more extreme dispositional inference. Finally, observers, compared with actors, tend to underestimate the importance of situational factors as causes of behavior.

SUGGESTED READING

Jones, E. E. The rocky road from acts to dispositions. *American Psychologist,* 1979, *34,* 107–117.

Jones, E. E., & Davis, K. E. A theory of correspondent inferences: From acts to dispositions. In L. Berkowitz (Ed.), *Advances in experimental social psychology* (Vol. 2). New York: Academic Press, 1965.

Jones, E. E., & Gerard, H. B. *Foundations of social psychology.* New York: Wiley, 1967.

CHAPTER 10

KELLEY'S ATTRIBUTION THEORY

ANN HAS just entered adolescence and spends much of her time hanging around with two friends, Betty and Cindy. Like many teenagers, the three friends spend much of their time listening to popular music. One evening the girls go to their first concert and see Paul McCartney, a popular rock star. Ann finds that she and her two friends are ecstatic at the concert. As an analytical person (somewhat unusual for a teenager), Ann begins to think about possible reasons for her positive emotional reaction. Was it because Paul McCartney is really great? Was it because she really likes music? Or are all concerts simply great? Over the next several months Ann and her friends see a potpourri of different performers in concert, listen to their records, and see them on television. Ann thinks back to her original question: Why did I like Paul McCartney's concert so much?

In pondering her question Ann first recalls that she and her friends were all ecstatic at the McCartney concert. But did she and her friends have a similar reaction to other performers? No, somehow they just didn't get the same feeling when they saw the Willie Nelson and the Leonard Bernstein concerts. Did she and her friends ever have this same ecstatic feeling from other musical experiences? Well, yes, when she and her friends listened to McCartney's records or saw him on television. But the three girls never had the same experience with the other performers. This information is summarized in Figure 10-1.

THE THEORY

In the two previous chapters we have considered how social inferences are made on the basis of a single behavioral episode. For example, in the chapter on self-perception theory we examined the inferences drawn about someone who signs a petition, writes an essay, or gives a speech. Sometimes, however, more complete information is available to observers. They might have observed the responses of several persons to the request to sign the petition. Or they might have seen solicitors representing a variety of causes approach the student. In such cases, in which multiple behaviors are involved, self-perception and correspondent-inference theories cannot be applied readily to the situation. The present framework, Kelley's (1967, 1971, 1973) attribution theory, provides an understanding of the inference process when the observer has multiple sources of information.

In our example above, how can Ann infer the apparent cause of the reactions of her friends and herself from the information she has? According to Kelley's attribution theory, she will try to identify the dimension with which these reactions or feelings are associated. This means that she will try to find a dimension that corresponds to changes in the emotional reactions of the three girls. To understand how she might do this, the example must be examined in more detail.

Dimensions of Attribution

As can be seen in Figure 10-1, we analyze all the events according to three dimensions: time/modality, consensus among persons, and entities.

Time/Modality The time dimension refers to the observer's experiences with the same object at different times; the modality dimension refers to the different ways in which the observer can interact with the object. For convenience, time and modality are normally treated as a sin-

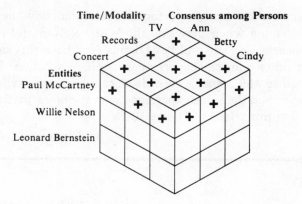

Figure 10-1.   An entity attribution. Note that the positive effects are associated only with Paul McCartney. Adapted from *An Introduction to Attribution Processes*, by K. G. Shaver. Copyright © 1975 by Winthrop Publishers, Inc. Reprinted by permission of the author and Winthrop Publishers, Inc., 17 Dunster Street, Cambridge, Massachusetts.

gle dimension, since it is difficult to keep their effects separate. This combined dimension gives us information about how consistent or reliable each person's responses are.

In our present example the three girls are exposed to the musicians at different times and through the modalities of concerts, records, and television. We note that changes in the time/modality dimension do not seem to be uniquely associated with the girls' emotional reactions. The girls continued to be excited about McCartney regardless of whether the exposure came through concerts, records, or television. Similarly, their unemotional reactions to Nelson and Bernstein were constant across the different modes of presentation. Therefore, the time/modality dimension may be ruled out as the apparent cause of the girls' reactions.

Consensus   What about the consensus dimension? This dimension refers to the reactions of the different observers. It gives us information about how widespread the reaction is among people. In our present example, the degree of consensus is determined by assessing the similarity of the individual reactions of the three girls—Ann, Betty, and Cindy. As we consider the three observers, we note that their emotional responses to each object are remarkably similar. This high level of agreement across observers suggests that the consensus dimension can be ruled out as the apparent cause of the girls' reactions. Only if consensus were low could we begin to talk about the role of this dimension, as will be illustrated in the next example.

Entities The entities are the objects (or persons) under consideration by the observers—in this case Leonard Bernstein, Paul McCartney, and Willie Nelson. We note that the emotional reactions of the three girls change when the entity changes. The girls always have a positive reaction to Paul McCartney (regardless of modality), and they do not have a similar positive reaction to the other performers. Since only the entities dimension is associated with the feelings of Ann and her friends, Ann will perceive that Paul McCartney, the entity that corresponds to her positive feelings, is the source of her emotional reaction. This can be seen in Figure 10-1: positive emotional reactions occur only in the top layer of the cube.

To summarize our discussion thus far, the observer first locates the behaviors under consideration along three dimensions. (1) *Time/modality* refers to the reactions to some object at different times and through different means of interacting with that object. (2) *Consensus* has to do with similarities in reactions of different observers to the same object. And by (3) *entities* we mean the different objects under consideration. The observer then tries to determine which dimension is associated with changes in the behaviors. That dimension is then inferred to be the cause of the behaviors.

Now consider a modification of the original example. Suppose that Ann observes that Cindy is ecstatic at the concert; Ann herself has a rather neutral reaction, as does Betty. In addition, Ann has observed that Cindy has similar reactions to the other musicians—Bernstein and Nelson. Finally, Cindy has positive reactions regardless of how she hears the performers—whether in concert, on television, or on records. Neither Ann nor Betty has such positive reactions to any of the performers, no matter how the music is heard. This information is summarized in Figure 10-2.

How would this situation be analyzed in Kelley's attribution theory? Once again, the observer's problem is to identify the dimension associated with the behavior (the emotional reaction). What about the time/modality dimension? The girls seem to have their respective reactions no matter whether the performance is in the form of concerts, records, or television. Time/modality can therefore be ruled out as an apparent cause. What about the consensus dimension? Only Cindy has positive responses to the performers. The other two girls have neutral reactions in all cases. The consensus dimension, then, is associated with the emotional response. Since there is very low consensus (that is, not everyone likes all the performers), we should infer that some trait of Cindy is responsible for her attraction to the musicians. In other words, she is not simply conforming

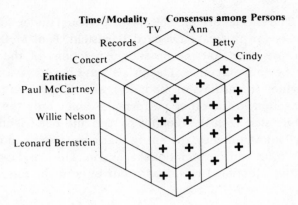

Figure 10-2.   A person attribution. Note that the positive effects are associated only with Cindy. Adapted from *An Introduction to Attribution Processes,* by K. G. Shaver. Copyright © 1975 by Winthrop Publishers, Inc. Reprinted by permission of the author and Winthrop Publishers, Inc., 17 Dunster Street, Cambridge, Massachusetts.

to a popular trend. Finally, the entities (the individual performers) do not seem to be a plausible cause of Cindy's behavior, for she likes all of them equally. Again, we cannot point to something external as a cause of her liking, and so it makes better sense to infer that some characteristic of Cindy is basic to her reactions to the performers.

In light of all this reasoning, Ann should infer that Cindy's basic love of music is the cause of her reactions. One can arrive at this conclusion graphically by reference to Figure 10-2, in which positive reactions appear only on the right side of the cube, corresponding to Cindy.

Once again, we have seen that the observer follows a straightforward inference process. The observer first classifies the behaviors along the three dimensions of time/modality, consensus, and entities. Next, the observer tries to identify the dimension associated with the behavior in question. If the behavior seems to go on no matter how a particular dimension changes, we can rule out that dimension as a possible cause. For instance, if hearing a performer on Tuesday or Saturday makes no difference in Cindy's reaction, time can be ruled out as a cause. If exposure to the performers in live concert or on television makes no difference, modality can be ruled out as a cause. If Cindy reacts the same way to all performers, this means that variation in the entity does not matter—that is, entities can also be eliminated as a possible cause. This leaves us with only the consensus dimension, and, to be sure, there is variation in the different girls' reactions. Given this variation, we can attribute Cindy's individual reactions to the fact of her being different from the other girls.

Before proceeding further, two observations should be made. First, Kelley's attribution theory deals both with self- and with other-attributions. Although the outcome of the previous example was a dispositional attribution about another (Cindy is a music lover), the example could easily be changed to lead to a dispositional *self*-attribution. This would simply require that Ann (the observer) experience the positive reactions to the performers, whereas Cindy would have the neutral reactions. In this case Ann would infer that something about herself caused the emotional reaction. Second, we saw in the two previous chapters that environmental and dispositional factors are the major causes inferred by observers to explain a single behavioral episode. These correspond respectively to entity and person attributions in Kelley's theory and were discussed in our first two examples. It should be clear that an attribution to an entity is a kind of attribution to an environmental factor and that an attribution to some unique trait of a person (the idiosyncratic Cindy) constitutes a person attribution. But we do not stop with a simple environment/person distinction in Kelley's attribution theory, for Kelley spells out two further kinds of attributions. We will illustrate these using variants of the opening example.

Circumstance Attributions   Suppose Ann notes that Cindy has a positive emotional reaction to the Paul McCartney concert. Imagine also that this is unusual—Cindy never responds to McCartney's television or recorded performances that way. Cindy also does not usually have strong reactions to other performers, whether in concert, on records, or on television. Finally, neither Ann nor Betty has a positive reaction to *any* performer, no matter what the medium. This case is illustrated in Figure 10-3. Note that the positive emotional reaction is not associated with *any* of the dimensions: it occurs only for Cindy listening to Paul McCartney in concert. In this case the effect is attributed to the special circumstances present for Cindy at this concert. This suggests that some unknown factor outside the analysis is probably causing Cindy's positive reaction. Perhaps Cindy overreacted at her first concert, Paul McCartney was unusually good that night, or Cindy was in an especially favorable mood. Since the cause is not clearly identified, it is difficult to predict when Cindy might have a similar reaction in the future.

Person-by-Entity Attributions   As an illustration of the final possibility, suppose Cindy likes Paul McCartney in concert, on records, and on television. However, she is neutral toward Willie Nelson and Leonard Bernstein, and her friends are neutral toward all three performers. This information is summarized in Figure 10-4. In this case the effect (liking)

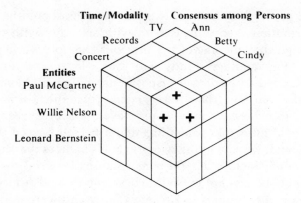

Figure 10-3.   A circumstance attribution. Note that the positive effects are not associated with any of the dimensions. Adapted from *An Introduction to Attribution Processes,* by K. G. Shaver. Copyright © 1975 by Winthrop Publishers, Inc. Reprinted by permission of the author and Winthrop Publishers, Inc., 17 Dunster Street, Cambridge, Massachusetts.

occurs only for the combination of a particular person (Cindy) and a particular entity (McCartney). This type of inference, called a "person-by-entity attribution," will often be made when the effect involves matters of taste or matters on which people have divergent attitudes. In such cases both the person and the entity must be specified to predict the effect (the positive emotional reaction). In the present instance we infer that Cindy has a unique liking for Paul McCartney's music.

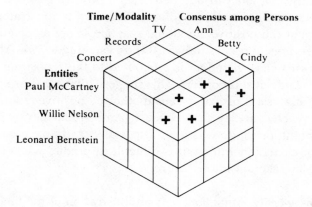

Figure 10-4.   A person-by-entity attribution. Note that the positive effects occur only for the combination of Cindy and Paul McCartney. Adapted from *An Introduction to Attribution Processes,* by K. G. Shaver. Copyright © 1975 by Winthrop Publishers, Inc. Reprinted by permission of the author and Winthrop Publishers, Inc., 17 Dunster Street, Cambridge, Massachusetts.

In summary, Kelley's attribution theory provides a very general framework for inferring the cause of a set of behavioral episodes. The effects taking place in each episode are the basic data from which we analyze. Effects include such things as behaviors (for example, aggression), attitudes, statements of liking, and emotional reactions. The observer analyzes the presence or absence of the effect in a number of contexts to determine the dimension with which the effect is associated. The effect may be associated with the entity dimension, leading therefore to an entity attribution, or it may be associated with the consensus dimension, implying a person attribution. If the effect is not associated with any dimension, the result is an attribution to special circumstances surrounding the event. Thus, according to the theory, the observer works in much the same way as a "naive scientist" who is seeking the apparent cause of an effect. Kelley's theory applies equally well to self- and other-attributions and assumes that one inference process underlies both types of attributions. Finally, attributions to a combination of dimensions (for example, person-by-entity) are possible, but they seem to occur less frequently in most situations than the simpler attributions to a single dimension.

RESEARCH EXAMPLES

Processing Complete Information

McArthur (1972) conducted a simple demonstration of Kelley's theory as applied to attributions about others. The subjects were given a number of simple vignettes. Each vignette presented an effect to be understood, and it conveyed whether the effect was associated with each of the separate dimensions (time/modality, consensus, entities). Consider the following effect (adapted from McArthur, 1972), which served as the focal point of subjects' attributions:

Kay thinks the stream is polluted.

Subjects were given potentially explanatory information relevant to each of the three possible dimensions:

1. Almost everyone who sees the stream thinks it is polluted.
2. Kay thinks almost no other stream is polluted.
3. In the past, Kay almost always thought the same stream was polluted.

The subject was then asked to decide what led Kay to conclude that the stream was polluted: Was it something about Kay (person attribution)? Was it the stream (entity attribution)? Was it some special circumstance—perhaps a herd of pigs had just passed by upstream (circumstance attribution)? Or was it some combination of these factors? For example, perhaps Kay had a unique belief that this particular stream was polluted every spring.

The effect to be considered in this example is the belief that the stream is polluted. We first observe that Kay and nearly everyone else think the stream is polluted, meaning that the effect is not associated with the consensus dimension. Second, we note that Kay has always believed the stream was polluted, so that the effect is not associated with the time/ modality dimension. Finally, Kay thinks that *this* stream is polluted but that most others are not. Therefore, the effect is associated with the entities (different streams) dimension. Since the effect has to do with the entities but not with the other two dimensions, the observer should attribute Kay's belief to the stream. In fact, 61% of McArthur's subjects who were given the problem above or similar ones, in which the effect was associated only with the entities dimension, attributed the effect to the entity. For other cases, in which the effect was not associated with entities, fewer than 15% of the subjects attributed the effect to the entity. Finally, when the effect was associated with the entity dimension *and* one or more of the other dimensions, fewer than 25% of the subjects attributed the effect to the entity. In short, when there were other plausible causes, subjects were less likely to perceive the entity to be the sole cause of the effect.

The results for the other types of attributions also followed the predictions of the theory. When the effect was associated only with the consensus dimension, 85% of the subjects attributed the effect to the person. Further, when the effect was not associated with *any* of the dimensions, 70% of the subjects made circumstance attributions. That is, when all dimensions could be ruled out as possible causes, subjects were left with only the possibility that special circumstances caused the effect. Finally, the more complex person-by-entity attributions occurred infrequently. Even under the "ideal" conditions illustrated in Figure 10-4, fewer than 40% of the subjects made person-by-entity attributions.

In summary, McArthur's experiment showed that subjects can make attributions that closely follow the predictions of Kelley's theory. When the effect was associated with only one dimension, attributions were made mainly to that dimension. This was true for both the consensus dimension (person attributions) and the entities dimension (entity attributions). If the effect was not associated with any of the dimensions, attributions were to the particular circumstances surrounding the event. Finally, the more complex person-by-entity attributions were not preferred to the simpler attributions under any of the information combinations.

Before proceeding further, some observations should be made about McArthur's experiment. In some ways this was the ideal situation in which to test Kelley's theory. The subjects were intelligent. They did not have to figure out whether each dimension was associated with the effect—they were given this information explicitly. The subjects also worked on a series of highly similar problems, which would give them considerable practice in using the information in a logical manner. Finally, the subjects were not motivated to justify their own behavior: they were simply trying to make accurate inferences about another person. All these factors would encourage logical inferences.

Processing Incomplete Information

In our analysis of the causes of the behavior of Ann and her friends, we assumed that the observer had complete information about the reactions of the three girls in all the possible situations. That is, the observer could, with confidence, assign a + (positive emotional response) or else not assign one to each cell of the cube. We also assumed that there were no reactions that were inconsistent with the general pattern. In Figure 10-1, if Ann had a neutral reaction to Paul McCartney's concert, thereby removing one of the pluses, the pattern would no longer be perfectly consistent with an entity attribution. How are such cases of inconsistent or missing information dealt with by the observer?

Three solutions to this problem have been suggested. One possibility (Kelley, 1967) is that observers will make more tentative attributions when information is inconsistent or missing. The patterns depicted in Figures 10-1 through 10-4 are "ideal" patterns expected for each of the attributional outcomes. As the actual pattern of effects becomes more and more discrepant from one of the "ideal" patterns, people's confidence in their inferences should decrease markedly. Subjects should be more confident about an entity attribution if they are given the case depicted in Figure 10-1 rather than the altered version in which Ann has a neutral reaction to Paul McCartney's concert. They might also be more reluctant to change their original entity attribution if they subsequently receive additional information inconsistent with this inference.

A second possibility is that subjects may fill in missing information so that it is consistent with the pattern suggested by the available information (Orvis, Cunningham, & Kelley, 1975). Suppose the observer has information that the effect is associated with the consensus dimension. This pattern suggests that the outcome will probably be a person attribution, and the observer is likely to fill in the missing information so that this pattern is completed. The guiding rule in filling in information, in this case, is that the effect should *not* be associated with either the time/modality dimension or the entities dimension. If it were, a more complex inference would be implied, and people seem to prefer the simplest attribution that is consistent with the available information.

A final method of dealing with missing information is for the observer to seek out situations that would supply the missing data (Kelley, 1967, 1975). The observer may set up an "attributional test" exposing the person to a situation in which the responses can be noted. If you observe a professor berating a student for incompetence, you might want to conduct such a test before reaching a conclusion. You might try to ascertain how this student performs in other contexts. Or you might observe the professor's interactions with other students, particularly those who are known to be highly competent. By seeking out such additional information, you can determine more confidently whether the behavior was due to the professor (is she a hostile person?), the student (is he in fact incompetent?), or the special circumstances surrounding the interaction (perhaps the professor or the student was having an unusually bad day).

In summary, the observer can deal with missing or inconsistent information in at least three ways. At the present stage of development of the theory, the conditions in which each of these methods will be used have not been specified. It is likely, however, that active information seeking will be most important when the observer must make accurate predictions about the person's future behavior.

SPECIAL TOPICS

The Role of Choice: Discounting

So far we have assumed that the people freely participated in each situation. The girls in our opening example freely chose to listen to the three performers. There were also no constraints on their emotional responses. Frequently, however, there are forces in the environment—rewards and punishments, rules, and the like—that encourage or discourage particular behaviors. How do such factors influence the attributional process?

To answer this question, it is helpful to proceed in two stages. We will first examine how environmental factors might influence the interpretation of each separate behavior; then we will consider how these interpretations might be combined to form an overall inference.

Let us return to our opening example. Suppose we discover that Cindy's parents will bankroll her concert attendance and record purchases only if she shows appreciation for "good music." Cindy dutifully attends a Leonard Bernstein concert and reports to her parents that she "really liked it." How would an observer interpret this effect?

Cindy's statement is less informative than the same statement made in the absence of parental coercion. Cindy may have really liked the Bernstein concert. She may also have made the statement simply to please her parents. Since there are now two plausible reasons for Cindy's statement, an observer would not infer that Cindy had strong positive feelings for the concert, but rather, weak positive feelings would probably be inferred, and such an inference would be attended by considerable uncertainty. This example illustrates Kelley's discounting principle: "The role of a given cause in producing a given effect is discounted if other plausible causes are present" (1971, p. 8). Hence, observers will interpret coerced positive (or negative) responses as *weakly* indicating that the actor's true feelings are slightly positive (or negative).

The second stage can now be specified. We need only assume that positive (or negative) effects that are discounted are treated in much the same way as missing effects. In attempting to isolate the dimension with which the effects are associated, the observer would treat freely performed behaviors as being highly informative and coerced behaviors as having less informational value. Hence, the observer could apply any of the solutions discussed in our section on processing incomplete information. The observer might form an inference based on the overall pattern of effects, but with diminished confidence if the behaviors in some conditions are coerced. Or if the coerced responses were consistent with one of the "ideal" patterns depicted in Figures 10-1 through 10-4, the observer might infer that the responses, even though coerced, were strongly indicative of the actor's true feelings. Finally, the observer might seek out other instances in which the actor performs the same behavior under more informative, free choice conditions. In short, the observer will give greater weight to freely performed than coerced behaviors in making the attribution.

Underutilization of Consensus Information

Although several studies have supported the predictions of Kelley's model, there is one troubling discrepancy that has appeared in a number of studies (for example, McArthur, 1972, 1976). This is the problem of underutilization of consensus information. In McArthur's (1972) study, described above, information about the responses of other observers ("Almost no one else thinks the stream is polluted" or "Nearly everyone else thinks the stream is polluted") made little difference in the inferences that were drawn. In contrast, subjects gave considerable weight to the knowledge that the person's responses were consistent (or inconsistent) over time and to the knowledge that the person had similar (or dissimilar) responses to different entities. Thus, although Kelley's model assumes that information about each of the three dimensions is equally important, subjects treat information about the time/modality and entities dimensions as more important than consensus information—in some circumstances. (Consensus information is underutilized when the effects under consideration are opinions, emotional feelings, or responses related to personality traits, such as extroversion or hostility. When the effects involve abilities, consensus information appears to be utilized readily, as will be seen in Chapters 11 and 15.) How can we account for this curious discrepancy?

Kelley's model assumes that observers use only the information provided in the problem. As we saw in our discussion of McArthur's (1972) experiment, the problems typically involve making inferences about the cause of the behavior of an unknown stranger. Since observers characteristically know nothing about this person, it is quite likely that they will rely heavily on the information provided about the person's responses to different entities and behavior over time. But the observer has another important source of information about the responses of others to the situation: observers can recall their own behavior in a similar situation or else imagine how they might behave in the situation. This additional source of information, which is not an integral part of the problem given to the observer, should be especially important because people often believe that their own behavior is more common than it actually is (Ross, 1977). Accordingly, if the consensus information is discrepant from observers' impressions of how they would behave in the situation, those same observers will tend to minimize the importance of the information. They might assume, for example, that the consensus information was not representative of a normal population, but was based on some group of oddballs who just happened to be selected. To the extent that the observer can be reassured that the information provided represents the responses of a normal or representative group, the impact of consensus information should increase (Wells & Harvey, 1977).

Consensus information may also be given little weight by observers because of the way it has been presented in most experiments. The information is typically given in abstract, summary form, as in our example: "Nearly everyone thinks the stream is polluted." When compared with the more vivid image of one's actual or imagined behavior, such abstract statements seem rather pallid, and it is not surprising that they are given little weight. However, if the consensus information could be presented in a more lively manner, its impact should be felt. Manis and Dovalina (1979) found that consensus information was readily utilized when pictures of a number of people were individually presented together with their accompanying attitudes. This procedure permitted the observer to form a concrete image of the collective attitude, thereby producing a strong consensus effect.

Manis and Dovalina's finding is potentially very important. Observers usually will not have abstract, summary information available, but rather will rely on concrete images of the behavior of persons recalled from memory, as in our opening example. Further, images of the behavior of individual persons recalled from memory are likely to be treated by the observer as being representative of the normal population (Ross, 1977). Consequently, in cases such as the opening example, in which the observer is analyzing a situation on the basis of personal experience, it is likely that each of the three dimensions will be given consideration in arriving at an attributional explanation.

The Problem of Bias

All the research examples discussed so far have focused on the inferences drawn by observers in rather mundane situations. Kelley's theory, however, is not limited to such mundane cases—it should apply equally well to involving situations in which actors derive inferences from their own behavior. And after our discussion in Chapter 9 it should come as no surprise that these personally involving settings are not adequately described by the simple version of Kelley's model described above. Rather, certain biases may enter the picture and seriously complicate the application of the model (Kelley, 1967).

One bias of interest to researchers is the "self-serving bias," defined as actors' taking credit for their successes and denying responsibility for their failures. Consider the following experiment by Stevens and Jones

(1976). Subjects worked on a number of sensory discrimination tasks, including matching different weights or different tones. These tasks constituted the entities. After each task, subjects were given bogus feedback indicating whether they had succeeded or failed. In terms of Kelley's theory, success and failure are simply effects, and one's successes should be interpreted in the same manner as one's failures. Subjects were then given information that indicated whether the effect (success or failure) was associated with the three dimensions of time/modality, consensus, and entities, and they were asked for the cause of their performance on the final visual discrimination task.

Contrary to Kelley's analysis, subjects who succeeded on the final task tended to attribute their performance to personal factors, whereas subjects who failed attributed their performance to the difficulty of the task (entity attribution) or to bad luck (circumstance attribution). We might try looking at this experiment in more detail: Consider the conditions in which the effect was associated only with the consensus dimension, a situation that should be highly conducive to a person attribution. This situation is analogous to our Figure 10-2: the person performed equally well on all the different tasks and also performed consistently on the two visual discrimination tasks, so that the effect was associated neither with the entities nor with the time/modality dimension. The person was also informed either that (1) he had succeeded on the final visual discrimination task even though most people had failed or (2) he had failed the final task even though most people had succeeded. In the first case 67% of the subjects attributed their success to personal factors, whereas in the second case, in which subjects failed, only 39% attributed their performance to personal factors. These results illustrate dramatically that the nature of the outcome influences the resulting self-attributions.

More specifically, whenever the behavior has implications for the subject's self-esteem or feelings of worth as a person, attributions will tend to be "self-serving." Rather than following the logical process postulated by Kelley's model, taking one in the direction of a logical inference, the person will attempt to arrive at attributions that maintain or bolster self-esteem. The person will strive to take credit for positive behaviors by making person attributions and to deny responsibility for negative behaviors by attributing them to the situation (entities) or to particular circumstances. Such self-serving attributions are particularly likely when accuracy is not important, as when the person does not expect to perform the same task again. Biased attributions are also to be expected more if the task is highly personally involving (Bradley, 1978; Miller & Ross, 1975; Snyder, Stephan, & Rosenfield, 1978; Zuckerman, 1979).

SUMMARY

Kelley's attribution theory provides a very general framework for understanding the inferences that will be drawn about a series of behaviors. According to the theory, the observer analyzes whether or not a given effect occurs in a number of situations and tries to isolate the dimension with which the effect is associated. If the effect is associated with the entities dimension, the result is an entities attribution; if the effect is associated with the consensus dimension, the result is a person attribution; and if the effect is not associated with any of the dimensions, it will be attributed to particular circumstances. Kelley's model may be applied with equal facility to self- and other-attributions.

Complications arise in applying the theory to more complex or involving circumstances. Among these are (1) missing or inconsistent information, (2) environmental coercion of responses, (3) the observer's bringing additional information or assumptions to bear on the analysis, and (4) bias entering the inference process. Most of these complications, however, can be understood with the addition of a few simple principles to Kelley's basic framework. Kelley's attribution theory has also been shown to be broadly applicable to a variety of social-psychological phenomena, including interpersonal attraction, interpersonal influence, and symptom interpretation, often providing a provocative alternative to theories built around motivational constructs.

SUGGESTED READING

Kelley, H. H. Attribution theory in social psychology. In D. Levine (Ed.), *Nebraska Symposium on Motivation* (Vol. 15). Lincoln: University of Nebraska Press, 1967.

Kelley, H. H. The processes of causal attribution. *American Psychologist,* 1973, *28,* 107–128.

Miller, D. T., & Ross, M. Self-serving biases in the attribution of causality: Fact or fiction? *Psychological Bulletin,* 1975, *82,* 213–225.

Shaver, K. G. An introduction to attribution processes. Cambridge, Mass.: Winthrop, 1975.

Snyder, M. L., Stephan, W. G., & Rosenfield, D. Attributional egotism. In J. H. Harvey, W. J. Ickes, & R. F. Kidd (Eds.), *New directions in attribution research* (Vol. 2). Hillsdale, N. J.: Erlbaum, 1978.

Zuckerman, M. Attribution of success and failure revisited; or, The motivational bias is alive and well in attribution theory. *Journal of Personality,* 1979, *47,* 245–287.

PART FOUR

SELF-EVALUATION
AND
SELF-EXPLANATION

The three notions discussed here, though highly divergent in their areas of application, have in common an emphasis on the human as a self-evaluator. The first two chapters have a common theoretical underpinning in that both invoke the assumption that humans need to evaluate themselves, no matter whether the evaluation takes the form of evaluating opinions, abilities, or even transitory bodily states. The third theory, operating in a much different context, assumes quite the contrary — that there is commonly a desire not to evaluate the self.

Social comparison theory (Chapter 11), beginning with the idea of a human need to evaluate opinions and abilities, has direct ramifications for a number of important interpersonal influence phenomena. For example, the theory addresses conformity as well as the effort to influence others — both of these being central topics in social psychology.

Schachter's theory of emotion (Chapter 12) has come to dominate psychological thinking about the onset of emotional states. Just like social comparison theory, the theory of emotions begins with an assumption of a need to evaluate — in this case to evaluate bodily states. It then goes on to argue that emotions are experienced to the extent that changes in bodily condition are explained in terms of feared objects, objects of lust, or other "emotional" stimuli.

The theory of self-awareness (Chapter 13) brings a new variable to a variety of social psychological phenomena. The variable is the degree of self-focused attention, and this concept is placed together with the idea that self-evaluation stemming from personal inadequacies is uncomfortable. The phenomena implied include reactions to the uncomfortable self-evaluative state (such as avoidance of settings that provoke self-awareness) and attempts to render the self better or more complete.

CHAPTER 11

SOCIAL COMPARISON THEORY

IT IS the spring of 1977, and the first United States execution in four years is about to get underway in Utah. A convicted murderer is to face the firing squad or hanging, and community opinion has become highly vocal. A group of men has convened in a barbershop, and all are expounding on the virtues of the execution as well as executions to follow: "What's the use in just locking 'em up? After five years they're paroled and out killing and raping again." Everyone in the shop is in agreement, and although all seem to be intent on expressing their accord with one another, none of them is very adamant in his arguments.

Then Smith drops into the shop. Smith is a regular part of the group, although he is known occasionally to harbor a maverick opinion. As soon as he senses the tone of the discussion, he volunteers his opinion: "Turn the poor guy loose! After fighting court battles for years, he's suffered enough."

The barbershop explodes into a flurry of opinion exchange. In concert, the group aims an all-out propagandizing effort in Smith's direction, refusing to allow him a chance for disagreement. The battle is long and hard, but Smith gradually comes to see the light and agrees that it is only just that one life be taken in exchange for another.

The newsboy, a local university student and known pacifist, suddenly drops by with the latest headlines on the capital punishment case and offers an offhand comment: "Turn the poor guy loose! After fighting court battles for years, he's suffered enough." The barbershop group looks askance, and a couple of men mutter something to the contrary, but there is no concerted effort to correct the error of the newsboy's opinion.

What are these phenomena all about? Festinger's theory of social comparison (1954) provides some unique answers, as will be shown below.

THE THEORY

The Drive to Evaluate

The theory's starting point is an assumption that humans have a drive to evaluate both their opinions and abilities. Why this drive? It is Festinger's thesis that inadequate appraisals of one's abilities and opinions can have immediate and sometimes disastrous consequences for behavior. If someone's opinion about the potential impact of a hurricane is totally out of fit with reality, the person could end up treading water beside an overturned boat. Similarly, it can be maladaptive to evaluate one's abilities inaccurately. The 16-year-old neophyte automobile driver, unrealistically cocksure of his abilities, might stray onto a Los Angeles rush-hour freeway where only those with real California driving skill are destined to live.

Festinger allows that our opinions and abilities can sometimes be evaluated by reference to nonsocial (physical) criteria. Some rather simple opinions are easily testable by reference to the nonsocial world—for example, an opinion about the number of teeth in a horse's mouth. One need only find a horse and proceed to count. (Indeed, the present authors have made this test, in order to answer the question once and for all. Typically, male horses have 40 teeth, independent of whether they have been castrated; mares have 36.) Simple abilities are also tested easily against physical reality. The question of whether we can touch the floor with our hands while standing with knees locked is best answered by trying.

The reader might imagine that Festinger was not interested mainly in these simple cases, and, to be sure, the theory comes into play when the opinion or ability cannot be tested readily through nonsocial tests and when we must therefore proceed to compare our abilities or opinions against those of others. The barbershop discussion of capital punishment is an example. Each person present felt that the murderer should be executed, but how could this opinion be evaluated by reference to physical (nonsocial) reality? Such a test is probably impossible, short of waiting to see whether renewed capital punishment has a long-range favorable impact on society. Accordingly, each person should turn to his fellow group members for evaluation of his opinion. Or should he? This depends on the nature of the group members, as we will see.

Similarity

Comparison with others' abilities or opinions occurs only to the degree that those others are similar to oneself. Festinger's 1954 meaning of *similarity*, as operationalized in his research, was exceedingly straightforward. He meant similarity on characteristics related to the dimension in question. Someone who arrives at an ice-skating pond for the first time will compare his initial skating efforts against the performance of other beginners. At the same time, his abilities on other dimensions will not enter the picture. No matter whether he is a football star, a javelin thrower, or generally inept in all sports, he will compare his ice-skating ability against that of other beginners. It is similar with opinions. In evaluating their opinions about capital punishment, the generally conservative members of the barbershop group will want to compare with other conservatives (such as Smith) but not with anyone so deviant as a pacifist student. By Festinger's reasoning, the conservative who can compare only with a pacifist will leave the situation with his opinion untested, or "subjectively" imprecise. In other words, the conservative barbershop customer would not stand to improve the clarity of his opinion or his feeling of correctness by comparing with the deviant student.

Importance of the Comparison Drive

Central to the theory is the idea that people compare because of a *drive* to evaluate. This means that the need to compare can rise and fall. The drive will be highest when the person is uncertain about the relative goodness of the opinion or ability, and it will decrease as the person gains progressively more evaluative input. If one of the regular barbershop customers had been away in the Canary Islands for a month, with no chance to discuss the opinion in question, he would have an especially strong need to seek out his comrades and become involved in discussion. This need would be independent of his need for a haircut. Just like the hunger drive, the need to evaluate should build as one is away from comparison opportunities.

Further, the need for comparison will vary as a function of the centrality of a given opinion or ability to the person. The novice ice-skater will find it highly important to compare abilities with other novices, but a non-ice-skater will have very little urge to engage in skating-ability comparisons.

Importance of the Comparison Group

Some groups are much more important to the individual, for comparison reasons, than other groups. In particular, Festinger argues that an attractive group is more appealing to the person as a comparison group. By this line of thought the highly cohesive barbershop group would be much more engaged in making comparisons than would a group of strangers, even if the strangers were initially in strong agreement with one another.

Measurable Outcomes of the Social Comparison Need

Someone who has no existing comparison group but who has the opportunity to select others as comparison persons will of course gravitate toward those who are similar. This much should be evident from what we have said thus far. But what happens when interactions are more constrained, so that mobility in and out of a group is impossible? Social comparison needs will then be reflected by attempts to increase the similarity between oneself and others, in either of two ways: persuading others to be more similar to oneself or changing to be more like them.

In the case of opinions, the person will tend either toward persuading others or toward being persuaded by them. In the case of abilities, the process is analogous but more cumbersome. If the potential comparison person is a somewhat better ice skater, social comparison theory implies that the person will try to perform better, in order to achieve comparability with the other's level of competence. This process is likely to surface in the form of competition. Or, if the other person is worse, the person desiring comparison will *lower* performance quality. Further, there might also be communications directed toward the other person, in an effort to persuade the other to raise or lower performance in the direction of matching one's own level.

Although the theory addresses itself equally to opinions and abilities, there is one crucial difference between the two in the dynamics of the way the comparing person functions: people generally strive upward in the case of abilities, whereas there is no such "upwardness" counterpart in the opinion comparison process. This means that the totally satisfactory state in ability comparison is to be just *slightly better* than one's comparison persons. Having achieved such a comparison, the individual's comparison needs (comparison with a similar other) as well as the need to be better (to strive upward) are satisfied.

RESEARCH EXAMPLES: THE THEORY APPLIED TO THE SMALL GROUP

Modes, Deviates, and Sliders

In 1951 Schachter reported an experiment that contained many of the same elements as our opening example. Schachter organized a number of clubs, each with about nine members. Club members did not realize that they were experimental subjects, and their ostensible purpose was to pursue discussion and action on a specified topic. The clubs were divided into the following topic groups: Movie, Radio, Editorial, and Case History. Each club actually met just once, during which time Schachter arranged for all clubs to discuss a common topic—the case of a certain "Johnny Rocco," a delinquent boy who is by now at least as renowned as any psychologist. The task, similar to that in the barbershop, was to make a decision about what sort of punishment Rocco should receive.

The discussion was highly structured. Members were initially asked for their judgments about the leniency or severity with which Rocco should be treated, then the discussion took place, and finally some clever measures of within-group liking and rejection were taken. It turned out that almost all club members thought that Rocco should receive lenient treatment. This means that any naturally occurring group pressures would have operated in a lenient direction.

Had each group with its regular members been left alone, there would probably have been little discord or influence. But in order to examine interpersonal influence pressures, Schachter planted three inauthentic members in each group. One of these played a straight, liberal role, always agreeing with the modal opinion of the group. He may be called the "Mode." Another confederate, called the "Deviate," was the antithesis of the Mode. He recommended the most severe treatment of Rocco at the outset, and no amount of discussion succeeded in liberalizing him. (One might surmise that the pacifist college student who entered the barbershop was an extreme case of a deviate, perceived as so disparate from the other members that they felt no need to try to compare with him.) A third confederate was labeled the "Slider." His counterpart in our example was Smith. It was the Slider's job to begin as punitively as the deviate but to shift gradually toward the group's modal, lenient position during the course of discussion.

After the 45-minute meeting, subjects were asked to nominate members to committees. As these committees varied in prestige (executive committee = high prestige; correspondence committee = low), it was possible to ascertain the relative popularity of the three inauthentic members (Mode, Slider, Deviate) by their committee assignments. It happened that the Deviate was generally assigned a less desirable committee position than the Mode. Further, the Slider's eventual conformity to the norm of leniency kept him from being excluded: his committee assignments from the group were no worse than those received by the Mode, just as with Smith in the barbershop.

The typical subject in this setting would have some concern about the correctness of his opinion. There was no reality test to be made; hence the only possibility for arriving at an opinion evaluation was social comparison, preferably with a similar other. Of course, in some objective sense we might say that the ordinary group member already had plenty of similar opinions with which to compare, independent of the Deviate's presence. Most of the other authentic members were largely in agreement with him. Nonetheless, the theory argues that comparison processes will operate in the direction of opinion uniformity in any case. It is as though the process does not cease until every conceivable comparison object is rendered similar or else ultimately rejected.

What comparison processes are realized in this context? The theory says that others will be preferred to the degree that they are similar with respect to the relevant opinion or ability. As we have seen, results of the committee-assignment measure showed overwhelming support for the theory, in that the Deviate was extremely likely to be rejected from the mainstream of the group by being placed on the correspondence committee, while the Mode and Slider had a strong record of nomination to more prestigious committees.

There is still more. It may be recalled that we listed two determinants of the social comparison process. (1) The process is set into action more *when the opinion or ability to be compared is important.* In half the groups (Case Study and Editorial), the Rocco case was central to group functioning. For the Radio and Movie clubs, the case was only peripheral. Indeed, the group's acceptance of "agreeing" members (Mode and Slider) and rejection of the Deviate were much more pronounced in the Case Study and Editorial clubs. Very simply, social comparison concerning Rocco was not an important matter in the Radio and Movie clubs, and social comparison needs were therefore not reflected in those groups to any marked degree.

(2) There is one further determinant. Festinger notes that the *importance of the particular group* as a source of comparison is also a determinant of whether comparisons occur. One determinant of group importance is within-group solidarity, or "cohesiveness." Schachter manipulated cohesiveness by assigning some subjects to groups that were inherently less attractive (Editorial and Radio) and others to the more appealing groups (Case Study and Movie). The result, according to Schachter, was the formation of less cohesive and highly cohesive groups, respectively. On the sociometric measure, the impact of cohesiveness was exactly as one would expect: the higher the group solidarity, the greater tendency to reject the Deviate.

In summary, Schachter's study tells us something important about several facets of group functioning. For one, someone who deviates at the outset but who eventually comes to "see the light" (Slider) is liked just as much as the person who continually conforms to group opinion (Mode). Second, the Deviate is eventually rejected no matter what combination of other variables is brought to bear on the situation. Third, the importance of the opinion to the group has a crucial impact: the Deviate is expelled with greater vehemence when the Rocco case is relevant to group functioning. Finally, a highly cohesive group is harsher toward a Deviate than a less cohesive group.

Who Communicates with Whom?

Social comparison processes, at least within the ongoing group, are likely to be mediated by individual members' attempts to persuade others. But we have not yet discussed the direction of communication. A small group experiment by Festinger, Gerard, Hymovitch, Kelley, and Raven (1952) went a long way toward dealing with this question.

All group members were asked to read some introductory materials about a labor-management dispute; then each member recorded his opinion—which would have fallen somewhere on the pro-management to pro-labor continuum. The individual subject was then led to think either that he deviated in opinion from the group norm or that he was in agreement with almost all members. The variable of interest was initiation of communications as well as the identity of the target of communications.

First, among subjects who believed themselves to hold the modal opinion, there was virtually no change in opinion during the group discussion. They simply froze at the mode. These subjects' communications were addressed largely to the extreme deviates rather than to deviates who were only slightly divergent from the group mode. Second, among subjects who believed themselves to be deviates, 23% changed, almost always in the direction of the mode. These same people were reluctant to address their persuasion efforts to members at the group mode; instead, their communications were to the person who stood partway between the majority unit and themselves. Deviates who changed toward the group also tended not to communicate very much. It is as though the relation between influencing others and being influenced were an either/or issue, whereby social comparison needs were met either through changing one's own opinion or changing the opinions of others.

What is the lesson of this experiment? Opinion change and attempts to persuade are not displayed by the same people. Those who are entrenched within a popular group position manifest social comparison processes by trying to persuade others to join, and further, their communications are most strongly directed toward members who are in extreme positions away from the mode. In contrast, people who begin at an extreme position are reluctant to try to influence others, especially others who have a good deal of social support. These same people are much more prone to change their own opinions as a reflection of the social comparison need.

What about rejection? In Schachter's study, in which interaction continued longer and was more interpersonally vivid, communication data suggested that modal members attempted to sway deviates over to the "correct" opinion and rejected them later when these attempts failed. It is likely that the interaction time was too brief in the study by Festinger et al. for rejection to surface. Members did not really have the opportunity to be sure that deviates were unpersuadable.

Comparison of Emotions

In a classic experiment by Schachter (1959), female subjects were led to expect some extremely painful electric shocks or else rather mild shocks. Having built these differential expectations, Schachter asked the subjects whether they would like to wait with someone else or alone. Most subjects in the high fear condition preferred to wait with others.

From social comparison theory, we may assume that emotions, much like abilities and opinions, need to be evaluated. A subject confronted with a highly threatening situation may not feel that her emotional reactions are "correct" and certainly would have a need to draw comparisons between her own state and that of others in the same setting.

A subsequent experiment by Wrightsman (1960) makes a still stronger case for the extension of social comparison theory to emotions. Subjects' anxiety was raised to a high pitch by threatening them with a series of painful injections that would ostensibly alter glucose levels. In a deviation from Schachter's procedure, some subjects were assigned to wait in groups. This waiting actually occurred, all group members waiting for the identical painful event.

One of the critical questions for Wrightsman was whether the group experience would serve simply to reduce anxiety level or whether the experience was one of trying to compare one's level of fright against that of other subjects. On a measure of anxiety reduction, over the period of time the group met, there were no differences between subjects waiting in a group and subjects waiting alone. However, there was some indication that subjects were engaging in social comparison processes: during the course of group discussion there was a clear "homogenization" of anxiety levels, so that group members resembled one another in anxiety more at the end of the session. This finding is highly reminiscent of the opinion convergence within the groups studied by Festinger et al. (1952). Therefore, it appears as though subjects, in some manner, compared reactions and "agreed on" an appropriate level of fear for the situation.

It seems evident that the comparison of emotional states works similarly to the comparison of opinions. Similar others are preferred for comparison, and further, within-group similarity increases during interaction.

Now that we have seen several illustrations of within-group comparison, we will move to a more recent paradigm, involving the individual's choice of a comparison group.

RESEARCH EXAMPLES: THE THEORY APPLIED TO SELECTION OF ANOTHER FOR COMPARISON

In recent years an exceedingly simple paradigm has evolved for examining social comparison theory. A subject is placed in a setting calling forth social comparison needs and then is asked to select one or more other persons with whom to compare. Many such experiments are reported by Latané (1966), but we will consider a more recent one that deals with comparison of abilities (Jones & Regan, 1974).

Subjects in one group were asked to take a test of "cognitive flexibility." In case the reader is unfamiliar with "cognitive flexibility," so were the subjects—it was designed to be a vague dimension. They received feedback about their performance, not knowing how their scores compared with the scores of others. Subjects then had the opportunity to take a second test of cognitive flexibility. Before this second testing they were supposed to choose a difficulty level from among ten levels. Subjects would have had very little basis for making up their minds, and the need for social comparison at that point should have been extremely high. Certainly any sort of comparison information would have been invaluable in reducing uncertainty. These subjects were then asked whether they would like to see normative information (information on how others performed) before deciding on a difficulty level. Not surprisingly, the great majority (93%) wanted to see the norms. Subjects in an additional group were treated similarly, except that they were asked to decide on difficulty level *before* having any chance to examine group norms. Following Festinger's reasoning, the drive for social comparison information should have been much less important for them, since the comparison information would have been useless in making up their minds. Jones and Regan were right: only 14% of this group wanted to see the scores of other subjects.

This experiment tells us that a comparison will be made if it is possible for the person to act on the comparison—that is, if the comparison is personally relevant. A second experiment by Jones and Regan addresses the issue of importance of the comparison group. We saw earlier, in the Johnny Rocco experiment, that a highly cohesive group elicited more social comparison behavior. In the present case group importance was defined in terms of how much knowledge the subject stood to gain from the group through comparison.

Subjects again took a "cognitive flexibility" test, but this time there was no immediate feedback. As before, subjects were told that they would now be allowed to choose a difficulty level for their second test. They also found that they could first talk to a "partner" (to be selected from two possible "partners") about aspects of the testing situation—and here is where Jones and Regan manipulated the importance of the comparison group. In the "low importance" condition, subjects found that the two potential partners would not be taking the second test and therefore obviously would know nothing about it. In the "high importance" condition, both potential partners had already taken the second test, and so obviously they knew something about it.

Subjects were then told that one of the potential partners had scored about the same as they on the first test and that the other potential partner had scored differently. As the dependent measure of the social comparison need, subjects were asked whether they would prefer the similar or the dissimilar partner or had no preference. The results were very much in keeping with the theory: preference for a similar, as opposed to a dissimilar, other was much more pronounced when the other was an important source of social comparison—that is, when he had already taken the second test.

The research of Jones and Regan makes two extremely basic points in the context of social comparison theory. If the need for clarity of information is great, the tendency toward comparison increases. Moreover, if the group is potentially informative and is therefore an important source of comparison, preference for a similar other increases. It is, of course, axiomatic that strong social comparison needs move in the direction of preference for similar others.

SPECIAL TOPICS

Preference for Dissimilar Others

In a recent chapter on social comparison, Goethals and Darley (1977) have proposed the most thoroughgoing revision of social comparison theory to date. Their analysis assumes quite literally, along with Festinger (1954), that people in need of social comparison are motivated to gain clarity about their opinions or abilities. Starting from this premise, Goethals and Darley proceed to show how social comparison considerations may be derived from Kelley's concepts (see Chapter 10). Although we do not have space here for a systematic presentation of their notions, we will look at a certain subset of their propositions.

Suppose that an 85-year-old woman has a highly favorable opinion of a quiet, lento movement of a piece of sacred music. She is interested in evaluating this opinion, and either of two persons drops by her house to listen to the sacred selection. (1) Another octogenarian listens attentively, immediately agreeing that the selection is terrific. (2) A 16-year-old also listens attentively and instantly expresses his highly favorable opinion. In which case does the subject's confidence in her opinion increase more? According to Goethals and Darley, the agreement from the 16-year-old, who at face value seems dissimilar, would instill more confidence. But how can this be? This seems contrary to social comparison theory.

The argument is this. If we like a given piece of music, part of our liking will owe to certain characteristic biases in our judgment style. Because of our values about music, we may have built up a habitual mode of processing sounds, such that only the calmest, slowest-paced pieces are labeled as worth listening to. Now, if we compare our opinion of a selection with that of someone who shares our values, that person is likely to be affected by the same kinds of biases. What this means is that a slow-moving composition would possibly be evaluated positively, even with its occasional flaws, owing to a value of "slow music is good." Therefore, if the 85-year-old has only another 85-year-old as a comparison person, she does not stand to gain much in the way of increased certainty of opinion.

What is the impact of the 16-year-old's agreement? This person, whose values are considerably different, will certainly not evaluate the music with the same set of biases as the senior citizens. If the younger person comes to a favorable opinion, our elder subject can be sure that the youngster's opinion is not a product of bias in perceptual style. More likely, she will attribute the young person's opinion to the qualities of the selection itself. As a result, she can now be extremely confident that her favorable opinion is correct.

This seemingly ironic chain of reasoning was tested by Reckman and Goethals (1973), and without going into detail, it can be said that a dissimilar other was indeed preferred, but only when *accuracy* of opinion was emphasized by the experimenter. Thus, subjects concerned mainly with accuracy of opinions evidence a realization that divergence of the basis for opinion, between themselves and others, can be quite helpful.

Although this experiment and its accompanying analysis clearly conflict with a fundamental derivation of Festinger's social comparison theory, we should keep in mind that the reasoning here is specific to the social comparison of *opinions*, or *beliefs*. Goethals and Darley's treatment of *abilities* leads to predictions in accord with the original Festinger statement. In addition, their analysis addresses primarily the *selection* of a comparison other rather than the broad spectrum of group processes stipulated in the original theory. Finally, Reckman and Goethals' study is the only one we have mentioned in which the person's main concern was accuracy. In settings in which accuracy is not of primary importance, one can expect results in keeping with the collected findings we have discussed.

Other Exceptions to Similarity

It is not difficult to find exceptions to the similarity postulate. Hakmiller (1966) noted a phenomenon of wanting to compare with someone of inferior ability, which he interpreted as a defensive process. Presumably people who are concerned about their own worth derive a certain pleasure by comparing against someone worse than themselves. A more general way of saying this is that other motives can sometimes outweigh the need for social comparison with similar others. On occasion we are pleased to note how poorly others have fared, and so we turn our attention toward people well below ourselves.

Another exception to similarity has been noted by Wheeler, Shaver, Jones, Goethals, Cooper, Robinson, Gruder, and Butzine (1969). If subjects had taken a test and did not know the range of scores, their first preference was to learn the range (that is, the extreme points) rather than the score of someone similar. This finding suggests a possible ambiguity in the original theory. Given that the motive is to arrive at a confident evaluation of one's own ability, it may be more confidence-inspiring to know one's relative place in the entire hierarchy than to know the score of some single adjacent person. This is the kind of specific detail that was omitted from the theory, and it is possible that Wheeler et al. are right. Indeed, most of the situations encountered in this chapter have included, at least implicitly, some knowledge of the range of abilities or opinions, thereby satisfying that initial desire to comprehend the spectrum of differences.

SUMMARY

Festinger's social comparison theory as originally stated has proved to be fundamentally correct in its predictions. Similarity of others, importance of the opinion or ability, and importance of the group as a source of comparison all operate to affect the comparison process.

For social psychology the effects of social comparison are central. The theory has a great deal to say about who joins what kind of group, and it says at least as much about communication and persuasion within ongoing groups. Still more, the implications for social comparison of emotional states have taken a central spot in social psychology.

The important exceptions to the theory have concerned the similarity postulate. When accuracy of opinions is the person's foremost goal, when the range of opinion is not known, or when the person is defensive about performance or abilities, certain kinds of dissimilar others seem to be preferred. Thus the social comparison need is not an all-fundamental desire that overwhelms all other motives, but is something to be considered in combination with other determinants of selection and influence of associates.

SUGGESTED READING

Festinger, L. A theory of social comparison processes. *Human Relations*, 1954, 7, 117–140.

Haisch, J., & Frey, D. *Die Theorie sozialer Vergleichsprozesse.* In D. Frey (Ed.), *Kognitive Theorien der Sozialpsychologie.* Bern: Huber, 1978.

Schachter, S. *The psychology of affiliation.* Stanford, Calif.: Stanford University Press, 1959.

Suls, J. M., & Miller, R. L. (Eds.). *Social comparison processes.* New York: Hemisphere, 1977.

CHAPTER 12

A THEORY OF EMOTION

PROFESSOR Bellows is an eccentric old faculty member. Nearly every afternoon he may be found around the psychology department, coffee cup in hand, drinking coffee and discussing psychological research with students and colleagues. He is known for incisive criticism, which he always delivers in a rather unemotional, professional manner. He never gushes over the brilliance of a student's idea, nor reacts to students with either disgust or contempt. Rather, he always attempts to point out the strengths and weaknesses of the idea and to suggest improvements.

One day the department head called Bellows in to inform him that some students had complained about his habit of drinking coffee in class and that he should immediately stop the practice. The next day Bellows downed two cups of coffee just before the seminar and appeared without the usual coffee cup. Some minutes later, upon hearing one of the better students propose an interesting idea, Bellows acted in an unusual manner. The professor walked over to the student, patted her on the back, and said "What brilliance! Why, it is perfectly clear that Irene here is the most outstanding student we have ever had at this university." After additional animated praise, Bellows called the usual 15-minute break and returned to the office, where he downed two more cups of coffee. When the class resumed, one of the weaker students presented a poorly thought-out idea, to which Bellows thundered "What garbage! Look, Sam, I don't know how they ever let you into this school." Let us leave Bellows shouting for the moment and digress briefly to consider the basic elements of a theory of emotion proposed by Schachter (1964, 1971; Schachter & Singer, 1962), which will help in interpreting this example.

THE THEORY

According to this theory, two elements are necessary for a person to have an emotional experience. First, the person must be in a state of physiological arousal. This is nothing more than general bodily excitement, which is reflected in such symptoms as a pounding heart, rapid breathing, sweaty palms, and a feeling of tenseness or nervousness. The heightened state of arousal will lead to a scanning of the immediate situation for an explanation of this bodily state. For example, if a woman were physiologically aroused and her archenemy then appeared, the villain would provide a cogent explanation of her arousal, and she would probably decide that she was angry. If, however she had been confronted with a ravishing young man, it is unlikely that she would decide on anger as an explanation for the arousal state. Rather, she would be more likely to decide that she was madly in love or in lust. Thus, emotion consists of two elements: (1) a state of heightened physiological arousal and (2) an explanation for the state of arousal.

In many "real world" situations, the actual source of the physiological arousal and the perceived source used to explain that state are one and the same. In the example above, the presence of an attractive and sensuous person of the opposite sex should increase physiological arousal, and the same stimulus would also be perceived as the cause of arousal. However, there are many interesting situations in which people may not be aware of the true source of their arousal. An example may be seen in the case of Professor Bellows.

Just before the class meeting described above, Bellows drank an unhealthy amount of coffee. Coffee is known to contain caffeine, which increases physiological arousal: the heart beats faster, breathing rate increases, and a feeling of general bodily excitement is experienced. Assume for the moment that Bellows is thinking about his class and has forgotten about the coffee as he enters the class. At this time the drug should not yet have taken full effect, and Bellows should not feel particularly aroused. However, as the class goes on, Bellows would experience an increasing state of bodily excitement, for which he may seek an explanation. At this point, brilliant Irene pipes up with a good comment, and Bellows "understands" why he is so excited. He is excited because of an insightful student who brings him nothing but cogent ideas. However, had dullard Sam spoken up before Irene (as he did during the second hour), Bellows would have "understood" his arousal as resulting from his contempt for an awful student. An explanation of these processes is quite simple: physiological arousal energizes the emotional behavior, but the cues present in the situation serve to direct it toward a particular emotion.

Although this analysis fits Bellows' behavior on the day of the seminar, it fails to explain his more usual nonemotional behavior. Recall that on previous days Bellows also drank coffee and was also presumably exposed to brilliant and dismal comments by students. According to the analysis that has just been presented, Bellows should act in an emotional manner as long as he is drinking coffee and is experiencing a state of physiological arousal. But why wasn't he emotional on those days when he brought his cup of coffee into class? This leads us to the second proposition of Schachter's theory.

Once people have an appropriate explanation for their physiological arousal, they will not search further for alternative explanations. People do not flit rapidly from happiness to anger to misery like cognitive butterflies. Instead, once they have found a satisfactory explanation of their physiological arousal, their search for an explanation stops immediately. New information that is encountered is likely to be ignored or reinterpreted in terms of the dominant emotional explanation. This proposition recognizes that once people have an interpretation of a situation, they do not easily change their interpretation, a principle that will emerge again in other chapters.

Recall that Bellows normally carries along a cup of coffee. This provides a strong, nonemotional explanation for his arousal (the coffee). Applying Schachter's second proposition, Bellows will not search further for alternative explanations, since he already perceives that the coffee is the source of arousal. As a result, he should respond to the students in a nonemotional manner, regardless of the nature of their comments. Only on the day of the seminar, without a prior explanation for his arousal, should he have an emotional reaction.

A final addition should be made to our example for the sake of completeness. Suppose that Bellows had drunk no coffee on the day of the seminar or that he had drunk 99% caffeine free Sanka. Would he have acted in the previously described emotional manner? According to Schachter, the answer is no, because there would have been no heightened physiological arousal and hence no need for an explanation for arousal.

To review, according to Schachter's theory of emotion two elements are necessary for the experience of an emotion: (1) a heightened level of physiological arousal and (2) an explanation for the arousal. If either element is not present, the person will not experience an emotion. Finally, a person who finds an explanation or has a preexisting explanation for the state of heightened arousal will not search further for alternative explanations.

RESEARCH EXAMPLES

Anger and Euphoria

Schachter and Singer (1962) conducted an experiment that in many ways parallels our example of Professor Bellows. The first element of the theory is physiological arousal, manipulated here by giving subjects an injection of either a saline solution or an adrenalin solution. The saline solution was a placebo, a drug with no physiological effects. Subjects receiving this drug may be assumed to be experiencing their normal level of physiological arousal. Adrenalin, however, increases heart and breathing rate, the amount of sugar available in the blood for emergency action, and feelings of nervousness or general bodily excitement. Subjects receiving this drug should experience a heightened state of physiological arousal.

The second element of Schachter's theory is that the search for an explanation of arousal should take place only when the subject does not have a preexisting explanation. If subjects were told that the drug would cause them to become aroused, they should not search for alternative emotional explanations for their arousal. But if they were told either that the drug would not lead to arousal or that the drug led to effects irrelevant to arousal (such as itchy feet), they would have no explanation for their increased level of arousal when the drug took effect. Consequently, when placed in an environment containing salient cues ("explanations") for arousal, they should "understand" their arousal as resulting from their emotional response to the situation.

Following this reasoning, Schachter and Singer informed half the subjects who had been injected with adrenalin that the drug led to symptoms of increased physiological arousal; the other half were informed that the drug would have no noticeable physiological effects. All placebo subjects were also informed that the drug would have no noticeable effects.

In their first experiment Schachter and Singer placed subjects in a room where the cues strongly suggested an emotion of extreme happiness, or euphoria. In other words, this was a situation in which a state of previously unexplained arousal might be interpreted as happiness. In this room a confederate acted in an ever-increasing silly manner, playing basketball with crumpled paper, throwing paper airplanes, building a tower of manila folders, and playing with a hula hoop. In the second experiment subjects were placed in a room where the cues strongly suggested an emotion of anger. The confederate and subject filled out highly personal and insulting questionnaires, and in the meantime the confederate reacted to these questionnaires in an increasingly angry and irritable way. In both experiments observers viewed the subject through a one-way mirror, recording any emotional behavior. The subject also filled out a questionnaire at the end of the experiment, concerning his physical and emotional state.

The results of the two experiments supported Schachter's reasoning. Subjects who experienced a state of arousal but who had no explanation for this state interpreted their arousal in terms of the cues provided by the environment. These subjects reported feeling joyful (experiment 1) or angry (experiment 2), depending on the behavior of the confederate. The record of the subjects' emotional behavior also showed a similar pattern. However, subjects who had a preexisting explanation for their physiological arousal (that it was due to the drug) did not have to search further for an explanation and therefore did not report emotional feelings or behave in an emotional manner. Subjects who had received the placebo injection also tended not to report emotional feelings or to behave emotionally, although these effects were not as clear-cut as the above findings. From these results one would think that both a state of physiological arousal and an explanation for that arousal are necessary for an emotional experience.

Fearful Rats

Singer (1963) extended the above reasoning to studies of emotion in animals. Paralleling Schachter and Singer's experiment, some animals were injected with adrenalin and others with a placebo. A third group of animals was injected with chlorpromazine, a tranquilizer that causes a decrease in physiological arousal. Of course none of the animal subjects was informed about the nature of the drug received. After allowing time for the drug to take effect, the animals were placed in a specially constructed fright box for 90 seconds. For some of the rats the box was inactive, and no unusual environmental stimuli were presented. For others, however, the box was activated, turning on a barrage of fear-producing stimuli, including buzzers, bells, and flickering lights. Since rats are known to respond to a wide variety of fear-producing situations with increased defecation, urination, activity, trembling, and face washing, these behaviors were recorded to provide a measure of fear.

Singer found that when the rats were in the neutral environment of the inactive fright box, they showed little evidence of fear regardless of which drug they had received. However, in the presence of the salient environmental cues provided by the active fright box, the animal's level of fear depended on its level of physiological arousal. Rats injected with adrenalin showed the highest level of fear, rats injected with the placebo showed an intermediate level, and rats injected with chlorpromazine showed the lowest level. Once again, emotion was shown to be dependent on both the level of physiological arousal and the emotional cues provided by the environment.

Misperceiving Sexual Pleasure

One of the more interesting aspects of Schachter's theory is his proposition that once a person has an appropriate explanation for a condition of physiological arousal, there will be no further search for alternative explanations. An intriguing implication of this proposition is that it may be possible to modify radically the emotional states resulting from naturally occurring physiological arousal by leading the individual to misperceive a nonemotional external agent as the source of arousal.

Hanson and Blechman (1970) induced married couples to take a placebo in the evening before retiring. The placebo, of course, would have had no physiological effect. However, some of the couples were informed that the drug was a stimulant, others that it was a tranquilizer, and a third

group that the drug would have no effect. The couples had been instructed to engage in sexual intercourse and then to fill out a questionnaire reporting on their experience.

Hanson and Blechman reasoned that the couples should (ideally) become physiologically aroused during intercourse. Normally (and when
they were told that the drug had no effect), couples should perceive correctly that their sexual experience was the source of their arousal and
report that it was an enjoyable experience. However, subjects who were
told that the drug was a stimulant should attribute a portion of their naturally occurring arousal to the drug. Consequently, like the subjects who
were informed of the effects of the adrenalin in Schachter and Singer's
experiment, these subjects should report that their experience was less
enjoyable than usual. Finally, subjects who believed that the drug was a
tranquilizer should expect a decreased level of arousal compared with
their normal level. As a result, they should perceive the sexual experience
to be the source of their higher-than-expected level of arousal and report
that it was an unusually enjoyable experience. The results were consistent
with this reasoning: subjects who were told that the drug was a tranquilizer reported more enjoyment of the experience than subjects who
were told that the drug had no effect; these subjects, in turn, reported
more enjoyment than subjects who were told that the drug was a stimulant. This experiment, then, indicates that it is possible to modify emotional reactions by leading subjects to misperceive a nonemotional
external agent as the source of their arousal. Other researchers have
found that such states as pain, fear, and anxiety can be similarly altered
by leading subjects to misperceive the source of their arousal (for example, Dienstbier & Munter, 1971; Nisbett & Schachter, 1966).

Transfer of Arousal from Exercise to Sex

Our discussion of Professor Bellows' behavior suggested that there
may be circumstances in which the person no longer remembers or perceives the source of still-existing physiological arousal. Under these circumstances, the remaining physiological arousal should facilitate
emotional responses if the person is subsequently presented with environmental cues that enable an "understanding" of the arousal. However, if
the person is reminded in some way of the actual source of arousal before
being presented with the cues, there should then be no emotional reaction: the arousal has already been explained.

Cantor, Zillmann, and Bryant (1975) showed such an effect in an intriguing experiment. Strenuous exercise leads to physiological arousal, as is evidenced by the feeling that one's heart is pounding and a general feeling of bodily excitement. Of course, immediately after completing a period of vigorous exercise, people perceive that they are aroused and also show elevated measures of arousal. But a person's perception of level of arousal may not always correspond to the actual level of arousal. Cantor et al. (1975) noted that 5 minutes after completing a period of exercise, subjects felt they had returned fully to their normal physiological state, even though they still showed evidence of actual increased physiological arousal—elevated pulse rate and heightened blood pressure. Just as with Professor Bellows in the seminar, these subjects should display an emotional response if presented with an appropriate cue with which to "understand" their arousal.

Taking advantage of this finding, Cantor et al. (1975) showed a group of subjects an erotic film *(Naked under Leather)* 5 minutes after a period of exercise, at which time they should no longer have perceived the exercise as responsible for their heightened level of arousal. These "5-minute" subjects reported being sexually aroused by the film. In contrast, subjects who were shown the erotic film immediately after the exercise period reported a much lower level of sexual arousal. These "immediate" subjects perceived that their high level of arousal was due to the exercise; they had no need to use the film as an "explanation." Finally, a group that had fully recovered from the exercise, and hence should have been at a normal level of arousal, also viewed the film. Their reported level of sexual arousal was rather low and was comparable to that reported by subjects who viewed the film immediately after the exercise period. This means that naturally occurring physiological arousal can facilitate other emotional responses only when people are no longer aware of the real source of their arousal.

Is a Heartbeat a Lovebeat?

Both the Schachter and Singer (1962) and Cantor et al. (1975) experiments showed that subjects who are unaware of the source of their physiological arousal will show a heightened emotional response to a suitable environmental cue. An interesting extension of these results may be proposed, which is that the degree of *perceived* physiological arousal, independent of *actual* arousal, may modify the person's reaction to an emotional stimulus. Even though their actual level of physiological arousal is at a normal level, people who believe that their level of arousal is high as a result of an emotion-related stimulus should infer that they have strong emotional feelings toward the stimulus.

Valins (1966) tested this idea in the following way: Male subjects were shown a series of *Playboy* nudes while hearing a beating noise. Subjects in the "heartbeat" condition were told that the noise was the amplified sound of their own heartbeat; subjects in the control condition were led to believe that it was extraneous machine noise. While some of the nudes were presented, the sounds remained at the "normal" level of 66–72 beats per minute. But for other nudes the sounds increased above the "normal" level, suggesting in the "heartbeat" condition that the subject was becoming physiologically aroused because of the nude.

Valins found that subjects rated the nudes to which their "heartbeat" had apparently increased as being more attractive than those to which their "heartbeat" had apparently remained constant. However, if subjects believed that the sounds were just machine noise, the manipulation of rate of the sounds made no difference. These results suggest that the *mere perception* of increased arousal is sufficient to produce an emotional response and that actual internal physiological change may be unnecessary.

The experiments cited above are representative of the major programs of research that have developed out of Schachter's theory of emotion. Each of the experiments explores a different facet of the theory, and taken together, they illustrate the wide range of empirical support enjoyed by the theory. The reader may also have noticed that the theoretical concepts were implemented in diverse ways in the various experiments, sometimes leading to a subtle shift in our understanding of the concept, especially in the case of "physiological arousal."

SPECIAL TOPICS

Does Schachter's Theory Apply to Animals?

Although Singer's (1963) experiment on rats was derived from Schachter's theory and the results were consistent with the theory, a major question can be raised about whether Schachter's theory can be applied to lower animals. The theory requires that the animal (1) perceive that it is aroused and (2) scan the environment for an explanation of its arousal. The animals in Singer's experiment acted "as if" they were attributing their arousal to the fear-producing stimuli, but it is unlikely that rats have the elaborate cognitive ability required by the theory. In addition, the situation in which Schachter's theory makes the most distinctive prediction, a condition in which the subjects are informed of the effects of the drug, could not be included in the design. Therefore, other, simpler theoretical explanations of the results cannot be eliminated.

For example, it may be assumed that the behaviors recorded by Singer are a syndrome of closely interrelated fear responses that are dominant in the active fright box. Other responses (such as tail washing) may be assumed to be subordinate in the situation. Now social facilitation theory (Chapter 2) may be applied: As arousal increases, the performance of the dominant fear responses should also increase, while the performance of subordinate responses should decrease. From social-facilitation theory it should be possible to substitute a grandstand of passive spectator rats for the adrenalin injection and obtain identical results. Of course, Singer's experiment was not designed as a test of social facilitation theory, and this means that all the difficulties of defining the dominant response in the situation (discussed in Chapter 2) apply.

Still, social facilitation theory does seem to offer a plausible explanation for much of the research on lower animals derived from Schachter's theory. Given the complex cognitive processes required by Schachter's reasoning, simpler, noncognitive explanations, such as that provided by social-facilitation theory, are preferred.

General versus Specific Physiological States

Schachter made the rather startling assumption that such diverse emotions as fear, anger, and elation have the same physiological basis—namely, the state of general physiological arousal. Some psychologists (for example, Averill & Opton, 1968; Plutchik & Ax, 1967) have criticized the theory on the basis of this assumption, pointing out that some studies have shown differences between emotions on physiological measures. For one, Ax (1953) designed conditions that elicited anger in one group of subjects and fear in a second group. He measured a variety of physiological responses and found subtle differences in the pattern of responses in the two groups. This research suggests that fear and anger have slightly different physiological bases, in contrast to Schachter's assumption of a general state of arousal underlying all emotions.

Nonetheless, a number of arguments may be raised in support of Schachter's assumption. First, suppose that Emotion 1 leads to an increase in pulse rate of 30 beats per minute and an increase in diastolic blood pressure of 14 mm. Emotion 2 leads to an increase in pulse rate of only 25 beats per minute but an increase of 18 mm in diastolic blood pressure. The experimenter, using sophisticated physiological measuring devices, can detect these differences and distinguish between the two emotions on the basis of the exact pattern of physiological responses. But can the subject, without these sophisticated measuring devices, detect such subtle differences? A number of studies (see Mandler, 1975) indicate that subjects are unable to perceive subtle physiological differences; however, they can perceive more general changes, such as those associated with a general state of physiological arousal. This means that from the subject's viewpoint Schachter's assumption of a state of general physiological arousal is correct.

Second, physiological researchers have not demonstrated that fear and anger (or any other pair of emotions) are generated by different physiological states, but only that these different states are associated or correlated with fear and anger. What would researchers have to do in order to lead us to question seriously Schachter's assumption of a general state of physiological arousal? They would have to show, in a constant situation, that inducing the specific physiological state underlying fear or underlying anger makes the subject more likely to report fear or anger, respectively. This has not been carried out, as such an experiment is beyond the current technology of physiological psychology.

Finally, even though one can demonstrate that slightly different physiological patterns do characterize different emotions, it has thus far been impossible to specify a process through which these physiological differences are related to subjects' reports of emotion and their emotional behavior. That is, there is no alternative theory that makes unique and testable predictions. As always in science, Schachter's theory will continue to be an important explanation of emotional phenomena until a more precise theory is proposed.

The Nature of Physiological Arousal

Schachter suggests that physiological arousal consists of (1) a general state of bodily excitement, which is (2) perceived by the individual. In Schachter and Singer's experiment, subjects were injected with adrenalin, a manipulation that would induce both of the components of arousal.

Similarly, Hanson and Blechman relied on sexual behavior, which would lead to both actual and perceived bodily excitement. However, two of the experiments cited above apparently satisfied only one component of Schachter's definition: the experiment by Valins, in which subjects were given false heart-rate feedback irrespective of changes in actual arousal, and the experiment by Cantor et al., in which subjects aroused by exercise no longer perceived that they were aroused. These last two experiments should be reexamined as evidence for the theory.

Valins' experiment manipulated only the perception of arousal, while the level of actual arousal was assumed to be constant in the "increased" and the "no change" bogus heart-rate conditions. As pointed out in the previous section, people are normally able to perceive changes only in the general level of physiological arousal; they cannot make fine discriminations between the separate components, such as heart rate and blood pressure. Further, the threshold for detecting changes in general arousal is relatively high (Mandler, 1975; Mandler & Kremen, 1958). These considerations lead to a very fitting interpretation of Valins' results: The *perception* of arousal, when it does occur, may be the powerful stimulus that sets the cognitive processes identified by Schachter into motion. Although a large increase in actual physiological arousal is normally needed before the person will perceive the change, Valins was able to short-circuit this step by giving the subjects ostensibly direct feedback about their level of arousal. As a result of their perception of increased arousal, subjects searched for an explanation, which in this case was the *Playboy* nudes. According to this view, actual arousal is important only in that it is normally necessary to produce the perception of arousal. It is the perception of arousal that triggers the search for an explanation.

But there is an alternative way to look at Valins' results. A number of studies (Goldstein, Fink, & Mettee, 1972; Hirschman, 1975; Stern, Botto, & Herrick, 1972) have shown that false heart-rate feedback also leads to changes in measures of *actual* physiological arousal. Not only does actual arousal lead to the perception of arousal, but the perception of arousal can also lead to actual arousal. This suggests that Schachter's original stipulation—that of *actual arousal*—may have been satisfied in Valins' experiment. The increases in the false heart-rate feedback may have led to corresponding changes in actual arousal, so that both perception of arousal and actual arousal were present.

Which interpretation is correct? As in our discussion of general versus specific physiological states, this is a situation in which it cannot easily be determined whether the changes in actual physiological arousal are necessary for the emotional response. Perhaps such changes are merely associated with this response. Regardless of which interpretation is correct, they both suggest that the *perception* of arousal may play a more important role in the theory than Schachter originally envisioned.

However, the experiment by Cantor et al. suggests that actual arousal can play an important role in emotion even if it is not perceived. In that experiment subjects were in a state of heightened actual arousal, but they did not perceive themselves to be aroused. In terms of Schachter's original definition, only one of the components—actual arousal— was present, and hence subjects had no reason to search for an explanation. However, these same subjects actually did report feeling more sexually aroused than the fully recovered control group. This experiment, then, suggests that the role of actual arousal needs to be strengthened within the theory.

We are clearly faced with a problem: to understand the results of Valins' experiment, we must assume that *perceived* arousal is the effective component of arousal, whereas to understand the results of the study by Cantor et al., we must assume that *actual* arousal is the effective component.

One possible way to resolve this problem is to suggest a slight modification of Schachter's theory. Though actual and perceived arousal normally occur together, the operation of two components may be distinguished in special situations (Cantor et al., 1975; Valins, 1966). *Perceived* arousal may lead to the active search for an "explanation" which Schachter's theory postulates and which we have discussed throughout the chapter. In support of this, Barefoot and Straub (1971) found that subjects receiving false heart-rate feedback who were not given adequate time to view a slide of a nude did not show the usual increased rating of the nudes to which their heartbeat apparently increased. Subjects who were given adequate time to view the nude showed the same results as in Valins' original experiment. Thus, subjects who were prevented from scanning the nude to find an "explanation" for their apparent heart-rate increase failed to show evidence of increased emotionality. This finding strongly suggests that the perception of arousal leads to an active search for an "explanation."

In contrast, *actual* arousal may have somewhat more complicated effects. Although actual arousal will often lead to perceived arousal that requires an explanation, as in Schachter and Singer's experiment with adrenalin, actual arousal probably has a further effect as well: that of enhancing the dominant response in the situation. This operation of active arousal is somewhat "cognitively passive," in that the direct impact of arousal on dominant-response tendencies does not require an active seeking after an explanation. The process is presumed to go on without cognitive work, just as described in the social facilitation chapter. The dominant response to be energized by arousal will not have an emotional flavor in every case, although the situations discussed in this chapter were ones that would elicit a particular emotional response. For example, the erotic film used by Cantor et al. would elicit sexual responses in the subjects who were first aroused by the exercise. Singer's active fright box would elicit fear responses in the rats that had been aroused by the adrenalin injection. This last example illustrates another advantage of the present view of actual arousal: the results in animal research can be interpreted as caused by arousal enhancing the dominant response (for example, fear), without recourse to the element of perceived arousal and its highly cognitive consequences.

In most situations, the active and the passive processes probably both operate. In addition, the two processes usually lead to the same predictions. It is only in the more unusual cases, such as those studied by Valins and by Cantor et al., that the two arousal processes can be distinguished and their unique implications explored.

Appropriate Emotional Stimuli

In the research we have discussed no mention has been made of how the investigator chose the particular stimuli that were to serve as the "explanation" for the subject's arousal. Certain stimuli (such as pictures of nudes or accident victims) do seem to serve as prepotent explanations for arousal, but it is clear that the choice of stimuli in each experiment depended largely on the experience and intuition of the investigator. The investigator's task is to identify situations that are (1) perceived by subjects as plausibly linked to physiological arousal and (2) interpreted by most of the subjects as reflecting the same emotion. If Schachter and Singer had placed their aroused subjects in a room with a sedentary St. Bernard, no consistent pattern of emotional responses could have been predicted: some subjects would have reported fear, others friendliness. Extending this example, if the stimulus object had been a bar of soap, it is unlikely that subjects would have reported experiencing any emotion unless they had been housewives acting in TV advertisements. In implementing the theory, the investigator has to be careful to use a situation that does not vary greatly in its meaning to the subjects and at the same time to ensure that the situation provides an "emotional" explanation.

SUMMARY

Schachter's theory of emotion proposes that both a heightened level of physiological arousal and an explanation for the arousal are necessary for a person to experience an emotion. If either the state of arousal or the explanation is not present, the person will not experience an emotion. Once a person has an explanation for the arousal, there will be no further search for other explanations.

Several issues are raised by the theory and by research relevant to the theory. These include the difficulties in applying Schachter's theory to lower animals, Schachter's assumption of an undifferentiated state of physiological arousal, actual and perceived changes in physiological arousal, and the problem of choosing stimuli to serve as appropriate explanations of arousal. If carefully implemented, Schachter's theory leads to clear-cut predictions that are among the most intriguing in social psychology.

SUGGESTED READING

Grabitz, H-J., & Gniech, G. *Die kognitiv-physiologische Theorie der Emotion von Schachter.* In D. Frey (Ed.), *Kognitive Theorien der Sozialpsychologie.* Bern: Huber, 1978.

Schachter, S. The interaction of cognitive and physiological determinants of emotional state. In L. Berkowitz (Ed.), *Advances in experimental social psychology* (Vol. 1). New York: Academic Press, 1964.

Schachter, S. *Emotion, obesity, and crime.* New York: Academic Press, 1971.

CHAPTER 13

SELF-AWARENESS THEORY

SONNY HAS grown up in a typical American city with normal middle-class parents, has been sent through school, has been confirmed in the church, and easily knows right from wrong. Nonetheless, like many other well-socialized citizens, Sonny is sometimes tempted to violate those earlier-instilled principles. Occasionally he cheats a few dollars from his business travel account, "forgets" to give back the overpayment when receiving too much change at the grocery store, and pockets stray money without making any attempt to return it.

This particular summer Sonny is vacationing at a European resort and one day decides to visit a famous, picturesque castle in the area. Unknown to him, the castle authorities have adopted a clever new money-making scheme. As visitors enter the castle they are discreetly pho-

tographed, and as they pass out the exit door they find their individual
pictures displayed plainly on a bulletin board. The tourists can then purchase the pictures or not, as they wish.

Just as Sonny is approaching the exit door, still inside the castle, he
sees a $20 bill fall out of an obviously wealthy man's pocket. As Sonny has
already sized up the man as obnoxious, he stuffs the money into his
pocket and doesn't give it a thought. Only seconds later, upon emerging
into the sunlight, Sonny is confronted with a photograph of himself in full
color. Oddly, he is suddenly seized with feelings of discomfort and re-
trieves the $20 from his pocket, returning it to its rightful (though obnox-
ious) owner. Why would the photograph have brought about this surge of
moral scrupulousness?

Psychologists are fond of thinking that humans have internalized a
great many values and that our behaviors, especially in the moral sphere,
are dictated by these internalized values. Psychologists are sometimes
right, but at the same time it is easy to point to instances in which values
seem to have little or no bearing on behavior. But why shouldn't these
values be operative all the time? The purpose of this chapter is to explore
this question, but first a laboratory analogue to the opening example will
be discussed—this time dealing with the value against cheating.

It has been documented that college students have quite definite
ideas about the immorality of cheating. According to a survey taken by
Goldsen, Rosenberg, Williams, and Suchman (1960), the vast majority of
students find cheating objectionable. Accordingly, if such students were
given the opportunity to cheat, they should do so rather infrequently. Diener and Wallbom (1976) provided one such opportunity. Their subjects
were taken into a testing room individually, given a test, instructed to stop
working after a 5-minute timer bell had rung, and left alone. As it was a
test of speed, the students could gain an advantage by working beyond the
time limit—that is, by cheating. The results provided unequivocal evidence that moral rules, as expressed on paper, are not necessarily strong
determinants of moral behavior: 71% of the students who were tested under the standard individual testing procedure cheated.

However, it was possible to effect a marked increase in moral behavior by means of a simple change in the testing procedure. Half of the
subjects (described above) were tested using the standard procedure, and
the others were confronted with a large mirror while they worked on the
test. The cheating rate in the latter condition was only 7%. Why should a
mirror or a photograph have such an impact on aligning behavior with
values?

THE THEORY

We will return to the phenomenon found by Diener and Wallbom shortly, after sketching out the rudiments of the theory of self-awareness (Duval & Wicklund, 1972; Frey, Wicklund, & Scheier, 1978; Wicklund, 1975, 1979). The theory begins with the concept of conscious attention. Attention, as we all know, can be directed toward different objects. A person may direct attention toward a rock, a house, another person, or any number of other objects in the environment. Conscious attention is also not easily divisible: it is nearly impossible to focus one's attention on two objects, such as a house and another person, at the same time. Finally, conscious attention sometimes gravitates toward some aspect of the self, such as one's body, personality traits, or behaviors. It is the phenomenon of self-directed attention that is central to self-awareness theory.

Self-awareness means simply that a person takes the self to be an object of attention, just as anything else might be viewed as an object of attention. The theory assumes that attention is directed sometimes on the self and sometimes away from the self and that the direction of attention is dictated by certain specifiable events. Very generally, self-focused attention is created by any stimuli that bring one's attention to bear onto one's self. Such stimuli include, for example, mirrors, the person's own tape-recorded voice, a photograph of oneself, or the presence of an audience staring at the person.

Is the person's attention continuously focused on the self while confronted with one of these self-focusing devices? Not necessarily. The only assumption necessary is that such stimuli increase the *proportion of time* spent in thinking about oneself. For example, in the absence of their tape-recorded voices, people might on the average have self-related thoughts about 40% of the time, but hearing their own voices could raise this figure—perhaps to 50%, perhaps to 100%. Theoretically, the precise amount of increase makes very little difference: all that is crucial is that the stimulus make some difference in proportion of self-focus.

There is a reverse side to the idea of self-focusing stimuli. There are also classes of stimuli, called "distractions," that move attention away from the self. It is relatively difficult to think about oneself while watching a house on fire, a dazzling touchdown run, or any other captivating event. Some self-awareness research has used such distractions to *decrease* the proportion of time people's attention is focused on themselves. For example, watching an involving television program or engaging in a simple but

involving motor activity (squeezing a handgrip, turning a record turntable) appears to decrease self-focused attention.

What does a person think about when attention is self-focused? The
theory makes the assumption that attention orients around whatever aspect of the self is most salient at the time. If someone is in the midst of a
conflict about whether or not to cheat, self-directed attention will highlight the self as cheater or noncheater. If a passer-by has just been examined critically by a band of sorority sisters, his self-directed attention will
have to do with his physical appearance. We now come to a crucial assumption, which has guided all the research relevant to the theory: no
matter what kind of stimulus instigates self-focused attention, that attention will quickly move toward the part of the self that is currently salient.
If one has recently flunked the final exam of an important course and
then hears one's own tape-recorded voice, attention will initially be directed toward the voice. However, the general orientation toward self-
observation that is created by the tape recording will quickly shift toward
a self-examination of intellectual ability. Similarly, in Diener and Wallbom's cheating situation, self-focused attention was created by the mirror,
thus immediately generating an awareness of the subject's own face.
However, given that a conflict over cheating was salient for the subject,
self-directed attention should have gravitated quickly toward a consideration of the self as cheater or noncheater. Further, and most important, the
amount of time spent thinking about one's own honesty should have been
greater in the mirror condition than in the control condition.

Thus far we have made the case that self-focused people come to
examine themselves on the salient self-related dimensions. What happens
next? The theory postulates that tension, discomfort, or negative affect
will be experienced to the degree that people find themselves to be unsatisfactory on the salient dimension. More generally, it is possible to characterize self-related dimensions according to whether the person has
discrepancies on those dimensions. A discrepancy is a difference between
the way a person would like to be (aspiration, or goal) and the way that
person is at present. The theory views the individual's tension state as a
joint function of the size of discrepancy and the proportion of time spent
in self-awareness. If a person is never self-focused, the size of existing
within-self discrepancies makes no difference. Therefore, someone who is
lacking in important human qualities will not suffer psychologically as
long as attention is turned away from these personal inadequacies. Once
the person becomes self-focused, the size of the discrepancy plays a crucial role.

To illustrate the causes of negative affect (discomfort), it will be useful to consider the cheater more carefully. Suppose that students in general hold a personal standard of not cheating. Not to cheat is a personal aspiration, or ambition. Once students are placed into a setting where there is some temptation, their behavior can match this standard, or it can stray from the standard in varying degrees, thus creating different sizes of discrepancy between actual behavior and the personal standard. If the non-cheaters come to focus on themselves, they will find no discrepancy between their personal standards and actual behavior, and so discomfort will be small or nonexistent. Or if people are able to avoid self-focused attention entirely, then no amount of cheating will cause any felt discomfort. However, if they are self-focused *and* have cheated, the discomfort experienced will depend on the amount of cheating: the greater the amount of cheating, the greater the resulting discomfort. This theoretical point has been documented in a study by Archer, Hormuth, and Berg (1979), in which some subjects expected to talk about their problems or failures, while others expected to talk about more neutral aspects of self. When self-awareness was raised by confronting subjects with their mirror images, the group that expected to disclose negative information about the self evidenced the strongest negative affect.

What happens when the person discovers a discrepancy and experiences the attendant negative affect? The first of two possibilities is that the negative affect can be eliminated readily by avoiding self-focused attention. Normally this will entail either of two reactions: (a) removing oneself physically from the self-focusing stimuli or (b) engaging in motor activities that will shift attention from the self onto the activities. The first process is illustrated in a study by Duval, Wicklund, and Fine (reported in Duval & Wicklund, 1972), in which some of the subjects came to experience a sizable discrepancy concerning their intelligence and creativity. The same subjects were placed in a small room and seated at a desk, half of them confronting an imposing mirror. All subjects were given license to leave the room after about 5 minutes. Subjects who were experiencing a large discrepancy *and* who were made self-aware were expected to leave soonest. The results showed exactly this: the large-discrepancy/mirror subjects left after about 6 minutes, whereas the large-discrepancy/no-mirror subjects left after about 8 minutes.

The other process, engaging in a motor activity to avert self-awareness, has never been tested directly. However, there is evidence in a study by Liebling, Seiler, and Shaver (1974) that the simple motor activity of smoking increases when smokers are placed before a mirror.

The second possible reaction to self-focused attention is called *discrepancy reduction*. Discrepancy reduction involves making efforts in the direction of attaining one's goals. Such efforts include working to perfect one's performance on a task, changing attitudes so that they correspond with objective or social reality, or coming to behave in line with one's moral values. By reducing the discrepancy, the self-focused person decreases the amount of experienced discomfort.

Before proceeding to discuss instances of discrepancy reduction, we should clarify the relations among discrepancy reduction, self-criticism, and avoidance of self-focused attention.

We have seen that the initial reaction is self-criticism, which is tantamount to *admitting* the existence of a large discrepancy. But how could discrepancy reduction go on simultaneously with self-criticism? Self-criticism and discrepancy reduction are almost opposites, in that self-criticism consists of an admission that there is some deficit within the self, whereas the process of discrepancy reduction eliminates or reduces the deficit. The solution, according to the theory, is the following: When a person first comes to focus on a discrepancy between aspired and actual self, the immediate reaction is self-criticism. The greater the discrepancy, and the larger the proportion of time the person is self-focused, the more the person will experience a personal shortcoming. But the person is also motivated to do something about the perceived discrepancy, and this motivated state leads to attempts to reduce the discrepancy. In other words, there is no contradiction between these two opposites: a person can be (and is) aware of shortcomings while trying to correct them. Whether we are able to observe both reactions, therefore, depends on the nature and the timing of the measurements we take. If we measure the person's self-evaluation, the result should be more self-criticism with increasing self-focused attention. But if we measure attempted discrepancy reduction, more efforts toward self-improvement should be found under self-focused attention. Finally, we should note one further important point: Once discrepancy reduction has proceeded sufficiently far, self-criticism on the improved trait should dwindle. Therefore, self-criticism will be found most easily immediately after the induction of self-focused attention.

Now, what is the relation between *distraction* and discrepancy reduction? Given that both distraction and discrepancy reduction are methods of reducing the discomfort created by self-focused attention, the theory indicates that the person will gravitate toward whichever of these is more effective in the situation. What is meant by "more effective"? To illustrate, reconsider the case of a cheater.

Suppose that Mary Lou has cheated throughout a final exam. Toward the end of the exam period, a number of other students realize what she is doing and therefore turn their stares toward her. The theory says that such circumstances will generate self-focused attention toward a salient personal aspect (the self as cheater), and in this instance there will be a self-critical reaction. How can the negative affect be reduced? For one, the cheater can try to escape the self-awareness. She might simply lay down her test and leave the lecture hall, thereby avoiding the stares of classmates. She may also seek distractions (go to a movie, play tennis, and so on) to take her attention further from the discomfort. In fact, in this example, escape is more likely than discrepancy reduction, for there is little that the student can do about the discrepancy between having cheated and the personal value against doing so. To reduce the discrepancy would mean to "revoke" the act of cheating, but that would be difficult. Consequently, the most effective mode of reducing the felt discomfort in this situation would be to escape from the self-focusing stares of classmates.

Diener and Wallbom's study, by contrast, was set up to *minimize* the possibility of escape and to maximize the utility of discrepancy reduction. Subjects were confronted with a mirror, from which they could not easily escape—and more important, they were made self-aware *before* the irrevocable act of cheating had occurred. Therefore, subjects in the mirror condition were able to anticipate the discrepancy that would result from an immoral act and to keep the discrepancy at a zero level by not cheating.

The idea to be gained from this example is the following: A mode of reaction to self-focused attention will be selected to the degree that it serves to reduce the negative affect immediately. If an avoidance strategy immediately eliminates self-focused attention, then avoidance is likely to be preferred. If discrepancy reduction can be brought about swiftly and completely, then it will tend to be preferred.

In summary, the outcomes of self-focused attention can be classified in the following way: (1) Self-criticism is an effect that is basic to avoidance and to discrepancy reduction. It is the immediate reaction to self-focused attention and underlies the two effects that follow. (2) Self-focused attention will result in either avoidance or discrepancy reduction, depending on which is the more immediate route to reduction of discomfort. In the research to be described next, all of which is concerned with discrepancy reduction, escape from self-awareness was made impossible, ensuring that subjects would engage in some form of attempted self-improvement.

RESEARCH EXAMPLES: DISCREPANCY REDUCTION

Personal Values and Aggression

Self-awareness theory postulates that self-focused people will attempt to change their behavior in the direction of their personal values. This general notion has an interesting implication: If people can be found who harbor highly aggressive values, they should act more upon those values when made self-aware. In comparison, the opposite counterpart, who holds nonaggressive values, should become increasingly nonaggressive when made self-aware. Carver (1975) has examined this implication in a pair of similar experiments.

He began by measuring students' feelings about punishing others. Students were asked whether they thought punishment helped in the learning process and whether they were generally willing to punish others. On the basis of these responses Carver identified two extreme groups: one group (high punitive) believed that punishment was an effective learning device, and the other (low punitive) was opposed to the use of punishment. Then these subjects were brought individually into the laboratory and were led to think that they were responsible for teaching verbal concepts to another subject. The other subject was in reality a male accomplice of the experimenter. Part of the teaching task involved punishment: each time the accomplice made a mistake, the subject was to give him an electric shock. The measure of interest was the intensity of that shock. The subject was allowed to deliver any one of ten intensities. (The accomplice did not actually receive any shocks.)

Half the subjects in the high-punitive group and half in the low-punitive group engaged in this teaching procedure while viewing their mirror images. The prediction from the theory is quite clear. In the presence of a mirror, people who have punitive values should act in an especially punitive way, and people who have nonpunitive values should display only minimal punitiveness. That is, the self-focusing stimulus (the mirror) should cause the intensity of shocks delivered by subjects to come into alignment with the subjects' personal values. The results were just as expected in each of two highly similar experiments.

It was also interesting that the high- and low-punitive groups did not differ in amount of shock administered as long as no mirror was present. It took the presence of a self-focusing device to bring out the behaviors that were implied by their values.

Consistency between Behavior and Self-Report

One of the problems plaguing personality psychologists has been the validity of their instruments. Self-report measures, such as personality tests and attitude scales, often bear little relation to the behaviors those measures are supposed to predict (Mischel, 1968; Wicker, 1969). For instance, if a person were given a simple self-report measure of sociability that included questions like "I usually take the initiative in making new friends," it would not be expected that actual sociable behavior could be predicted accurately from the person's answers. In Mischel's review, it becomes evident that correlations between self-report measures and actual behavior are very low, usually in the range of .10 to .30. Thus, there is normally only a weak positive relation between self-reports and behavior. Why should this be?

It is conceivable that people giving self-reports are seldom motivated to create consistency between their reports and the relevant behaviors. Self-reports are often gathered in settings that are not conducive to self-examination: these measures are often given in large, anonymous groups in which there are numerous potential distractions. Such situations will tend to decrease self-focused attention, so that the person should have difficulty in contemplating the consistency between self-report and behavior. Self-awareness theory proposes that self-focused people will try to make themselves internally consistent—whether the consistency is between values and behaviors, between values and other values, or between behaviors and self-reports about those behaviors. In the present instance, the theoretical derivation is quite easy. Given that some trait, such as sociability, is salient, self-focused attention will motivate people to try to align their behaviors and self-reports into a consistent pattern. Accordingly, if people are brought into self-awareness while responding to a sociability questionnaire, they should make increased efforts to report accurately on their normal level of sociability. Moreover, the self-report should have stronger predictive power than if the motivation to be consistent were missing.

An experiment to examine this derivation was conducted by Pryor, Gibbons, Wicklund, Fazio, and Hood (1977). Undergraduate males were first asked to fill out a simple, 16-item sociability questionnaire. For the most part, the items asked the subject about his reactions upon encountering a member of the opposite sex for the first time. In line with the theoretical reasoning, half the subjects filled out this form while looking at themselves in a mirror. This group of subjects should have been especially motivated to bring their self-reports into line with their usual level of sociability with members of the opposite sex.

Since the theoretical question asks about the relation between self-report and *behavior*, an index of overt behavioral sociability was required. In other words, how does the subject get along with a stranger of the opposite sex? This requirement was satisfied by asking subjects to return two days later, at which time they had an unstructured 3-minute interaction with an attractive undergraduate female. The index of behavioral sociability was composed of the number of words the subject initiated in her presence plus her subjective rating of his sociability. In line with Mischel's pessimistic conclusions about the accuracy of self-report measures, it was found that subjects who filled out the scale in the absence of a mirror did not attain a high level of consistency between self-report and behavior. The self-report/behavior correlation for that group was only .16, a very weak relationship. When a mirror was introduced during the sociability questionnaire session, subjects evidently became increasingly interested in giving a self-report that was consistent with their behavior: the correlation for that group was .62, a much stronger relationship.

A highly informative parallel should be noted between this and the previous research on aggression. In Carver's experiment the self-report was made in the absence of any self-focusing device; then, during assessment of behavior, self-awareness was introduced for some of the subjects. That procedure results in relatively high correspondence between behavior and the earlier-stated value for the subjects who are self-aware; the non-self-aware subjects do not show a similar level of value-behavior correspondence. In the experiment by Pryor et al., the self-awareness manipulation came during the self-report and before the behavior, and this procedure also resulted in increased consistency between behavior and self-report. The point is simple: no matter whether the self-report or the behavior is subject to the effects of self-focusing, the end result seems to be an enhanced inner-self consistency.

A SPECIAL TOPIC

Conflicting Directions for Behavior

The research represented here has been simple and uncluttered, in that the "direction" taken by self-aware subjects was always clear. People on the verge of cheating who became self-aware and who were generally inclined to abide by an anticheating norm reduced their cheating. Similarly, in the research on validity of self-reports it seemed evident that discrepancy reduction could mean only one thing: reporting one's trait in a way that better reflected actual behavior.

However, by adding just a bit more complexity to the self-awareness-producing situation, we can find instances in which self-aware people might take alternative directions, thereby throwing a fly into the ointment regarding predictions.

1. Suppose that the achievement and honesty ethics are brought into conflict. A person is strongly motivated to achieve success but can do so only by cheating—and at the same time is presumably bound by a moral principle that would inhibit cheating. Will an increment in self-focused attention bring the achievement value or the moral principle to the fore? The answer presumably depends on the nature of the situation. A research project by Vallacher and Solodky (1979) indicates that the self-aware person tends to push aside the moral principle in favor of pursuing achievement, although it seems rather likely that other situations could be devised in which the moral principle would predominate. Had the subjects been devout churchgoers and the experimenter their minister, one would suspect that the outcome of the study would have been quite different. These examples serve to remind us that when two prominent guides for action collide, we must be more cautious in our predictions.

2. When confronted with pressure to conform, is the self-aware individual more inclined to buckle under the conformity pressures or to hold fast to preexisting personal values and beliefs? Again, there are two opposing directions one can take, and in individual experiments there are examples of both. An experiment by Wicklund and Duval (1971) demonstrated increased conformity with self-awareness, as did a study by Duval (1976), but a variety of other experiments show that self-aware people act more on their *own* values (see Carver, 1975; Gibbons, 1978). Who is right? In this instance it seems to be a question of how salient a personal belief is that would form the basis for taking a given action. If the personal belief is rendered highly salient through recent actions, it overrides external conformity pressures—a point documented by McCormick (1979).

3. Is the self-aware person basically cognitive and rational—always following closely a principle for correct action—or can self-focused attention also stir up the emotions? Again, this is a conflict of directions which usually does not surface in research but which can be brought about rather easily. Take the instance of someone who is provoked through arbitrary insults and grows angry. Then self-awareness is induced. Will the person follow a personal rule about the virtues (or nonvirtues) of aggression, or will the anger simply increase? We have already seen, in Carver's 1975 experiments, that without the presence of anger, people who are made self-aware are much more likely to abide by their personal beliefs

about aggression. But if anger arousal is added to this situation, the whole picture changes. Under self-awareness, subjects disregard their cognitive standards about the appropriateness of aggression, and overall they *increase* anger and aggression (Scheier, 1976). An analogous finding, such that the emotion of fear becomes more intense, is reported by Scheier, Carver, and Gibbons (in press).

Which Direction When?

Fortunately there may be a general theoretical solution to this seemingly perplexing issue of "Which direction does the self-aware person take?" Wicklund and Frey (1980) have offered the following solution: Suppose a person has recently acted on a given standard, conformed to a given group, or been responsive to some particular emotional state. That standard, source of conformity pressure, or emotion will then take precedence when the person becomes self-aware, because it *recently* had an impact. Note that the extreme case is when a standard or emotion is presently having an influence. Thus, if someone is currently displaying an emotion, the behaviors stemming from the emotional state will dominate over potential behaviors that are steered by moral standards or other rules—because the emotion is more recent, or immediate, in its effect on the person. Similarly, if someone has just recently (perhaps 2 minutes ago) behaved in a highly benevolent fashion and is then confronted with the conflict of acting benevolently again or abiding by social pressure to behave unscrupulously, self-awareness should push the person toward acting benevolently.

In summary, the solution to the issue of "Which direction?" is potentially not too difficult. First assess (or manipulate) which aspect of the self has recently influenced the person's behavior, and then place other self aspects in competition with that recently influential one. The self-aware person's behavior should then be guided more by the first than by the second source of direction for behavior.

SUMMARY

The theory of self-awareness, with its implications for discrepancy reduction, has developed in a variety of directions. Not only have cheating, aggression, and self-report/behavior consistency been explored, but other forms of discrepancy reduction, such as speed on simple tasks and cognitive dissonance reduction, can also be affected by self-focus. The implications of the theory are broad, in that self-focused attention should play a positive role in any process whereby a person has a potential disparity between an aspiration and actual behavior or, more generally, a disparity between any two components of the self. With reference to other chapters in this book, there is research indicating that that achievement-oriented behavior, dissonance reduction, restoration of equity, emotions, and even performance in the "helplessness" situation would be affected by self-focused attention.

SUGGESTED READING

Duval, S., & Wicklund, R. A. *A theory of objective self awareness.* New York: Academic Press, 1972.

Frey, D., Wicklund, R. A., & Scheier, M. F. *Die Theorie der objektiven Selbstaufmerksamkeit* (The theory of objective self awareness). In D. Frey (Ed.), *Kognitive Theorien der Sozialpsychologie.* Bern: Huber, 1978.

Wicklund, R. A. Objective self-awareness. In L. Berkowitz (Ed.), *Advances in experimental social psychology* (Vol. 8). New York: Academic Press, 1975.

Wicklund, R. A. The influence of self-awareness on human behavior. *American Scientist,* 1979, 67, 187–193.

PART FIVE

ACHIEVEMENT AND LEADERSHIP

The thread drawing these three chapters together is the idea that many instances of complex behavior are influenced by the interrelation between personality dimensions and the difficulty of succeeding in some given situation. It is interesting that both achievement and leadership, which are to some degree related and are also highly valued by society, have been approached theoretically from the perspective that we must know something about the personality of the person involved and that we must also understand the person's likelihood of success in a given setting.

The theory of achievement motivation (Chapter 14) begins by viewing the human as having either a preponderance of achievement orientation or else a preponderant tendency to avoid failure. Once the person is classified, it is possible to make predictions about how the person will respond to varying ranges of probabilities of success. For instance, a major ramification of the theory is that the achievement-oriented person prefers, and works hardest at, the task that carries a moderate chance of success. The striking contrast is provided by the person who is dominated by a fear of failure, for this person seeks out either the excessively easy or the especially hard tasks.

Chapter 15 brings the ideas of attribution (see Chapters 8–10) to the domain of achievement motivation. A primary purpose of this theory is to show how particular attributions (for example, to effort, ability, or luck) influence the kinds of achievement behaviors documented in Chapter 14.

The contingency model of leadership (Chapter 16), like the theory of achievement motivation, begins by drawing a distinction among leaders. The distinction is between two types, such that some leaders may be cast as oriented mainly toward the task, whereas the dominant interest of others is in the smooth operation of the social milieu. Having posited this distinction, the theory then considers the ease with which a group can be led and predicts an intriguing relation between type of leader and group performance. For instance, the task-oriented leader is said to function best with groups that are quite easy to lead or else difficult to lead, but the socially oriented leader performs more effectively if the group poses only moderate problems for leadership.

CHAPTER 14

A THEORY OF ACHIEVEMENT MOTIVATION

IT is spring and an elite group of undergraduate seniors who call themselves "Student Lawyers Incorporated" is meeting to discuss common legal interests. All the members are outstanding prelaw students who have 3.9 grade-point averages and scores above the 95th percentile on the Law School Admissions Test. Each student has received acceptances from a variety of law schools, and so the conversation on this particular evening is dominated by concerns about which school to select. Mary opens the conversation by discussing her options:

> I got admitted to three schools. First, there's Ivy University back east. It's a real fine school—they have some programs I really like—but I hear they flunk out 90% of their freshman class. Then there's Midwestern State University. They have some good programs, and I feel that I would probably be successful there—they flunk out only 50% of their freshman class. Finally, I

got accepted at that Learn by Night school out west. They are brand new, and I don't know how good their programs are, but they keep nearly all their students—they flunk out only 10% of their freshmen. All things considered, though, I guess I'm going to choose Midwestern State.

Several other students talk about their choices, and their stories sound similar. In each case the student appears to have considered the attractiveness of the school and the odds of being flunked out, and everyone seems to have chosen a school where the chances of making it through the first year are neither overwhelmingly good nor totally unfavorable. In terms of personal subjective probabilities, each student's chance of successfully completing the program at the chosen school is about 50% among this group of Student Lawyers Incorporated.

At this point a few other students begin to discuss their choices. Their comments differ in two important ways from those of the first students. For one, they admit that they would prefer not to go to law school at all; their wealthy parents have pushed them to pursue a law career. And second, their remarks sound like this:

> I was admitted to the same law schools as Mary. I just don't know if I could make it at Midwestern State, and I know I would feel terrible if I flunked out. Ivy University seems OK—I wouldn't feel bad if I failed there, since nearly everyone flunks out. And that Learn by Night school out west would be fine, too, since I would be sure to make it through their program. I don't know, I haven't been able to decide between Ivy University and Learn by Night. I'll give it some more thought, but if I can't decide, I'll just flip a coin.

As it turns out, the behavior of these two sets of students can be accounted for rather well if we know that the first group is highly achievement-oriented and that the second group is concerned with fear of failure. Here is the theory that explains these phenomena.

THE THEORY

The Achievement Motive

In 1943 Murray published a clever test that enabled psychologists to tap into a great number of human needs. The test requires the person to examine a number of pictures—such as two men in a shop working on a machine, or a young boy sitting at a desk—and to create a story about the situation. Subsequently the story is examined for certain kinds of themes—for example, achievement themes—and the person can then be given a score for achievement. This test is the Thematic Apperception Test, or "TAT."

The test is a "projective" test, so called because people are assumed to project their salient needs or motives into the fairly contentless pictures and subsequently tell a story that reveals something about the self. For example, if someone looks at the picture of the young boy and says "He's thinking about sex," we would say that the subject has read a sex motive into the picture. If the subject reports "He's contriving a method whereby he can be president of General Motors," we might say that the subject has projected an achievement theme into the picture. In general, achievement themes include "thoughts about performing some task well, of sometimes being blocked, of trying various means of achieving, and of experiencing joy or sadness contingent upon the outcome of the effort" (Atkinson, 1977, p. 30).

It is this type of theme that was all-important to McClelland and his coworkers (McClelland, Atkinson, Clark, & Lowell, 1953). McClelland instigated the work in achievement motivation, drew many interesting implications from the concept, and even found ways to compare entire nations' levels of achievement motivation. Further, it was McClelland et al. (1953) who validated the TAT measure of achievement motivation. That is, they showed that people who were placed in an achievement-eliciting situation showed a comparatively high level of achievement imagery when taking the TAT.

Taking this test as a starting point, Atkinson (1957) proceeded to develop a theory of achievement motivation. The theory includes some ingenious mathematical calculations that help clarify its predictions. The reader is cautioned that these calculations should not be taken literally, but are only an indication of the *relative* level of motivation in different situations. Let us begin by examining Atkinson's formula for a person's immediate tendency to pursue achievements. We will call this tendency "Approach Motivation."

$$\frac{\text{APPROACH}}{\text{MOTIVATION}} = \frac{\text{achievement}}{\text{motive}} \times \frac{\text{expectancy}}{\text{of success}} \times \frac{\text{incentive value}}{\text{of success}}$$

In explaining these four terms it is best to start with the "achievement motive," which is conceived of as a fairly stable personality trait, measured by the number of achievement themes in the person's TAT stories. Each person can be assigned a number determined by the test outcome, although the absolute size of the number is not all-important. The size relative to someone else is the crucial issue. For the sake of illustration Atkinson uses arbitrary values, such as 1 or 2.

The achievement motive lies dormant until it is set into action by the situation, and for Atkinson, the significant parts of the situation are the next two terms in the equation: "Expectancy of success" is nothing more than the probability of success (P_s) at a given task. From our opening example the expectancy of success with Learn by Night was .90, and with the top Ivy University it was only .10. "Incentive value of success" is the degree to which success is valued by the person. Taking some ideas from Escalona (1940) and Festinger (1942), Atkinson assumes that success is attractive, or of high incentive value, when it is hard to attain. Thus, the incentive value of attending Learn by Night is very low, and the incentive value of attending Ivy University is nearly maximal. Mathematically, it is easy to calculate the incentive value: just subtract the P_s from 1.00. This means that the expectancy of success and the incentive value of success will always add to 1.00, which is convenient in dealing with the theory.

The left side of the equation is the end result, called "Approach Motivation" which means the behavioral tendency to try to achieve success. In order to exercise the formula, we might try some different values for P_s to see what happens to the size of the Approach Motivation.

First, take the case of the new (easy) law school and assume we are dealing with a student whose measured achievement motive is 1. By inserting the numbers appropriately in the above equation, we find the following:

$$\text{(Learn by Night)} \quad \text{APPROACH MOTIVATION} = 1 \times .90 \times .10 = .09$$

Or if the school is the Midwestern state school,

$$\text{(Midwestern State)} \quad \text{APPROACH MOTIVATION} = 1 \times .50 \times .50 = .25$$

Finally, for the top Ivy League school,

$$\text{(Ivy University)} \quad \text{APPROACH MOTIVATION} = 1 \times .1 \times .90 = .09$$

Three points are extremely important. Only the *relative* size of these numbers is of interest, not the absolute size. Second, note a certain symmetry. As we move away from the P_s of .5 in either direction, the student's Approach Motivation declines, and it would eventually reach 0 if the P_s were either 0% or 100%. Third, note that a P_s of .5 maximizes the Approach Motivation, by which we mean the behavioral tendency to strive toward success.

proach Motivation, by which we mean the behavioral tendency to strive toward success.

What does all this mean for behavior? First, there will be a strong preference for goals that have about a 50% chance of attainment. Second, if someone is already involved in the pursuit of some given goal, there will be more persistence when the P_s is near .5. We will focus on the first kind of effect in our forthcoming research examples.

Fear of Failure

Atkinson's theory deals with more than just one motive. Atkinson also speaks of a motive that has to do with fear of achievement situations, and the personality trait that is relevant is called "fear of failure." Fear of failure works in opposition to the achievement motive and is best viewed as a tendency to run away from challenges. Just as with the achievement motive, we can draw an equation that describes the circumstances leading to Avoidance Motivation:

$$\text{AVOIDANCE MOTIVATION} = \frac{\text{fear of}}{\text{failure}} \times \frac{\text{expectancy}}{\text{of failure}} \times \frac{\text{incentive value of}}{\text{avoiding failure}}$$

Starting with "fear of failure," which is conceived of as a chronic trait, all we have to worry about is the measurement. Normally, this has been handled by the Mandler-Sarason (1952) Test Anxiety Questionnaire (TAQ), which asks the person about worries and physiological reactions (for example, uneasiness, accelerated heartbeat, perspiration) in testing situations. Just as with the TAT achievement-motivation measure, we can assign numbers to people on the basis of their answers to the test. Again, Atkinson assigns arbitrary numbers, such as 1 or 2, to indicate the relative level of this trait when dealing with examples.

The achievement motive and fear of failure can be measured in more comparable ways. Heckhausen (in press) has developed a measure of fear of failure that uses the same TAT device that is used to measure achievement motivation, and Mehrabian (1978) has developed a questionnaire that yields measures of both the achievement motive and fear of failure.

"Expectancy of failure" is nothing but the probability of failure (P_f). This value is 1 minus P_s, so that, for example, if P_s were .7, P_f would be .3. The "incentive value of avoiding failure," conveniently, is identical to the P_s. The incentive value of avoiding failure and the expectancy of failure therefore add up to 1. This notion of the incentive value of avoiding failure makes a certain intuitive sense. If the P_s is quite high, then it is psychologically dangerous to fail, for the conclusion then is that one is incompetent. In other words, when the task is easy, people who are concerned about their images have to be careful not to fail. But when the task is impossible, everyone would be expected to fail. With impossible tasks failure is not a reflection of personal worth, so that there is less reason (incentive) to try to avoid failing.

The left side of the equation is the resultant "Avoidance Motivation" that is set into motion by the combination of the three terms on the right. If we may assume that the measured value of fear of failure for some given individual is 1, then we arrive at the following values for the avoidance-eliciting power of each of the three law schools.

(Learn by Night)   AVOIDANCE MOTIVATION $= 1 \times .10 \times .90 = .09$

(Midwestern State)   AVOIDANCE MOTIVATION $= 1 \times .50 \times .50 = .25$

(Ivy University)   AVOIDANCE MOTIVATION $= 1 \times .90 \times .10 = .09$

Note the similarity to our first set of equations. The only numerical difference is that the values of the expectancy and incentive terms are reversed, but of course that does not matter when we multiply the terms together.

There is an important observation to make here. Fear of failure is maximized when there is a 50% chance of failure, which means that the 50% area will be avoided. At the same time, this was the level that led to an especially high Approach Motivation. Thus, we seem to be talking about two opposing motives. Which one wins out?

The answer depends on which of the two motives, achievement motive or fear of failure, is stronger. We arbitrarily assigned a value of 1 to each of them, but it turns out that it is possible to categorize people according to which of the two traits dominates. We will see how this is done in the research to follow. This classification into achievement-oriented and failure-oriented people turns out to have great consequences.

Going back to the example of Student Lawyers Incorporated, we might try assuming that the students in the first group are achievement-oriented. Arbitrarily, we will say that their achievement motive score is 10 and their fear of failure score is 1. From the equations it turns out that this preponderance of achievement motivation will be maximized in the case of Midwestern State, and therefore these students will tend to be most highly motivated to attend such schools and not schools that are either extremely stringent or extremely lenient.

Just the opposite is found for the second, more fearful group. Assume that their achievement motive score is 1 and their fear of failure score 10. Again from the equations, it is apparent that they will be motivated to avoid Midwestern State, and given that they must go *somewhere*, they will move toward *either* of the extreme categories. This last implication, that failure-oriented people will select either extremely easy or extremely hard tasks and will avoid achievement settings generally, is one of the most intriguing aspects of Atkinson's theory. We will now give some examples to show how the principle works.

RESEARCH EXAMPLES

Risk Preference in Ring Toss

The contrasting behaviors of achievement-oriented and failure-oriented people was noted by Hamilton (1974) in a paradigm that had already become classic several years earlier in a study by Atkinson and Litwin (1960). The apparatus was composed of a peg about 12 inches tall, ten large rings to be pitched in the direction of the peg, and a "throwing field" marked off at intervals between 1 and 18 feet from the target. The subjects were high school males.

Hamilton devised a unique method of determining each subject's subjective probability of success (P_s). Each person was given a good number of chances to throw rings from various of the possible distances, and after this practice the experimenter analyzed the performance with him, to be sure that the subject had a feeling for his P_s at each of the distances. Once these different P_s values were completely clear to the subject, he was given ten "free" throws, with no directions about the appropriate distance. The average distance selected by the subject was the main dependent measure.

Now to the mathematical question. Earlier, Hamilton had obtained achievement motive scores and fear of failure scores from his subjects, but as two very different kinds of personality measures are involved, there is no way to compare the two scores directly. Accordingly, to arrive at a group of achievement-oriented subjects, Hamilton just selected people who had a high achievement score (compared with other subjects) and whose fear of failure score was low (compared with other subjects). The reverse procedure was used to obtain a group of failure-oriented subjects. This same procedure has been followed in the other research relevant to this theory, as there is simply no way to take the mathematical aspects of the theory completely literally.

The results showed that the achievement-oriented subjects clustered their preferences for throwing distance around the distance corresponding to a 40% chance of success, whereas the failure-oriented subjects gravitated very much toward the far end of the playing field, where the P_s was only .1. True to Atkinson's model, the achievement-oriented group sought out a challenge with a moderate probability of success, and the failure-oriented people pursued extreme probabilities—in this case the extremely low probabilities. It is almost as though they were trying to fail.

Vocational Aspirations

It is common on a university campus to meet a student who aspires to be a lawyer or doctor yet whose standard scores on entrance exams are only in the 30th to 40th percentile. The reverse is also common—the so-called underachiever with brilliant potential who is content to drive a taxi-cab or collect garbage. Atkinson's theory offers an excellent analysis of these phenomena, as illustrated in a field study by Mahone (1960).

The subjects, male college students, were asked to respond to measures of achievement motivation, fear of failure, and vocational aspiration. Nothing more was required of the subjects, and the remainder of the procedure consisted of a clinical analysis of subjects' aspirations and abilities.

The clinical analysis was carried out by two trained clinical psychologists who were experts in vocational counseling. These psychologists analyzed the vocational potential of each subject, taking into account such things as the student's college entrance exam scores and grade-point average. The subject's vocational potential was compared with his actual choice of a future vocation, and a judgment was made on whether his occupational aspiration was too low, realistic, or too high. Mahone then partitioned his subjects into "realistic" and "unrealistic"; the latter category included people whose occupational aspiration was either too low or too high. Presumably a "realistic" student is one whose aspiration involves some risks but not too many—that is, a midrange P_s. An "unrealistic" student is one whose aspiration implies very low or very high risks, such as an "A" student who plans to be a janitor or a "D" student who plans to be an astrophysicist.

The subjects were divided into achievement-oriented and failure-oriented in much the same manner as Hamilton's. The results were compelling. Of the achievement-oriented subjects, only 6% showed unrealistic occupational hopes, while an overwhelming 83% of the failure-oriented did. Noteworthy, and parallel to the finding of Hamilton, is that almost 100% of the unrealistic aspirations were overaspirations. Thus, among failure-oriented students there was again a distinct flavor of trying to fail.

Shifts in Risk Performances Following Success and Failure

The preceding examples have shown that achievement-oriented people prefer tasks at which they initially believe they have about a 50% chance of success. But what happens if the person is in fact successful or unsuccessful at the task? Returning to our opening example, suppose Mary is successful during her first semester at Midwestern State. It appears that she initially underestimated her probability of success (50%), and she would therefore need to revise her estimate upward. She might now think, for example, that she has a 90% chance of completing the program at this school. Her new confidence would be likely to generalize so that she might now perceive a 50% chance of completing the program at Ivy University and a 100% chance of completing the program at Learn by Night. More generally, the perceived chances of success across all schools should increase following success and decrease following failure.

Suppose that after completing her first semester at Midwestern State, Mary is given several opportunities: she can transfer either to Ivy University or to Learn by Night, or she can remain at Midwestern State. By the theory, Mary should now be more attracted to Ivy U. Although she originally thought the Ivy League school was too hard, she would now believe her chance of success to be closer to the 50% level. And as noted above, it should be the challenging 50% probability of success that will attract the achievement-oriented person.

But what about the failure-oriented group? Suppose that under pressure from his alumnus-father, a student from this group attends Midwestern State U. He also successfully completes the first semester and then is given the opportunity to transfer to one of the two other schools or to remain at Midwestern. In light of his classroom experiences he comes to think of the Ivy League school as not that hard after all—he now estimates his chances of success there at 50%. Interestingly, this is exactly the probability of success that would keep him from transferring, whereas earlier, when the odds of success seemed more like 10%, he was prepared to go. It is the midrange of probabilities that is especially frightening to the failure-oriented person.

A study by Moulton (1965) illustrates these contrasting shifts in risk preferences following success and failure. Using the now familiar procedure, achievement-oriented and failure-oriented boys were selected. The boys were shown three anagram tasks and were asked to select one of them to work on. One of the tasks was easy (the subjects were told that they had a 75% chance of completing it successfully), another was of medium difficulty ($P_s = 50\%$), and the final task was hard ($P_s = 25\%$). Instead of being allowed to work on the task they had selected, the boys were first required to work on the medium task. Irrespective of their performance, some of them were given fictitious feedback that they were successful, and others were told they had failed. Subjects were then asked to pick one of the two remaining tasks, either the difficult task or the easy task, as their final task to work on.

These choices were quite interesting from the perspective of Atkinson's theory. The achievement-oriented boys nearly always chose the hard task following success and the easy task following failure. The failure-oriented group showed an entirely different pattern: following success, many of them chose the easy task; following failure, many chose the hard task. In terms of the theory, both groups revised their subjective probability of success according to their outcome on the first task. The achievement-oriented subjects chose the task that they *now* perceived to be of medium difficulty ($P_s = $ about 50%), whereas failure-oriented subjects *avoided* the task they now believed to be of medium difficulty, instead choosing the most extreme available task (P_s near either 0 or 100%).

In summary, the model predicts with considerable success, but there is some suggestion in the first experiment (Hamilton, 1974) that $P_s = .4$ is more empirically correct than $P_s = .5$, an issue we will take up in the next section. Further, it is striking that the failure-oriented group moved almost exclusively in the direction of extremely low P_s, even though the theory suggests that they might be expected to go to *either* extreme. But, to be sure, there are also studies in which both extremes are sought by failure-oriented groups (Atkinson & Litwin, 1960; de Charms & Davé, 1965). Finally, P_s is adjusted upward after success and downward after failure, and it is the person's current P_s that should be used when applying the theory. As was shown, these adjustments in the P_s can lead to some unusual-appearing shifts in the risk preferences of failure-oriented people.

SPECIAL TOPICS

Other Motives

Thus far we have considered only two motives, the achievement motive and fear of failure. People have other motives—needs for sex, needs for approval, needs for power. Do these other motives have any effect on the person's risk preferences? From experimental research, the answer to this question is no. Other motives will have no systematic impact on risk preferences unless they vary together with the P_s.

In the opening example, suppose that Mary had a strong need to affiliate with others and, further, that she heard that some of the law schools had atmospheres highly conducive to socializing with fellow students. For this reason she would gravitate toward those law schools, but we would still expect her to show a predominant interest in schools where the chances of success were 50%. The optimal solution, given her achievement needs *and* need for affiliation, is to find a friendly school where the chances of success are moderate.

But in other cases the satisfaction of other motives may depend on the probability of success for each of the tasks. Imagine that a crowd of the subject's friends is watching him perform in the ring-toss experiment. It is unlikely that the subject would gain much approval for trying the easy distances. Rather, he is likely to gain more approval from his friends for trying the challenging distances. They may even dare him to stand 15 feet back from the peg. Thus, it is likely that the level of Approval Motivation would be higher when the P_s is small.

In cases in which Approval Motivation is important, the symmetrical qualities of the theory would be altered. Failure-oriented people would prefer very difficult tasks (low P_s), in which Avoidance Motivation would be minimal and Approval Motivation high. Success-oriented people, in contrast, should prefer tasks at which the P_s is slightly lower than .5. This would be the point at which the combination (summation) of Approval Motivation and Approach Motivation is highest.

This analysis may provide some insight into the deviations from the theory that we noted in our research examples. Several psychologists (for example, Rosenberg, 1969) have suggested that subjects tend to have high needs to gain approval from the experimenter in a laboratory experiment. If we consider our ring-toss research example in this light, the results become less surprising. Failure-oriented subjects gravitate to the far end of the ring-toss field, since this is where Avoidance Motivation is lowest and Approval Motivation is highest. Achievement-oriented subjects choose a distance where $P_s = .4$, ostensibly because that is where the sum of Approach Motivation and Approval Motivation is highest. Indeed, Heckhausen (1968) notes that achievement-oriented subjects quite regularly prefer tasks that are slightly more difficult than $P_s = .5$. However, if a situation could be devised in which the subject's approval motivation were 0, achievement-oriented subjects might then prefer tasks whose probability of success is .5, as predicted by Atkinson's theory.

A Broader Time Frame: Inertial Tendencies

The theory as we have discussed it thus far treats achievement behaviors as sets of isolated episodes. It is as though the person is sitting, inert, waiting to be confronted with a task associated with a set of probabilities before the motivational processes go into gear. More recently, Atkinson (1964, 1977; Atkinson & Cartwright, 1964) has drawn attention to what may be called the "inertial tendency." Once the motivational process is set into motion, whether an achievement-oriented state, a social-approval-oriented state, or any other motivated condition, that condition will tend to persist and add to or subtract from the person's subsequent motivations. For instance, if someone fails at a moderately difficult task (thereby becoming more motivated to achieve), the same person will be all the more persistent when later confronted with another, moderately difficult task.

The crucial idea here is that separate tasks or separate achievement-related situations are not really psychologically independent of one another. Two persons, both with high achievement motivation and low failure anxiety, might be expected to perform quite differently if one of them has just come from a setting that has set off a desire to achieve—or a setting that has suppressed or satisfied the need to achieve.

A Broader Time Frame: Contingent Achievement Situations

A useful line of analysis developed by Raynor (1974) approaches the issue of sequential achievement-relevant activities. Take, for example, someone who has to succeed at one risky activity before being able to proceed to the next, more important, risky activity. A good case in point would be the world of tennis tournaments, in which the player must win the first match in order to play in the second. Raynor describes such situations as "contingent," in that being able to take part in the second achievement-related activity is contingent on success at the first one. To be sure, the isolated achievement experiments of subjects in the laboratory are not especially related to any future activities, but in the real world of ego-involving achievements, one normally goes through a number of steps, always progressing from one challenge to the next, as long as the first challenge was met with success.

According to Raynor's thinking, the level of motivation on an early task is a function of the number of later activities that are contingent on it. It is one thing if a laboratory subject is told that the ring-toss game is a one-shot affair, with no further implications, but it is quite a different thing when success at a ring-toss game means a chance to try out for further competition. Arousal of achievement motivation during the ring-toss game will be greater if entering into further challenges is contingent on success at ring toss.

There is a further noteworthy implication of Raynor's thinking. The .5 P_s level that seemed to be sought by achievement-oriented experimental subjects might be too risky when we are dealing with successively contingent achievement activities, because it is important to be able to go on to the next activity, and little is to be gained by creating too great a challenge for oneself on any given activity. By Raynor's reasoning the achievement-oriented person is attracted to tasks for which the probability of successfully completing the *entire series* of steps is .5.

Motivation and Performance

The combination of achievement motivation and failure anxiety has been shown to affect preferences for intermediate tasks rather than easy or difficult ones. Persistence in actual *working* is affected in a parallel fashion: achievement-oriented people persist longer at tasks of intermediate difficulty, whereas failure-oriented people persist longer at impossible tasks (Feather, 1962). But there is also a more practical question that may be raised with regard to achievement motivation. Who is the most efficient or most successful worker in general? Is it the person characterized by high achievement motivation or someone with high fear of failure?

A well-known idea in psychology, existing well before the advent of achievement motivation theory, describes an intriguing relation between the motivation to perform and the actual quality of performance as reflected in such measures as the percentage of correct responses or

creativity of responses. This law indicates that there is a curvilinear relation between motivation to perform and quality of performance. That is,
performance is best when motivation is somewhat *less* than maximal, so
that one should be careful not to overmotivate people, but at the same
time, one must ensure that they are motivated enough (Yerkes & Dodson,
1908). Extending this idea to achievement motivation, we might think that
people who are highly achievement-oriented could, on occasion, have too
high a level of motivation, and hence the quality of their performance
would suffer.

An experiment by Smith (cited in Atkinson, 1977) supports this line
of reasoning. Subjects were asked to solve complex arithmetic problems
under a variety of conditions. In one case several features were present
that should have contributed to an extremely high level of motivation: the
situation was competitive, there were proctors who could have served as
sources of approval or disapproval, and a monetary prize was offered for
superior performance. Under these circumstances the subjects whose
measured achievement motivation was high performed worse than the
low achievement motivation group.

The implication of this experiment is clear: when the person's motivation (that is, measured achievement motivation) is already high, the addition of further motivating conditions may serve only to bring the person
beyond the optimal point of motivation—and just as noted by Yerkes and
Dodson, this overmotivated state can result in performance decrements.

Personality Measurement

Three of the theories in this book are highly dependent on the measurement of stable differences in personality between people, otherwise
known as "individual differences." One is the leadership theory of Fiedler,
another is the present, and the final is the Weiner formulation. Although it
is not crucial to define degrees of achievement motivation and failure anxiety in terms of a scale, this has been almost exclusively the approach
taken in testing the theory. Why should the personality-measurement approach be problematic?

The main issue that concerns us is "What psychological trait is measured?" In general, any one scale or projective personality test may be
said to measure a number of different entities. For instance, suppose one
found that people scoring high on the TAT achievement motivation measure also happened to be above average in intelligence (see Entwistle,
1972). Does one then say that achievement motivation is basic to the seek-

ing after .5 probability situations or that IQ is the crucial factor? Fortunately, it is possible to control for level of IQ and still find predicted differences as a function of measured achievement motivation (Atkinson, 1977). But the general point still remains: one must always be on the lookout for possible alternative meanings of a given personality measure.

Manipulating Achievement Motivation

Since the measures of achievement motivation and fear of failure presumably tap general psychological states, it is reasonable that one might also be able to create the same states experimentally. To be sure, the early validations of the TAT measure of achievement motivation employed experimental inductions of achievement motivation, but the Atkinson theory per se has been approached by means of personality measures in virtually every case. One exception is a seldom-cited study by Shaban and Jecker (1968). Subjects were given either favorable or unfavorable feedback about their social skills, on the assumption that positive feedback would generate an achievement orientation (that is, they would become achievement-oriented, at least with respect to social skills) and that failure would produce a failure-oriented set. These subjects then had a chance to pick an evaluator from among a group of evaluators who varied in the harshness of their criticism of social skills. Paralleling the first two experiments we discussed, the failure-dominated group gravitated toward selecting a harsh critic, thus maximizing the probability of failure.

This experiment is potentially very important, for it shows that Atkinson's reasoning goes beyond the personality-difference definition of achievement orientation. We can now conceive of the two psychological states in a more general way, defined either by chronic measured differences or by the immediate situation.

Differences between the Sexes

For the first time in this book we find a body of literature that is based almost entirely on research with one sex. With the exception of a field study in public schools by O'Connor et al. (1966), virtually none of the research reported in the classic literature includes female subjects. Why should the whole field of achievement motivation be limited to males?

Early in the development of achievement measures it was found that the TAT measure of achievement could not be validated with females (McClelland, Clark, Roby & Atkinson, 1949; Veroff, Wilcox, & Atkinson, 1953).

It turned out that under relaxed conditions women's achievement scores were no lower than men's, but under conditions that should have led to the arousal of achievement motivation, only men reflected that arousal in the TAT measure. In other words, women did not appear to respond to achievement-eliciting situations.

This finding, as one might expect, is not totally universal. For instance, Heckhausen (1963) reports that women in other nations (particularly Brazil, Japan, and Germany) do indeed seem to respond to achievement-arousing circumstances. He adds that this could be due to a selection factor, whereby college women (who are usually the subjects in this research) might be unusually high in achievement motivation in non-American countries, since relatively few women are permitted to attend universities in some of those countries.

Assuming that there are indeed important sex differences in responding to achievement situations, one can find at least two interesting reasons for the difference (Deaux, 1976). One of these assumes that women are just as aroused in achievement settings as men are but that the target of their achievement strivings is different. Men respond to the *stereotypic* achievement settings we have seen in the research, having to do with occupational or academic success and competition in general. But women, according to this position, are more responsive to social challenges, and their achievement motivation is said to blossom in the area of social skills.

A second answer comes out of the work of Horner (1968), who has introduced the concept of "fear of success" into the achievement literature. Basically, the idea is that women are apprehensive about pursuing success because of the potential consequence of losing favor in others' eyes, especially the eyes of men. In order to test this notion, Horner developed a method of assessing the presence of fear of success. A character in a story is described as achieving success, and subjects are asked to complete the story, describing the consequences. Characteristically, female subjects indicate that the consequences of a female's achieving success would be negative affect, success-generated conflict, or social rejection. Male subjects exposed to stories about successful men are much less inclined to mention negative consequences stemming out of success. In short, it looks as if men were much less concerned about the potential negative side effects of success, particularly in the social realm.

Although Horner's idea provides a possible insight into the sources of sex differences in achievement motivation, the concept awaits further development. The precise connection between fear of success and achievement, as well as the measurement of fear of success, remains to be established in a convincing way (Zuckerman & Wheeler, 1975).

SUMMARY

The joint functioning of two motives—to achieve success and to avoid failure—produces a fascinating complex of behaviors that would be quite unexpected without the help of Atkinson's theory. The striving behavior shown among those with high achievement is not just isolated behavior associated with the personality trait of high achievement; instead, such striving depends a great deal on the difficulty of the task. Similarly, the running away from striving that is associated with people high in fear of failure is not a general finding at all: their avoidance of achievement tasks depends completely on the task difficulty.

The important distinction Atkinson has drawn is between achievement motivation and fear of failure. Rather than simply being opposite ends of a single continuum, these are viewed as independent dimensions, and because the theory is constructed in this way, it is possible to arrive at some of the ironic predictions we have seen. Most of the research we have discussed has been of the "one-shot" or "one-situation" variety, but it is also important to recognize recent developments in the theory that view the human as guided by longer-range estimates of probabilities of success in future settings.

The theory discussed in the next chapter—the attributional approach to achievement—should in no way be viewed as a replacement for Atkinson's system, for many of the novel effects we have reported here are associated uniquely with the combination of the need-to-achieve and fear-of-failure motivations.

SUGGESTED READING

Atkinson, J. W. Motivation for achievement. In T. Blass (Ed.), *Personality variables in social behavior.* Hillsdale, N. J.: Erlbaum, 1977.

Atkinson, J. W., & Feather, N. T. (Eds.). *A theory of achievement motivation.* New York: Wiley, 1966.

Heckhausen, H. *Fortschritte der Leistungsmotivationsforschung.* In H. Thomae (Ed.), *Handbuch der Psychologie* (2nd ed.). Göttingen, Federal Republic of Germany: Hogrefe, in press.

McClelland, D. C. *The achieving society.* New York: Van Nostrand, 1961.

CHAPTER 15

AN ATTRIBUTIONAL MODEL OF ACHIEVEMENT MOTIVATION

READER'S DIGEST and other chronicles of Americana often print biographical stories about successful people. Nearly always included in these stories are the famous persons' thoughts about the reasons for their success experiences. The all-star baseball pitcher recalls having a strong arm, good control, and a major-league fastball even in high school. The crusading congresswoman reports that she had a strong speaking voice, superior organizational skills, and an ability to shake up bureaucrats from her earliest years. However, the successful will also recall expending great effort to achieve their successes. The pitcher describes how he threw baseballs hour after hour through an old tire in his back yard. The congresswoman reports wearing out numerous tape recorders while she practiced her speeches into the wee hours of the night. The people central in these examples would no doubt fall into the category of "high achievement motivation," as discussed in the previous chapter. And in line with that concept of the highly achievement-motivated person, who accepts challenges and risks, one would think that ability and hard work are basic to the end result in baseball or politics and that such successful persons view ability as being central.

Magazines are much less likely to print biographical reports of people low in achievement motivation. It is nonetheless interesting to speculate on the way such people are likely to talk about their successes and failures. How does the failure-oriented person account for athletic or occupational successes? We might imagine such a person, asked why he won the position of president of his senior high school class, responding with "It was just luck" or "You win some, you lose some." A failure-oriented woman who wins a seat on the city council might reply with "Fine, but I would never expect to win a second time, given my abilities" or "I won primarily on the weaknesses of my opponents."

The last chapter presented a motivational analysis of challenge-seeking and failure-avoiding behaviors. By "motivational" we mean that the object of study has been the dynamics of the approach (achievement) and avoidance (fear of failure) motives. The present chapter focuses on people's cognitive workings within achievement settings, as viewed from the perspective of attribution theory. The present attributional analysis (Weiner, 1974, 1978b; Weiner, Frieze, Kukla, Reed, Rest, & Rosenbaum, 1972) proposes that failure-oriented and achievement-oriented people make different inferences about the causes of their success and failure. These inferences, in turn, are assumed to be of critical importance in determining future performance.

THE THEORY

Perceived Causes of Behavior

The cornerstone of Weiner's approach is a unique classification of the potential attributions that people can make for achievement-related behavior. Weiner recognizes that the number of possible perceived causes is considerable, but at the same time he assumes that four potential causes are the central ones. Like other attribution theorists, Weiner begins with the distinction between factors inside the person and factors external to the person. However, he proposes a finer breakdown of the internal and external factors, naming two of each type.

Inside the person are ability and effort. Ability is used as an explanation when we think that a person's performance is due to a factor that is constant over time; effort is invoked to explain outcomes that might vary. The stability/instability distinction also applies to Weiner's two outside factors. Task difficulty is relevant when we are trying to explain why performance is relatively constant with a task, and luck is inferred when performance on the task varies. As the reader can see in Table 15-1, Weiner has added a "stability" dimension to the usual dimension of internality/externality. The four perceived causes represent every possible combination of stable/unstable and internal/external.

Some Determinants of Attributions

An experiment by Frieze and Weiner (1971) pinpoints some of the issues involved in sorting out perceived causes in an achievement setting: how do people decide which of the four factors caused someone's success or failure? Subjects were to imagine that a person (or, in a second experiment, they themselves) had performed a task several times, and they were given information that should have been relevant according to Kelley's attribution theory (see Chapter 10): how often the person had succeeded in the past on this particular task (consistency over time), how often the person had succeeded on other, similar tasks (entities), and how often others had succeeded on this particular task (consensus). The idea was to examine the impact of this information on the subjects' use of the four causal factors listed in Table 15-1.

**Table 15-1. Weiner's Classification Scheme
for the Perceived Determinants
of Achievement Related Behavior**

Location of Causal Factor	Stable	Unstable
Internal	ability	effort
External	task difficulty	luck

From "Perceiving the Causes of Success and Failure," by B. Weiner, I. H. Frieze, A. Kukla, L. Reed, S. Rest, and R. M. Rosenbaum. In E. E. Jones, D.E. Kanouse, H. H. Kelley, R. E. Nisbett, S. Valins, and B. Weiner (Eds.), *Attribution: Perceiving the Causes of Behavior*. (Morristown, N. J.: General Learning Press, 1972). Reprinted by permission of the Silver Burdett Company.

Consider first the internal/external dimension. When the target person's performance is consistent with the performance of others, it is clear from Kelley's theory that personal factors are largely irrelevant—the behavior does not vary across different people. This means that the two internal factors, effort and ability, can both be ruled out. Could the performance be the result of luck? No, luck would not lead everyone to behave in the same way. This leaves only task difficulty, and that is just what Frieze and Weiner found: performance under these circumstances was perceived to be largely the result of the ease or difficulty of the task.

What if the target person's performance is unique relative to the performance of others? When there is a lack of consensus, the subjects should look to personal factors as an explanation. As expected, both of the internal factors of Table 15-1, ability and effort, were then given central causal ascription. External factors were ascribed only minimal causal roles, luck being rated slightly more influential than task difficulty.

Let us turn now to the stable/unstable dimension. Attributions to effort and luck should result when the target person performs inconsistently over time. Indeed, subjects ascribed the target's performance to good luck and high effort when the person succeeded after a number of past failures and to bad luck and low effort when the person failed after a series of past successes.

Taken together, these results show clearly that people use the four attributional categories in the manner postulated by the theory.

Attributions by Achievement-Oriented and Failure-Oriented People

In our opening example, we saw that successful and unsuccessful people cite different kinds of reasons for their successes. Although people may generally use the attributional categories in the logical manner specified by Frieze and Weiner (1971), the achievement- and failure-oriented evidently diverge from this purely rational process, particularly when their own behavior is involved. This divergence from strictly logical thinking is an important ingredient of the attributional model.

An illustration of this point is found in an experiment by Kukla (1972). Achievement-oriented and failure-oriented subjects participated in a task that involved guessing which number would come up next in a sequence. The order of the numbers was arbitrary, so that some subjects did well and others did poorly simply as a result of chance. After performance feedback, the subjects were asked to what degree each of the four potential causal factors—ability, effort, luck, and task difficulty—was responsible for their performance.

Not surprisingly, all subjects inferred that their ability was higher following a successful performance than following an unsuccessful performance. However, the achievement-oriented subjects inferred a higher level of ability following success than the failure-oriented subjects. Also consistent with Weiner's reasoning, failure-oriented subjects tended to attribute their failure more to lack of ability than achievement-oriented subjects. Further, the achievement-oriented subjects, compared with the failure-oriented group, perceived high effort to be an important factor in their success and lack of effort to be an important factor in their failure. The experiment thus underlines a very central point, which tells us something about the attributional bases for the differences between achievement-oriented and failure-oriented people: the achievement-oriented tend toward finding ability explanations for their own successes, but the failure-oriented are less likely to do so and are also particularly inclined to cite lack of ability as a cause for failure.

Consequences of Attributions

How do the attributions people make for their successes and failures influence achievement-related behavior?

Recall that the four possible causal explanations can be classified along two dimensions: stable/unstable and internal/external. Weiner proposes that each of the dimensions will influence behavior in a different way. The location of an attribution on the stability dimension will influence the person's expectancy of success on the task, whereas the location of an attribution on the internal/external dimension will influence the person's affective reaction to success and failure. Let us examine each of these links in turn.

Stability and Expectancy of Success   In the last chapter, we saw that the person's subjective probability of success (P_s—the perceived chance of succeeding) is related directly to performance and to choice of task. We also saw that P_s shifts upward following a success and downward following a failure. Weiner has taken this analysis one step further by pointing out that the magnitude of the shift in P_s will be determined by the attributions the person makes about the reasons for performance. For example, suppose a person attempts a moderately difficult task (initial $P_s = .5$) and succeeds. If the person ascribes this performance either to high ability or to ease of the task, there should then be an expectancy of doing well on future similar tasks, and P_s should shift to a substantially higher value. However, if success is attributed either to good luck or to a high expenditure of effort, the person should be less likely to alter the P_s. Note that since the person does have some control over the amount of effort expended, an effort attribution should lead to a greater increase in P_s following success than would a luck attribution (Weiner, Nierenberg, & Goldstein, 1976). And more generally, we should expect more dramatic expectancy changes when tasks have to do with skill, rather than with chance.

Following failure, just the opposite shifts should occur. Attributions to the stable factors of ability or task difficulty should lead to a sharp reduction in expectancy of future success, whereas attributions to effort or luck should lead to a much smaller downward shift in P_s.

Internality and Affect   In addition to holding expectations about future success, people also have affective reactions to their performance outcomes. Often the person reports feeling good following success—experiences of pride and accomplishment should be common. Following failure, shame or guilt is the likely outcome. But situations can also be identified in which people seem to have little emotional reaction to the outcome of their performance, depending on the attributions given for performance.

For affect, it is the internality dimension that is important. If people attribute success to the external factors of good luck or ease of task, they cannot really take credit for success and hence should experience little pride in their performance. However, if they attribute success to a high level of ability or to hard work, they will experience pride. Further, since one has more control over the amount of effort expended than over ability, the greatest amount of pride will be experienced when success is explained as the result of hard work.

The effects of attributions for failure mirror their effects for success. Attributions of failure to bad luck or task difficulty lead to less shame than attributions to the internal factors of low ability or lack of effort.

In summary, attributions to a stable factor (ability or task difficulty) produce stronger shifts in the expectancy of future success than attributions to an unstable factor (effort or luck). Attributions to an internal factor (ability or effort) lead to a greater affective reaction of pride and esteem-related feelings than attributions to an external factor (task difficulty or luck). Because the person has the greatest control over the amount of effort expended, attributions to effort should lead in particular to affective reactions.

The Link to Behavior   Following the lead of Atkinson (see the previous chapter), Weiner proposes that the person's expectancy of success and affective reaction jointly determine performance. By Weiner's reasoning, the pattern of attributions made for success or failure will directly affect expectations for subsequent performance. The achievement-oriented person is said to react to failure by citing insufficient effort as the cause, whereas the failure-oriented person will be more inclined to blame poor abilities. Accordingly, a failure should not affect the achievement-oriented person's expectancy about success to any marked degree, and such people should continue to persist following failure (Weiner, 1978b). But failure will bring forth a tendency to give up among failure-oriented people, simply because their expectancies for success have been lowered by viewing lack of ability as the cause of failing.

In one of the few studies to investigate the connections between attributions and achievement behavior, Weiner and Sierad (1975) proceeded within a framework resembling the work of Schachter (Chapter 12). Subjects were first divided into achievement-oriented and failure-oriented groups on the basis of test scores. Some of the subjects in each group were asked to take a pill; others in a control condition received no pill. The pill was actually a placebo and had no physiological effect, but subjects in the "pill" condition were told that it impaired eye/hand coordination, an aptitude that just happened to be quite relevant to the task the subjects were about to undertake.

Subjects then went ahead with the task, which involved substituting the symbols Y, λ, λ, λ, Y, Y for the digits 1–6, respectively. For instance, whenever subjects saw a 2, they were to write down a λ. After each of four separate timed trials on this task they received failure feedback. The question for the experimenters was what effect the pill would have on subjects' performance over the series of trials.

Recall from our discussion of Kukla's (1972) experiment that achievement-oriented people normally attribute their failures to lack of effort—an unstable, internal cause. The pill provides a salient alternative explanation for their failure, but one that is external and stable. Therefore, these subjects should have a low expectancy of future success, so that there will be little motivation for improved performance.

Failure-dominated people, in contrast, typically attribute failure to lack of ability—a stable, internal cause. Attributing failure to the pill—a stable, external cause—decreases their affective response to failure. Consequently, they should no longer be upset over their lack of ability, something they can do nothing about, and hence should be able to perform at a higher level than normal.

The results were as predicted: the pill facilitated the performance of

the failure-oriented subjects but *reduced* the performance of achievement-oriented subjects. This experiment, then, provides the final link between attributions and performance in Weiner's analysis of achievement-
related behaviors.

SPECIAL TOPICS

Extensions to Other Settings

Weiner (1978b) has recently suggested that his attributional analysis
can be extended to a number of nonachievement settings. Among the phenomena he cites as being amenable to attributional analysis are helping
behavior, parole decisions, affiliation and loneliness, learned helplessness
(see Chapter 18), and hyperactivity in children. Caution must be exercised
in these applications, however, since the important attributional dimensions may vary from situation to situation. For example, an analysis by
Michela and Peplau (1977) of the reasons for social failure suggested that
a third dimension of causes—controllable/uncontrollable—was important in addition to the usual two dimensions (internal/external and sta-
ble/unstable).

One interesting extension of the analysis is to the effects of schedules
of reinforcement on extinction (Weiner, 1972; Rest, 1976). In this problem,
subjects are given reinforcements for performing the correct behavior according to a schedule set up by the experimenter. For example, they might
receive a reinforcement every time they make the correct response, or
every fifth time, or at fixed time intervals of one minute. The question is
how long it takes for subjects to stop responding when reinforcements are
no longer provided.

According to Weiner, the person uses information about the schedule
to make attributions concerning the roles of ability, effort, luck, and task
difficulty in bringing forth reinforcements. Using these attributions, one
develops an expectancy about future reinforcement, which in turn determines whether or not responding should be continued. Thus, if a person
attributes lack of reinforcement to one of the stable factors (lack of ability
or task difficulty), responding will cease. However, if the attribution for
nonreinforcement is to luck or to lack of effort, continued responding is
likely.

To illustrate one application, consider a subject who is given continuous reinforcement in comparison with a subject who receives random re-

inforcement. The former subject is more likely to attribute success to ability, the latter to luck. When reinforcements are withdrawn, the subject who has received continuous reinforcement will quickly cease responding, sensing that the task has changed in some important respect and that the formerly effective ability is no longer adequate for the task. In contrast, the subject who has received random reinforcement will continue to respond longer, since it will not be abruptly clear that the nature of the task—that is, the relation between performance and reward—has changed. A number of results have now been obtained in this area that are consistent with Weiner's analysis. At the same time, it should be noted that a variety of simpler theories (see, for example, Amsel, 1958; Humphreys, 1939) also account for much of the same data. These simpler theories are often preferable because intermittent-reinforcement results have also been found in lower animals—organisms that presumably are not capable of the complex reasoning required by Weiner's approach.

Perceived Causes of Behavior Revisited

A number of recent studies have begun to examine more closely the perceived causes of achievement-related behavior. In one study (Frieze, 1976) subjects were allowed to list freely the possible causes of several hypothetical successes and failures. Although subjects frequently listed the familiar four causes cited by Weiner, they also listed other causes, such as mood and other people in the situation.

Studies have also suggested that the placement of each potential cause on the stability dimension can vary from situation to situation. For example, effort can be conceptualized either as an unstable factor that will change from trial to trial or as a stable personality characteristic of the individual ("He is a hardworking person"). Similarly, task difficulty can be thought of as stable if the person works on a series of highly comparable tasks or as unstable if the tasks vary in character (Frieze, 1976; Valle & Frieze, 1976).

Weiner argues that these problems highlight the need for a careful analysis of the subjective meaning of the causes to the person in each new situation. However, the theoretical and empirical guidelines for determining the important subjective elements in a situation are not yet specified.

Affect Revisited

Weiner originally proposed that internal attributions (ability and effort) lead to stronger affective reactions than external attributions (task difficulty and luck). Further, he proposed that of the two internal attributions, effort generates a stronger affective reaction than ability. However, several recent studies have suggested that the second part of Weiner's proposal may not be correct. For example, Sohn (1977) found that subjects reported more unhappiness when failure was attributed to lack of ability than when it was attributed to lack of effort.

Weiner, Russell, and Lehrman (1978) recently conducted a study that probed more deeply into the link between attribution and affect. Subjects were given a series of little stories such as the following:

> Francis studied intensely for a test he took. It was very important for Francis to record a high score on the exam. Francis received an extremely high score on the test. Francis felt that he received this high score because he studied so intensely. How do you think Francis felt upon receiving this score? [Weiner et al., 1978, p. 70]

In each story, the main character either succeeded or failed, and a perceived cause for the outcome (*effort* in the story above) was specified. Subjects were then given a rather lengthy list of affective responses that the character in the story might have displayed and were asked to indicate how much each of the responses applied. Weiner and his colleagues then identified the affective reactions that were most characteristic of Weiner's original four perceived causes, plus several others that have been identified in recent studies (Elig & Frieze, 1975; Valle & Frieze, 1976). Each attribution and its associated affect are listed in Table 15-2, separately for success and failure.

The data may be summarized by the observation that people expect different affective responses to be associated with the different possible attributions for success and failure. For instance, pride was clearly associated with internal attributions for success, and shame with internal attributions for failure. However, the second part of Weiner's proposal was not supported: effort attributions did not exceed ability attributions in producing the affective reactions of pride and shame.

Some Costs of Generality

From the previous sections it is clear that efforts are underway to extend the generality of Weiner's model. The model is now applied to non-achievement situations, other possible causal explanations for success and failure are being explored, and the links between this expanded set of causal explanations and a wide range of affective responses are being spelled out. This work is beginning to provide a detailed description of the conscious experience of people in achievement (and other) settings.

Table 15-2. Attributions and Associated Affects for Success and Failure

(a) Attributions and Most Characteristic Affects for *Success*

Attribution	Affect
unstable effort	activation, augmentation
stable effort	relaxation
own personality	self-enhancement
other's effort and personality	gratitude
luck	surprise
ability vs. task difficulty	competence vs. safety

(b) Attributions and Most Characteristic Affects for *Failure*

Attribution	Affect
ability	incompetence
unstable effort; stable effort	guilt
personality; intrinsic motivation	resignation
other's efforts; other's motivation and personality	aggression
luck	surprise

From "Affective Consequences of Causal Ascriptions," by B. Weiner, D. Russell, and D. Lehrman. In J. H. Harvey, W. J. Ickes, and R. F. Kidd (Eds.), *New Directions in Attribution Research* (Vol. 2). Copyright 1978 by Lawrence Erlbaum Associates, Inc. Reprinted by permission.

But the reader might have noticed a shift in focus between Weiner's original theory, presented in the first part of this chapter, and his emerging theory, presented in the last few sections. Weiner's original theory followed a logical progression from success/failure experiences to attributions to expectancy and affect and finally to achievement-related behavior. The links between successive stages were specified, and definite predictions could be made about achievement-related behavior. Although Weiner's major emphasis has never been on behavior, a few studies (Chapin & Dyck, 1976; Kukla, 1972; Weiner & Sierad, 1975) have shown that altering the causal ascriptions for success and failure (particularly those made to effort) leads to changes in performance on achievement-related tasks.

The concentration of the emerging new theory on the person's conscious experience has led, at least at present, to a shift away from achievement-related behavior. Although the attributions that can be made in a variety of achievement settings have been extensively catalogued, no research to date has shown that altering attributions to the newer categories, such as "other's personality," has any effect on performance. It is possible that the newer attributional categories can be classified on the internal/external and stable/unstable dimensions so that their effects may be explained within the structure of the original model. However, additional problems are raised by the complex links between attributions and affect recently suggested by Weiner and his colleagues. In the original model, the internality dimension leads to a simple affective reaction on the dimension of pride/shame. The current theorizing permits an array of affective responses to be associated with a variety of possible attributions; there is apparently no simple set of dimensions underlying the person's affective response. Further, the links between affective reactions—such as gratitude, aggression, and surprise—and achievement behavior have not yet been specified conceptually. Thus, increased generality has led to a more complex theory in which the links between several of the elements have yet to be defined.

Questioning the Theoretical Assumptions

Two very broad assumptions underlying the theory have to do with the implications of the theory for behavior. First, it is clear that an observer, noting an actor's behavior impartially, can arrive at the kinds of attributions for performance predicted from the present model, but one should ask whether the process will work similarly for behaving actors. As it turns out, the theory has no special provision for a difference between involved and uninvolved subjects. Second, the even broader issue of how we get from attributions to behavior requires special theoretical assumptions, and these assumptions remain short of being totally specified. We will take up these two points in turn.

Personal Involvement   It has been assumed in many experiments that presenting uninvolved subjects with a brief description of an achievement-related scene will produce the same cognitive workings that would occur if the subjects were actually confronted with a highly challenging achievement task. However, as we saw in Chapter 9, actors (those who are actually involved in a situation) and passive observers tend to make different attributions for the actor's performance. Actors generally have more information about the situation than observers. Further, their attention tends to be focused on the situation, whereas observers focus their attention on the actor's performance (Jones & Nisbett, 1971). The result is that actors attribute their performance to external (situational) factors more often than observers. Consistent with this reasoning, a recent study by Bar-Tal and Frieze (1976) showed that involved actors attributed their outcomes on achievement-related tasks more to the external factor of task difficulty, whereas observers were more likely to ascribe the outcome to the internal factor of effort. This study raises serious questions about Weiner's frequent use of uninvolved observers to investigate the cognitive processes of involved actors in achievement settings.

Expectancy and Behavior   What is the relation between shifts in expectancies for success and actual behavior? This is a two-faceted question: one aspect is the form of the relation between expectancies and performance, and the other is whether attributions in general have much bearing on performance.

With regard to the first aspect, a critical question arises about the precise pattern of connections between expectancies for success and actual achievement behavior. As noted by Heckhausen (in press), Weiner has continued to work within the general expectancy × value tradition of Atkinson and has not explicitly redefined the workings of Atkinson's Motive, Incentive, and Probability factors (see Chapter 14) in attributional terms. One might say that Weiner's framework could be used *within Atkinson's theory* in order to arrive at subjects' attribution-based expectancies, assuming, of course, that attributions are basic to expectancies.

However, Weiner (1978a) proposes explicitly that achievement-oriented people exhibit performance increments and persist in goal-directed action after failure. Failure-oriented people, being the opposite counterpart, are supposed to be "relatively hampered" by failure and consequently give up when the goal is not attained. However, something is missing here: Since Atkinson's theory is not brought into direct comparison with the attribution model, it is difficult to know whose ideas about the expectancy/behavior link to use. And the issue is important, for the two conceptions differ in their implications. For instance, in Atkinson's scheme, failure-oriented people should *persist more* when the P_s is low. In fact, Feather (1962) has provided evidence for this implication in a study that compared the performance of achievement-oriented and failure-oriented subjects on a virtually impossible task. What would the attribution model predict? The failure-oriented group should have tended to *give up* in the face of adverse odds—more so than the achievement-oriented group.

Although one cannot find a complete answer to this dilemma, the literature does contain some comparison between the expectancy-behavior predictions of these two approaches. An insight about the way they might fit together is offered by Weiner, Heckhausen, Meyer, and Cook (1972). The basic idea is that attributions may mediate the relation between P_s and performance intensity within Atkinson's framework. Specifically, Weiner et al. suggest that attributions to effort may make a great deal of difference when the P_s is approximately .5 but that effort is of negligible significance when the probabilities are extremely low or high. Since tasks with a P_s of about .5 should bring forth the inference that effort is a salient determinant of performance, effort expenditure will be maximal in that midrange of probabilities. Thus we have at least a start toward an integration, but the question "whose rules to use for linking expectancy and behavior" remains in large part intact.

The second aspect of the question posed in this section is whether attributions directly affect behavior. There is no question that expectations about future success or failure can influence performance, but there is a more central question to be asked of any attribution theory. This is the simple, all-too-obvious question whether attributions have any direct, systematic connection with future behaviors.

One way to try to answer the question is to look at one study mentioned above that seems to tell us that attributions do have bearing on subsequent performance. The failure-oriented subjects of Weiner and Sierad (1975) who could attribute failure to a placebo pill showed better subsequent performance than their counterparts who could make no such attribution. There is also good evidence in research by Weiner, Heckhausen, Meyer, and Cook (1972) that speed of performance on a digit-symbol substitution task is affected substantially by the pattern of attributions made for previous performance.

At the same time, it is fair to note that the evidence on this point is mixed. Especially informative is a study by Diener and Dweck (1978), in which subjects encountered repeated failure experiences. The subjects who met these failure experiences by trying to augment their performance (analogous to what we would expect from the achievement-oriented) showed a conspicuous *absence* of any specific attributions for previous failure. Rather, their focus was more on alternative task-solution strategies—not on a retrospective account of their own performance. Closely akin to this finding is one by Hanusa and Schulz (1977), showing that subjects tend not to generate spontaneous explanations for their failures. At least, they do not generate explanations that take the form of attributions to any special cause. Finally, a field study by Covington and Omelich (1979) indicates that attributions have little relation to later performance.

In short, one begins to wonder how prevalent the tendency to attribute is and, further, whether the attributions—if made—have a direct impact on later behavior. If we are to take Bem (Chapter 8) at face value, we should question very seriously whether conscious rumination about causes of one's own behavior is more a determinant of behavior or simply a backward glance at what one has been doing.

SUMMARY

In implementing and interpreting the present approach to achievement, it is useful first of all to view the model as stemming out of Atkinson's formulation. The general notion that achievement performance stems from expectancies for success/failure is central both in Atkinson's original approach to achievement and in Weiner's approach, and the critical contribution of this newer model lies in its focus on attributions as sources of expectancies and expectancy shifts. There is a certain appeal in the fourfold classification of attributions for performance—a tidiness that makes one think there must be some definite self-attributions following performance feedback.

The basic attributional analysis has been expanded in at least two important respects. For one, the model makes some assumptions about the relation between expectancies and performance, and these assumptions await a further integration or comparison with the counterpart assumptions in Atkinson's achievement-motivation theory. Second, the attribution model now goes well beyond the simple fact of the attributional explanation and talks also about the affective, or emotional, accompaniments of the attributional account of one's own behavior. Thus, the concept inherent in attribution theory, that of a human with the analytic capacity for a backward interpretive glance at behavior, has been carried forward considerably in the direction of a notion about the determinants of overt behavior and affective experiences.

SUGGESTED READING

Weiner, B. (Ed.). *Achievement motivation and attribution theory.* Morristown, N. J.: General Learning Press, 1974.

Weiner, B. Achievement strivings. In H. London & J. Exner (Eds.), *Dimensions of personality.* New York: Wiley, 1978.

Weiner, B., Frieze, I. H., Kukla, A., Reed, L., Rest, S., & Rosenbaum, R. M. Perceiving the causes of success and failure. In E. E. Jones, D. E. Kanouse, H. H. Kelley, R. E. Nisbett, S. Valins, & B. Weiner (Eds.), *Attribution: Perceiving the causes of behavior.* Morristown, N. J.: General Learning Press, 1972.

CHAPTER 16

A CONTINGENCY MODEL OF LEADERSHIP

THORNTON Price has recently graduated from a well-known automotive technical institute and has been selected for its prestigious managerial-training program. As part of this program, the trainees are exposed to a number of work situations within the auto industry. The trainees occupy each leadership position for 3 months and then are rotated to a new assignment. Price is outgoing and friendly and believes that worker morale is the key to success in business. He manifests this belief by always trying to develop good relationships with the workers.

Price's first assignment is to serve as team leader for a group that has the task of designing a new bumper. This is not a clear-cut task: bumpers can be designed in many shapes and made of all sorts of materials, and they have to meet safety and economic requirements that are often contradictory. This position is also difficult because the workers have nothing but contempt for a leader who is still "wet behind the ears." Unfortunately, Price also discovers that his position has little power—he has no way of rewarding the workers who are doing a good job or punishing those who are not trying. After 3 months in this position, Price discovers that both the quality and quantity of the work of his unit have fallen off dramatically from their previous output.

Price is then given the similar task of serving as the leader of a team that is deciding on the ideal speaker placement in new cars equipped with stereos. Once again, he discovers that the task is not clear-cut, since the design requirements are sometimes contradictory—for example, speakers should be well placed acoustically yet must not interfere with shifting. He also finds that this leadership position has little power. In sharp contrast, though, he is pleased to learn that the workers are behind him: working relationships are ideal. After 3 months in this position, the work of his unit improves so dramatically that the president of the company sends Price a congratulatory letter and a key to the executive washroom.

Finally, Price is put in charge of a unit of workers whose job is to construct molds for the bolts for next year's car. This is a totally clear-cut, structured task: there is only one way of performing it, and each man knows how to do his job. Price's relationship with the workers is also very good, and he has considerable power to reward the workers who perform well and punish those who perform poorly. Given this very favorable leadership position, Price is surprised to discover that the performance of his unit falls off over the 3-month period. He and his men get along well, but the men just don't produce up to their capability.

The preceding example illustrates some of the complexities associated with trying to match leaders to groups. Especially perplexing is the oft-observed phenomenon of leaders who fit some settings perfectly, while in other situations their leadership appears to crumble. The purpose of this chapter is to show how Fiedler's (1964, 1967, 1978a, 1978b; Fiedler & Chemers, 1974) contingency model of leadership deals with these intricate problems. But first, as a lead-in to the theory, a touch of background on the "great person notion" will be helpful.

THE GREAT PERSON NOTION

When we think about leadership, great political and military leaders such as John F. Kennedy, Golda Meir, Winston Churchill, and General George Patton come to mind. These individuals were charismatic leaders who were able to get the best possible performance out of their followers. In thinking about them, it is easy to conclude that there should be a set of personality traits that are characteristic of the great leader. If only we could identify these traits, we could then select leaders who could best motivate their followers.

Yet, attempts to isolate the personality traits characteristic of leaders have been consistently unsuccessful (Mann, 1959; Stogdill, 1948). Nearly every study reveals a few traits that are related to leadership, but each new situation studied has produced a different set of leader traits. For example, popularity might turn out to be an important leader characteristic in one situation, but adaptability would be critical in another. A few traits, such as intelligence and extroversion, are characteristic of leaders in many situations, but the relation between these traits and leadership ability is surprisingly weak. And even these traits do not seem to be characteristic of all leaders.

On further consideration, a possible reason for this failure to establish a relation between personality factors and leadership becomes apparent. Typically we see great leaders in only one situation. Leaders such as Churchill and Patton were outstanding in the wartime situation with which we are familiar. However, during peacetime both men were ineffective leaders. So it seems as if people with certain personality types may be great leaders only within a specific situation.

An illustration of this point is provided by Fiedler (1966). Belgian naval officers had to lead teams of men in several tasks. One task was to write a recruiting letter urging men to join the navy. In another task, the teams had to route ships to ten ports in the most efficient manner. And in still another task, the leaders had to teach their units, without speaking, to disassemble and reassemble an automatic pistol.

The great person notion would lead us to expect that good leaders would elicit good performances on all the tasks, whereas groups with poor leaders would perform inadequately on all the tasks. However, performance on one task was unrelated to performance on a second task. Few leaders did well or poorly across all tasks. Rather, the typical pattern was that the teams did well on some tasks and poorly on others. Thus it appears that certain types of leaders are able to stimulate good performance, but only in specific situations.

This conclusion leads to another approach to the study of leadership. Rather than simply identifying the characteristics of great leaders, we must identify the personality characteristics of leaders and the characteristics of situations which, *in combination*, produce the best performance by the group members. It is the contingency, or match, between the leader's characteristics and the nature of the leadership situation that is the cornerstone of Fiedler's theory.

THE CONTINGENCY MODEL

Fiedler's model consists of two general components. First is situational control, which provides an index of the degree of control and influence the leader can exert in the situation. Second is the person's leadership style—whether the leader is normally focused on accomplishing the task or on maintaining good relationships with group members. To understand the predictions of the model, we will need to consider both components in some detail.

Situational Control

Fiedler views situational control as composed of three parts: leader-member relations, task structure, and position power.

Leader-Member Relations   The most important part of leaders' influence is how well they get along with group members. If workers like the leader, they are more likely to help the leader meet goals and less inclined to sabotage or otherwise disrupt the project. How can leader-member relations be assessed? The researcher can measure the members' liking for the leader or the leader's liking for the group members. As an example of Fiedler's methodology, a measure called the "Group Atmosphere scale" is typically used to assess the leader's feelings about the group. The leader is asked to describe the work team on a series of scales, such as pleasant/unpleasant, friendly/unfriendly, and bad/good. Leader-member relations are considered "good" if the leader's score is above average on the scale and "poor" if the leader's score is below average.

Task Structure   The next most important aspect of the leader's influence is the extent to which the work task has clear-cut requirements and a method of solution. Some tasks, such as that of a barrel drainer who "empties water from barrel that has been inspected or weighed by rolling barrel onto a stand and pulling bung from hole by hand" (Fiedler, 1967, p. 291), are highly structured. By comparison, the task of a social-welfare research worker who "performs research to facilitate investigation and alleviation of social problems" (Fiedler, 1967, p. 288) is considerably less structured. To the extent that the task is structured, the leader can give specific instructions and provide an objective evaluation of the workers' performance. Thus structured tasks provide a more favorable situation for the leader.

Task structure is typically measured by examining a number of task characteristics and forming an overall evaluation of the structure. Some of the characteristics examined are the specificity of job requirements, the number of ways the problem can be solved (the fewer, the more structured the task), and whether the solution can be evaluated objectively. Once again, task structure is considered "high" if it is above average and "low" if it is below average.

Position Power   The final determinant of leaders' influence is their ability to evaluate the performance of their workers and to give them rewards or punishments. Clearly, a leader who can make recommendations on salaries or promotions has considerably more influence than a leader who does not have these powers. A scale has been developed for use in business organizations (Hunt, 1967), but Fiedler and Chemers (1974) have proposed a much simpler method of classifying position power. Managers, foremen, supervisors, and other autocratic leaders are assumed to have high position power, and committee chairs and leaders of groups of equal-status people are said to have low position power.

The Situational-Control Index   Now that we have examined each of the three parts of situational control, how can these parts be put together to form a rough index of the overall control of the situation? Fiedler proposes a simple yet elegant method. Each of the parts (leader-member relations, task structure, position power) has been classified as being either high or low. Putting these three components together logically produces eight combinations, as shown in Table 16-1.

Table 16-1. The Eight Situational-Control Combinations

Situational Control	Combina- tion	Leader-Member Relations	Task Structure	Position Power
high	I	good	high	strong
	II	good	high	weak
	III	good	low	strong
	IV	good	low	weak
moderate	V	poor	high	strong
	VI	poor	high	weak
	VII	poor	low	strong
low	VIII	poor	low	weak

Combination I shows that when leader-member relations are good, task structure is high, and position power is strong, then situational control is considered to be high—the leader can exert considerable control and influence. With Combination VIII, relations are poor, task structure is low, and position power is weak. Here the leader will be able to exert little influence. In general, situational control is high to the extent that each of the factors is positive.

In Table 16-1 the three factors have been combined in a particular orderly fashion that gives the factors different degrees of importance in determining situational control. For instance, in order for situational control to be high, leader-member relations must necessarily be good. It is not necessary that task structure be high, nor is it crucial that position power be strong. Therefore, if one wants to alter a setting so that situational control is maximal, it is best to start by worrying about whether leader-member relations are good and then to consider the task structure. Position power, the least important component, should then be analyzed in order to complete the picture.

Leadership Style

The second major element of Fiedler's model is the leader's style or personality. Some leaders are predominantly task-oriented; they discourage irrelevant comments, demand participation from group members, and make or receive a number of critical comments. Other leaders are more concerned about having good social relationships in the group. They are less directive, are concerned about the satisfaction of the group members, and try to reduce the level of group tension. Fiedler proposes that this dimension of task-oriented to relationship-oriented leadership style captures the most relevant aspects of the leader's personality.

The leader's standing on this dimension is typically measured by giving leaders a scale asking them to describe the worker with whom they have worked *least* well. This scale, known as the "least-preferred-co-worker scale," asks leaders to rate this difficult worker on a number of traits, such as pleasant/unpleasant, rejecting/accepting, boring/interesting, and self-assured/hesitant. Since task-oriented leaders focus primarily on the worker's performance, they have difficulty admitting that poor workers may have positive, non-task-related qualities. In contrast, relationship-oriented leaders, who make an effort to get to know their workers, are likely to discover that even the difficult worker has some positive qualities. Hence, relationship-oriented leaders will rate their least preferred coworker more positively than task-oriented leaders. This scale has been used throughout Fiedler's research program and has been shown to be a good predictor of group performance.

Interaction of Situational Control and Leadership Style

Although Fiedler's early research showed that the leader's score on the least-preferred-coworker scale was frequently related to group performance, the direction of the relation was never certain. Sometimes task-oriented leaders are able to stimulate their groups to superior performances, but at other times the relationship-oriented leaders elicit the better performance. This puzzling set of results was untangled when Fiedler considered the leadership style and situational-control dimensions as contingent on each other. In general, task-oriented leaders perform well when the situation is either very favorable or very unfavorable. In contrast, relationship-oriented leaders are able to elicit good performance when the situation is moderately favorable. This idea is illustrated in Figure 16-1.

Returning to our opening example, we note that Price was a relationship-oriented leader. His first assignment was to a setting in which situational control was low—leader-member relations, task structure, and leader position power were all poor (Combination VIII in Table 16-1). In these conditions the group performed poorly under his leadership. He was then switched to a position in which situational control was moderate: leader-member relations were good, but the task was unstructured and there was little position power (Combination IV). Price's relationship-oriented style was just right for this situation, and he was able to generate a superior performance from the group. Finally, situational control was high in the last position because his relations with the workers were good, the task was structured, and he had the power to reward and punish the workers' efforts (Combination I). Unfortunately, his relationship-oriented style was not suited for this situation, and the group's productivity plummeted. Alas for Price, great leaders are not born; instead, their leadership style is correctly matched to the situation. If only he had possessed a task-oriented style, his workers would have performed better in the final situation.

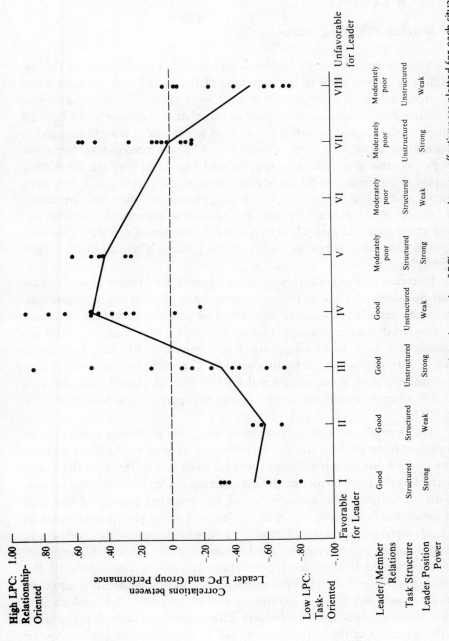

Figure 16-1. Correlations between leaders' least-preferred-coworker (LPC) scores and group effectiveness plotted for each situational-control combination. From *A Theory of Leadership Effectiveness*, by F. E. Fiedler. Copyright 1967 by McGraw-Hill, Inc. Reprinted by permission.

229

RESEARCH EXAMPLES

Religious Bargaining Groups

A bargaining study by McGrath and Julian (1963) illustrates the importance of taking each of the elements of the model into account when studying leadership. Four-person groups were created for the purpose of discussing such controversial topics as whether the Bible should be read in public schools and whether the federal government should give aid to parochial schools. The topics were especially controversial for these groups because the members represented churches holding conflicting viewpoints on these issues: each group contained a Catholic, a Southern Baptist, and a Unitarian. As in any bargaining situation, the members were expected to advocate the position of their organization (church), but at the same time the group had to reach a consensus of opinion. The leaders, who were the fourth members of the groups, obviously had a challenge before them.

In terms of the contingency model, this is a situation in which task structure is low—religious disagreements have no well-defined solutions. The leader also has no power to reward or punish the group members, meaning that leader position power is low. Leader-member relations, however, did vary: in some groups leader-member relations were quite good, and in others they were unfavorable. Therefore, when leader/member relations were good, situational control was moderate (Combination IV). But when relations were poor, situational control was low (Combination VIII).

The group's solution to a series of religious problems was rated by clergymen from each of the three faiths and by impartial judges. The extent to which the group solution received high scores from all the raters was the basis for a measure of the overall constructiveness of the solution. Consistent with the contingency model, the constructiveness of the solution depended both on the style of the leader and on the favorableness of the leadership situation. When leader-member relations were good, giving rise to a moderately favorable leadership situation, groups having relationship-oriented leaders produced relatively constructive solutions. But when leader/member relations were poor and the leadership situation therefore unfavorable, the groups that had task-oriented leaders produced the most constructive solutions. This study illustrates that changing just one element of the situation can lead to radical shifts in the requirements for the type of leader who will be most effective.

Military Cadets

Much of Fiedler's work has involved studying leadership in real-world situations. Studies in actual settings give us confidence in the usefulness of the model, but they typically do not allow the researcher to create or manipulate the levels of the situational variables. Instead, the researcher can only classify situations according to their score on the measurement scale for each component of the model. The different situations, moreover, may vary in a number of other ways that make it difficult to pin down the exact source of the effect. Group members might like their leaders better when the group is functioning smoothly and effectively. Or task-oriented leaders might be more experienced than relationship-oriented leaders in some situations. Consequently, our confidence in the model is greatly increased by laboratory experiments that allow greater control over each element of the model, thus ruling out other explanations of the findings.

Chemers and Skrzypek (1972) constructed four-man work groups composed of West Point cadets who worked on two tasks. One task was highly structured, consisting in drawing plans for a barracks building from detailed specifications. The other task was rather unstructured—the group had to discuss and develop a plan to interest overseas enlisted men in world politics. The groups were composed of a leader and either three of his close associates or three people he disliked, a variation that should have promoted good and poor leader-member relations, respectively. Finally, leader position power was manipulated by having the leader in the high-power condition assign a grade at the end of the exercise to be put in each subordinate's permanent record. In the low-power condition, the leader was not given authority to grade the group members. In summary, all eight possible combinations of good and poor leader-member relations, structured and unstructured tasks, and high and low leader position power were created.

As usual, task-oriented and relationship-oriented leaders were identified by their scores on the least-preferred-coworker scale. Group performance was assessed by the accuracy of the barracks drawings in the first task and ratings by trained judges of the quality of the proposal for the enlisted men in the second task. As shown in Figure 16-2, the results closely followed the predictions of the model. When situational control was high, groups with task-oriented leaders performed better than groups with relationship-oriented leaders. In contrast, when situational control was moderate, relationship-oriented leaders were able to stimulate a better performance from their group than task-oriented leaders.

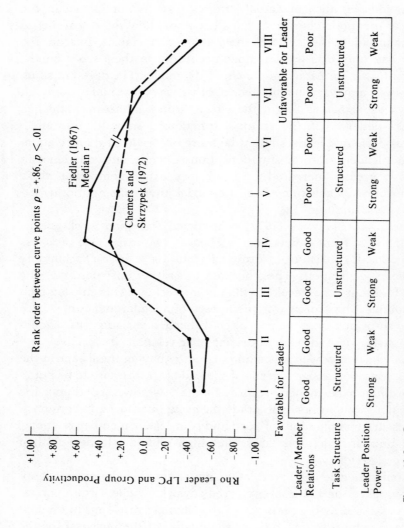

Figure 16-2. Comparison of predicted and obtained curves for LPC and group effectiveness. From "An Experimental Test of the Contingency Model of Leadership Effectiveness," by M. M. Chemers and G. J. Skrzypek, *Journal of Personality and Social Psychology*, 1972, *24*, 172–177. Copyright 1972 by the American Psychological Association. Reprinted by permission.

Finally, in Combination VIII, in which the leadership situation was very unfavorable, groups with task-oriented leaders once again outperformed groups with relationship-oriented leaders.

Leadership Training

Business and industry invest heavily in sending their managers and leaders to leadership-training programs. These training programs teach leaders specific skills for structuring the task and resolving interpersonal disputes. Yet, the few studies that have evaluated these programs have failed to demonstrate any positive effect of leadership training on group performance (Campbell, Dunnette, Lawler, & Weick, 1970; Stogdill, 1974).

The contingency model offers an intriguing explanation for this paradoxical effect. The main effect of leadership training should be to help the leader organize a more favorable leadership situation. The more the leader can structure the task and promote good relations with group members, the more favorable the leadership situation. But a more favorable leadership situation is not always conducive to better group performance.

Suppose a task-oriented leader is functioning well in a setting with little situational control—leader-member relations are poor, the task is unstructured, and there is little leader power (Combination VIII). After taking leadership training, the leader works on leader-member relations and smooths everything out. Task structure and power are still both low, but now leader-member relations are good (Combination IV). However, the situational control is now moderate, and this is the type of setting in which task-oriented leaders do not perform particularly well. Consequently, the group's performance should decline in spite of the improved relations between the group members and the leader. Ironically, then, leadership training in some cases should actually hamper group productivity.

This effect was demonstrated in a study by Chemers, Rice, Sundstrom, and Butler (1975) in which groups worked on a code-deciphering task. Each group had to solve a series of cryptograms such as the following:

gkkw gk mw wqk cwmwrft wdkcomz gfvtrtj
- - - - -- - - - -- s - - - --- - - -s - - - - --r----

r brss nk ovkccko rt m nsmlh fxkvlfmw
- --ll - - - -r-ss-- -- - -l - -- ---r-- - -

(The solution is "Meet me at the station Tuesday morning/ I will be dressed in a black overcoat" [Chemers et al., 1975, p. 405].)

Some of the leaders were novice codebreakers for whom this task was rather ambiguous and unstructured. Other leaders were given a brief lesson in deciphering messages. These "trained" leaders were informed about such facts as letter frequencies, distribution of vowels, and common endings and were given a set of procedures to facilitate codebreaking. The result of this training was to change the situation from unstructured to structured for this latter group of leaders.

The researchers did not give the leaders any power, and an assessment of leader/member relations using the Group Atmosphere scale (see p. 236) indicated that relations were poor. This implies that the situational control was low (Combination VIII) for the untrained leaders and moderate (Combination VI) for the trained leaders. As the contingency model predicts, groups with untrained leaders correctly deciphered more messages when the leader was task-oriented than when he was relationship-oriented. After leader training, however, groups having relationship-oriented leaders performed better than groups having task-oriented leaders.

In summary, the effect of traditional leadership training depends on whether the change in situational control matches the person's leadership style. If the leader can change the favorableness of the situation to match his style, the group's performance should improve. However, if a change in situational control leads to a less favorable match with the leader's style, performance will decline. Only if leaders are selected for training programs on the basis of both their leadership situation and their personal style can positive results be expected.

Leader Match

In response to the problems of traditional leadership-training programs, Fiedler, Chemers, and Mahar (1976) have recently developed their own unique program called Leader Match, which is based on the principles of the contingency model. In this program, leaders learn about the contingency model and how to assess the components of the model using the standard scales: they administer the least-preferred-coworker scale to themselves to ascertain their leadership style and then use other scales to measure each component of situational control—leader/member relations, task structure, and position power.

With this information, the leaders can determine whether there is a good match between their leadership style and the amount of situational control. If the match is poor, leaders can take action to change the amount of situational control and hence improve the group's performance. A task-oriented leader confronted with a setting in which situational control is moderate (and thus inappropriate for a task-oriented style) could become more available to subordinates or request more routine assignments. These changes should increase the amount of situational control and lead to increases in leader effectiveness. Conversely, a relationship-oriented leader in a setting with high situational control should maintain more formal contacts with subordinates or request less-structured assignments. These changes should decrease the situational control from high to moderate, again leading to increases in leader effectiveness.

The reader may find it ironic that leaders would often be obligated, through Leader Match strategies, to *reduce* the general favorability of the situation to be led. For instance, a relationship-oriented leader should try to reduce a highly favorable situation to one of moderate favorableness. The only issue here is a practical one: would a leader readily allow a reduction in quality of the situation?

Early assessments of the Leader Match program (Fiedler & Mahar, in press) have been quite favorable: leaders trained using the Leader Match program have outperformed untrained leaders in a variety of settings. Although some problems have been noted in motivating the leaders to complete the course and in assuring that they comprehend the Leader Match principles, Leader Match appears to be a promising new approach to leadership training.

SPECIAL TOPICS

Measurement of Situational Control

Situational control provides a rough index of the leader's potential control and influence over group members. The leader can exert considerable influence in Combination I, where all the factors are conducive to effective leadership. In contrast, little influence is to be had in Combination VIII, since none of the factors is conducive to effective leadership.

Throughout his writings, Fiedler has identified leader-member relations, task structure, and leader position power as the most important determinants of situational control. But he has also acknowledged other factors that influence situational favorableness, and occasionally these have been incorporated into his research. For example, in his study of Belgian naval officers and enlisted men, Fiedler (1966) included cultural background similarity of the leader and group members as a determinant of situational favorableness. Other studies have considered such factors as leader status (Rice & Chemers, 1973) and leader experience (Csoka & Fiedler, 1972) as determinants of situational control. Further, Fiedler and Chemers (1974) note that the relative importance of the three standard factors in determining situational control is not fixed. As one illustration, in many military settings leader position power may be more important than either leader-member relations or task structure. Fiedler argues that it may be necessary in some cases to include additional factors and/or to alter the relative weighting of the three standard factors in order to determine the degree of situational control.

Although these possibilities increase the range of situations to which the model can be applied, they do so at a considerable cost to predictiveness of the model. How can we know *in advance* exactly what factors to include or how to weigh them in determining situational control? At this point in the development of the model, Fiedler and his associates provide no concrete guidelines. As a result, one researcher might decide that experience is central in a situation and that leader position power is really the most important factor, while another researcher might decide that the same situation calls for Fiedler's *original* model. Considerable ambiguity arises from this lack of specification in attempting to use the model.

A second problem related to the measurement of situational control derives from the use of the Group Atmosphere scale as a measure of leader-member relations. Characteristically, this scale is given to the leader only after the task is accomplished; by this time the group has either succeeded or failed. It is therefore likely that groups that perform well are given a good Group Atmosphere score by the leader, whereas groups that perform poorly will be given a low Group Atmosphere score (Graen, Alvarez, Orris, & Martella, 1970). In other words, the leader's assessment of the group will be based on the group's performance, rather than group performance stemming from an independent leader assessment of the group. Laboratory experiments such as Chemers and Skrzypek's (1972) investigation of leadership in military cadets rule out this possibility by manipulating leader-member relations, but it is a problem that plagues most of the field studies.

A final problem with situational control is that there is little independent evidence that leaders do in fact exert power and influence in the more favorable situations. One would expect to find members rating the leader as being more influential when situational control is high rather than low or to find evidence of leader behaviors exemplifying greater control (see Ashour, 1973). Yet, such evidence is very scarce. Perhaps situational control represents the *potential* for influence rather than actual control. Good leaders may not always need to exert the potential control that they do have.

Clearly, one of the main tasks facing the contingency model is to develop a better understanding of situational favorableness. Some attempts have been made to specify how other variables affect the three primary factors of leader-member relations, task structure, and position power (Chemers & Rice, 1974; Fiedler & Chemers, 1974), but considerably more detail is required before the contingency model can be applied in a straightforward manner.

What Does the LPC Scale Measure?

Thus far we have proceeded as if the least-preferred-coworker (LPC) scale had been specifically designed to differentiate between task-oriented and relationship-oriented leaders. In fact, this is not the case: the LPC scale was originally part of a scale devised to measure interpersonal relations between therapists and clients. Only later, when it was serendipitously discovered that leader LPC scores were related to group task performance, did the LPC scale become an important tool for use in leadership research. Given the central importance of the LPC scale in research on the contingency model, it is important to ask "Exactly what does the LPC scale measure?"

Fiedler argues that the LPC scale measures some fairly stable characteristics of the person. When someone is given the LPC scale on two separate occasions, the two scores tend to be about the same (median r = .67; Rice, 1978b). As with any test, the agreement between the two scores decreases the farther apart the testing occasions are, but reasonable reliabilities have been reported over periods of 15–30 months. There is, however, one major exception to this consistency: people who have dramatic, new leadership experiences such as executive or military training will often show marked changes in their LPC scores. These changes probably reflect a basic change in the person's leadership style rather than a lack of reliability of the measure. For people performing in routine leadership situations the LPC score does seem to be a reliable measure of a relatively stable characteristic.

Exactly what the least preferred coworker scale measures is less clear than its reliability. Fiedler (1957) once viewed the LPC scale as a general measure of psychological closeness. People scoring low on the LPC scale were believed to be psychologically distant from others. At another time, Foa, Mitchell, and Fiedler (1971) proposed that the LPC scale was a measure of cognitive complexity. According to this interpretation, people who score high on the LPC scale make finer differentiations among the components of a situation and the personality attributes of the group members than people who score low. Finally, Fiedler and his associates have at various times interpreted the LPC scale in the general manner we described earlier: leaders with high scores are mainly relationship-oriented, and leaders with low scores are mainly task-oriented.

At present most of the available evidence supports the third interpretation (Rice, 1978a). Leaders with high scores on the LPC scale value interpersonal relations in the group. They are more attuned to information about interpersonal relations and become more favorable toward the group and the task when the relations have been harmonious. Their behavior generally reflects this value: they try to include all members of the group in the planning of the task and provide the group members with emotional support. In contrast, leaders with low scores on the LPC scale value task success. They are more attuned to task-relevant information and judge the members of the group according to their competence at the task. They develop more favorable attitudes toward group members and themselves when the group is successful at the task. Finally, these leaders typically behave in a manner consistent with this value. They speak frequently, coordinate the group, establish dominance, and are strict in running the group. This means that the original description of leaders with high LPC scores as relationship-oriented and leaders with low LPC scores as task-oriented seems to be the most appropriate interpretation of this measure.

Why Does the Model Work?

Why are task-oriented leaders more effective in either highly favorable or highly unfavorable situations, while relationship-oriented leaders are more effective in moderately favorable situations? What goes on that makes these particular leaders effective in these situations? Paralleling the numerous interpretations of the meaning of the LPC score, several hypotheses have been suggested that attempt to answer this question.

Leader Needs   One hypothesis focuses on the needs of relationship-oriented and task-oriented leaders (Fiedler, 1964, 1967). According to this hypothesis, both types of leaders attempt to satisfy their needs through the group. The relationship-oriented leader's dominant concern is with promoting positive interpersonal relations. When situational control is high, interpersonal relations are already satisfactory, and so the relationship-oriented leader should be satisfied. Consequently, this leader will not feel compelled to exert much influence, with the result that the group's attention may wander from the task, leading to less than optimal performance. When situational control is moderate, the leader's needs for good interpersonal relations are threatened by either poor existing leader-member relations or a lack of structure and position power that may undermine good relations when they do exist. To meet these threats, the leader will be interpersonally responsive in interacting with group members. These actions will facilitate the flow of ideas, which is critical to successful performance on the kinds of creative tasks that are often found in the moderately favorable situational-control conditions. Finally, when situational control is low, the leader's attempts to promote good relations lead to an almost complete withdrawal from the leadership role. The leader will seek emotional support and fail to provide appropriate structure and direction for the group. Hence, the performance of the group is quite poor in this situation.

The task-oriented leader, in contrast, is concerned primarily with task success. This leader will also be generally satisfied when situational control is high. Any deviation from high performance will be met by restructuring the task and punishing ineffective group members, keeping productivity high. However, when situational control is moderate, often defined by creative tasks and committee work, concern with accomplishing the task will tend to inhibit the free expression of ideas and discussion necessary for successful performance. Finally, when situational control is low, attempts to focus the group's efforts on the task will distract the members from their disagreements and the difficulty of the task. Consequently, the group is again likely to be productive.

Cognitive Complexity   Another hypothesis interprets the LPC scale as a measure of cognitive complexity, such that high-LPC leaders make finer discriminations among situations and personality characteristics of group members than low-LPC leaders. The situations in which leaders with low LPC scores are more effective are rather simple: settings in which situational control is high have all positive factors (leader-member relations, task structure, and position power), and settings in which situational control is low are composed entirely of negative factors. Settings where situational control is moderate are more complex, being composed of both positive and negative factors. Hence the success of the high-LPC leader in moderately favorable situations may represent a match between the complexity of the situation and the cognitive complexity of the leader. Considerable evidence for this position is presented by Chemers and Rice (1974).

Other Considerations Groups having relationship-oriented leaders tend to have more relaxed, less physiologically aroused members than groups having task-oriented leaders (Fiedler, 1967). As we saw in Chapter 2, arousal facilitates performance on simple tasks and interferes with performance on complex tasks. Accordingly, relationship-oriented leaders may be able to elicit superior performance when situational control is moderate, particularly when creative ideas are called for, since such leaders do not overarouse the members.

A further observation may be made about the leader's own task performance. If we separate the leader's work *on the task itself* from that of the group members, the leader's performance characteristically parallels the performance of the entire group. In fact, the relation between the leaders' LPC scores and their own task performance is even closer than the relation between the leader's LPC score and the performance of the entire group (Rice, 1978a). On many laboratory and some field tasks, the leader's work may represent an important contribution to the group's overall performance, meaning that the leader's own high (or low) level of productivity on the task may account in large part for the high (or low) level of group productivity.

SUMMARY

The study of leadership has always been one of the most difficult and confusing areas of social psychology. Fiedler's model is an important contribution to this area because it has helped organize a mass of disparate findings. Beginning with observations of the relation between the LPC measure and group performance, Fiedler inductively developed the contingency model to provide the best possible fit to the existing data. Subsequent research has focused largely on verifying the accuracy of the contingency model by comparing its predictions with new data.

We now know that the contingency model is able to predict leadership effectiveness with reasonable accuracy in a variety of situations ranging from basketball teams to brainstorming groups. It has also been useful in answering a number of practical questions faced by organizations, such as "Why is leadership training often unsuccessful?" and "What are the effects of rotating leaders to new positions?"

At the same time, we have noted a number of weaknesses in Fiedler's model at a more conceptual level. After 25 years of research with the LPC scale, its interpretation is still somewhat ambiguous; the factors that determine situational favorableness also need additional specification. Further, the exact reasons why the contingency model works are far from clear. Several explanations have been proposed to account for the relation between leadership style and group performance, each explanation receiving some empirical support. Thus, Fiedler's model is very useful in an applied sense: it provides a framework with which organizations can identify the most effective types of leaders for a wide variety of situations. However, its usefulness as a basis for understanding the processes underlying successful leadership appears to be limited at present.

SUGGESTED READING

Fiedler, F. E. *A theory of leadership effectiveness.* New York: McGraw-Hill, 1967.

Fiedler, F. E. Recent developments in research on the contingency model. In L. Berkowitz (Ed.), *Cognitive theories in social psychology.* New York: Academic Press, 1978.

Fiedler, F. E. The contingency model and the dynamics of the leadership process. In L. Berkowitz (Ed.), *Advances in experimental social psychology* (Vol. 11). New York: Academic Press, 1978.

Fiedler, F. E., & Mahar, L. The effectiveness of contingency model training: A review of the validation of Leader Match. *Personnel Psychology,* in press.

Graen, G., Alvarez, K., Orris, J. B., & Martella, J. A. Contingency model of leadership effectiveness: Antecedent and evidential results. *Psychological Bulletin,* 1970, 74, 285–296.

PART SIX

REACTIONS TO LOSS OF CONTROL

"Control" is a concept pervading much of personality and social psychology. One can find elements of control, especially as defined in terms of free choice, in numerous of the theories throughout this book (Chapters 6, 8, 9, 10, 14). This section contrasts two theories about control that focus exclusively on the freedoms and nonfreedoms of people who are trying to maintain control over the end results of their actions. Although the control concept is central for both these theories, the interesting point is the seeming opposition between them.

Reactance theory (Chapter 17) is a set of ideas about the human as an active agent who reasserts threatened or eliminated freedom. A person's expectation about freedom can vary from activity to activity, but given that a person has a clear expectation about being able to pursue a freely chosen course of action, infringements on that freedom lead to "negativism," refusing to obey, and becoming attracted to the hard-to-obtain. *Reactance* is a term that captures the psychological state of someone who is motivated to restore a threatened or lost freedom.

Learned helplessness theory (Chapter 18) considers the opposite side of the human (as well as other organisms). With repeated loss of control, a condition of "giving up" ensues, entailing a lowered motivation to perform, deficits in cognitive abilities, and also depression. These various outcomes are all considered to be indicators of helplessness. We treat learned helplessness theory in a unique way among the theories in the book, for the state of the art of learned helplessness theorizing affords us the opportunity to examine the evolution of a theory, giving attention to the myriad of issues that arise in the course of developing a theoretical concept.

CHAPTER 17

REACTANCE THEORY

REACTANCE theory (Brehm, 1966) is a broad theoretical approach to the question of what happens when a person's freedom is threatened or eliminated. Humans quite often, if not most of the time, expect a degree of freedom of choice in their activities. We take for granted that we are free to select among possible items to drink or eat, that we have freedom to select among various potential friends, and that we have some power of decision over which profession to pursue. Not only can overt decisions be free, but we also expect freedom to express and feel a number of internal states, such as attitudes and emotions.

What does it mean for a freedom to be threatened? If we are free to choose any of several selections on a restaurant menu, a freedom is threatened when we find that there is only a limited supply of one item—such as onion soup. Imagine a person who is pondering over the selections and is informed by the waitress that the kitchen may have run short of onion soup. Such a threat to this particular behavioral freedom (eating onion soup) will create "psychological reactance," a state in which the person tries to reassert or reestablish the threatened freedom. The result is not difficult to measure: Our restaurant customer should tend to become increasingly interested in the onion soup, which means a greater likelihood of ordering it and an enhanced attraction to it. This should be true even if onion soup was not initially the customer's first preference on the menu.

THE THEORY

Brehm (1966) has described a number of variables that influence the course of reactance, and we will discuss these in some detail below, together with illustrative research. For now a brief summary of these variables will be helpful as an introduction to the theory.

First is the question of threat. Threats to freedom can vary from minimal (there is only some hint of onion soup not being available) to maximal (the kitchen has already run out of the soup). Second is the variable of freedom. If the restaurant customer were on a highly restricted medical diet and had no expectation of choosing exotic foods such as onion soup, the unavailability of onion soup would generate no reactance. Third is importance of the freedom. A freedom is important when the choice alternatives are associated with the satisfaction of important needs. If a customer were rather hungry and also characterized himself as a gourmet, it would be highly important to make up his mind about what to eat. Hence reactance would stand to be quite high. But if he did not care for French food and was satiated anyway, the freedom would be of little importance.

The domain of reactance theory is twofold: Much of the application has been to cases analogous to the restaurant setting, in which a person expects freedom to choose among any of several distinct alternatives. In such situations reactance is created when one or several of the alternatives is threatened with elimination. The other application of the theory is to social influence settings. Considering once again the restaurant customer, reactance can be created when some person attempts to convince the customer to make up his mind in a certain way. This "social influence" source of reactance always involves the attempted influence of another person as the source of threat to freedom. The stronger is this attempt at influence, the more reactance is created.

To illustrate the workings of the theory in these two domains, we will move on to two examples, both taken from research on the theory. The first example illustrates a nonsocial source of reactance; the second deals with social influence as a source of threat to freedom.

A customer walks into a record store with the intention of perusing the local selections. In particular, she is interested in purchasing some music by Bach, Mozart, Scarlatti, or Vivaldi. As it happens, this is a small store, and the present stock does not include anything she wants to buy. Nonetheless, the customer knows that new shipments arrive frequently, and she is assured by the owner that something very appealing by each of the above-named composers will be represented in the next shipment. A week later, after the shipment has presumably arrived, the customer returns and finds that the owner was 75% right: the new shipment has a fine variety of Bach, Mozart, and Vivaldi but no Scarlatti. Changing this description into theoretical language, the customer's freedom to choose among any of the four has been seriously threatened, and in such a case reactance theory predicts an increased interest in the missing alternative. Were we capable of measuring the customer's feelings about the four composers, she should now be more interested than before in Scarlatti records. In fact, something akin to such an effect is reported by Brehm, Stires, Sensenig, and Shaban (1966) and will be discussed below in more detail.

As the second example, suppose that a college student feels he has some expertise in the area of personnel selection. He is assigned the task of selecting, from among two candidates, the better-qualified person for the position of dormitory adviser. Before making his decision, this student is fed bits of information about the two applicants—home town, education, and other related matters. As the student proceeds through these data, he gradually comes to favor one over the other, and at some point before his deciding it is possible to measure the degree of his preference of Candidate A over Candidate B. Then, also before the decision, a peer of this student tries to influence him. In one case the peer simply says "Candidate A is the best adviser," and in the second case his remark is stronger: "There is no question about it. Candidate A is the best adviser."

After this attempt at social influence, the student's opinion is measured once again. The issue here is whether the two remarks—mild and severe—will have different effects on opinion change. To answer this question we can appeal to the results of an experiment by Wicklund and Brehm (1968), which was highly similar in format to this example. It happened that the mild influence attempt had no impact on opinion change, whereas the severe one caused a significant change in the direction *opposite* from the peer's influence attempt. Otherwise stated, the "there is no question about it" language created a "boomerang" effect—that is, opinion change opposite from what was intended by the communicator.

It is useful here to offer a very brief interpretation of this effect: Subjects felt free to select either of the two candidates, and further, they felt sufficient expertise to make up their minds for themselves. When the peer indicated that Candidate A should be selected, the student's freedom to make up his own mind was threatened. The threat was magnified when the influence attempt carried the pressure-laden "no question about it." In response to this threat to freedom, the student became motivated (through reactance) to reassert his freedom to make up his mind for himself. This motivation surfaced in the form of taking issue with the source of influence and moving in the "boomerang effect" direction.

It should now be possible to have some feeling for the way reactance theory is applied. At this point we will move on to a more detailed consideration of the conceptual issues.

Area of Application

The crucial prerequisite for reactance arousal is the condition of freedom of choice. It is easy to think of instances in which most of us expect the freedom to choose as we please, and every one of these situations is potentially ripe for reactance. Every day we select people with whom to associate, clothing to wear, routes to travel to work or school, varieties of entertainment, and food to eat. At the same time, there are also classes of behavior over which we exert no freedom of choice. We do not expect to choose which telephone company to deal with, nor do we expect to choose whether or not to pay our income tax. These are instances in which the potential for reactance approximates zero, for there is no freedom to be threatened.

It can be seen that reactance theory does not deal with "free" as opposed to "unfree" individuals. Each person is viewed as having some areas of behavior that are freely chosen, while behavior in other areas is not so freely chosen. The application of the theory is straightforward, once it is established that a person expects freedom of choice over a given area of behavior.

Thus far we have devoted most of our discussion to the freedom that consists in choices between distinct behavioral alternatives. However, it is also possible to speak of freedom of choice over "internal" events, such as attitudes or emotions. There are two points worth noting in taking reactance theory into this realm of "internal" events: (1) Freedom in internal matters is ordinarily not defined in terms of discrete alternatives. Instead, one can imagine an infinite number of possible attitudes that might be held on a particular issue or an infinite number of shades of a given emotion that might be felt. This feature of "internal" freedoms does not make the application of reactance theory difficult. The nature of predictions and influence of theoretical variables is exactly the same as with choices among discrete behavioral alternatives. (2) There is probably no such thing as *not* expecting freedom or control with respect to one's attitudes and emotions. There is no physical means by which an influence agent can interfere with the course of these internal events; hence we are always free to feel a variety of attitudes and emotions, and we are always in a position to experience reactance when social influence is directed toward those internal processes.

One more point should be made regarding the appropriate area for application of reactance theory. The operation of reactance assumes a viable freedom—one that has not been totally usurped by external forces or by oneself. If we have already decided about a certain matter, we are no longer in a position to experience reactance about that particular choice, because the freedom has at least momentarily been forgone. Returning to the case of the onion soup, the customer glancing over the menu is in full possession of his freedom of choice. He deliberates, engages in mock choices, reverses preferences, and stares at the alternatives for some time before actually choosing. During all of this predecisional period he is entirely free and fully open to the influences of reactance. It is during this time that he should be maximally motivated to protect the freedom. But if the customer has elected to try the vegetable soup and is halfway into it before the waitress announces a shortage of onion soup, reactance will not be aroused, simply because the decision has been made and the freedom that was once there to protect has been temporarily set aside.

Effects of Reactance

Reactance is a state that directs a person's energies toward reasserting freedom. This means that the person whose freedom is threatened or eliminated will act in the direction of regaining that freedom. If the Scarlatti record is overpriced, we should witness an increased tendency to purchase the record along with an increment in the record's attractiveness. If the record is actually missing, we cannot very well measure its increased sales popularity, but there should still be evidence for reactance in the form of enhanced attractiveness. In short, the person experiencing reactance will show an increase in desire for whatever behaviors are threatened with elimination, no matter whether that desire is measured behaviorally or by subjective ratings.

In conceptualizing freedoms, it is important to realize that the freedom to choose Scarlatti is not the only one tampered with in the preceding example. The freedom *not to* choose the other records is also threatened. To make the example more extreme, a music fan might walk into a record store only to discover that a Vivaldi record is the only available one that she might conceivably buy. Certainly in this case the freedom *not to* purchase the Vivaldi record is threatened. What is the result? Obviously a derogation of Vivaldi should take place, which is the manifestation of reassertion of freedom not to choose Vivaldi.

The analysis of threats to freedom of internal states (attitudes and so on) is also uncomplicated. Normally the threat will arise from a source of social influence, who will be trying to pressure the person's attitude in a certain direction. To manifest reactance is to show tendencies to shift in the opposite direction. Suppose a high-pressure communicator insists that his audience vote for the Democratic party in a presidential election. The freedom threatened is the freedom to be favorable toward the Republicans. Consequently, to reassert that freedom means to shift one's attitude in the direction of the Republicans and away from the position of the high-pressure communicator.

Theoretical Variables

Strength of Threat   It should already be implicit in our remarks that reactance is produced in proportion to the strength of the threat. In empirical terms, strength of threat means the following. In the record store a relatively weak threat would have resulted if the owner had expressed some doubts about receiving Scarlatti records in the shipment. As it happened, the threat was considerably stronger, in that the records did not arrive at all. Moving to the attitude-change context, it is a useful tack to define strength of threat in terms of the amount of perceived intent to influence. One can imagine a gradation of communications, beginning with a neutral presentation of facts, then moving to a presentation of facts coupled with a conclusion, then a conclusion plus a strong recommendation, and then—still more extreme—all of the foregoing plus an adamant demand that everyone must without exception agree. At this last stage the perceived pressure should be strongest, and the resulting reactance would be greatest.

Freedom   A classic empirical effort to examine the variable of freedom is reported by Brehm et al. (1966). The paradigm of the experiment was almost an exact parallel to our record-store example, except that the study took place in the laboratory. Further, some of the subjects were told at the outset that they would have complete freedom to choose among one of four records, whereas others found that the experimenter intended to assign them one randomly. Subjects first listened to and rated four selections of music and were told that when they returned for a second session, they would receive one of the four. It should be remembered that some of these subjects expected freedom to choose any of the four at the second session, and others expected no such choice.

On returning for the second session, subjects in a control (no freedom elimination) condition were asked only to rate the records again. These control subjects were from the group that expected freedom of choice. All the remaining subjects discovered that one of the records (the selection they had originally ranked third) had not been included in the shipment. This elimination should have aroused reactance for subjects who expected freedom but not for those who expected no choice. The dependent measure for this experiment was the change in rated attractiveness of the critical record, and the results were quite consistent with the theoretical reasoning. If there was no elimination, there was no change in attractiveness. However, if subjects initially felt free and the record was eliminated, there was a sizable increase in the record's attractiveness. In contrast, if no freedom was expected, the elimination actually caused the record to decline in rated attractiveness. This latter effect, which is sometimes called "sour grapes," is commonly observed in the absence of reactance forces. That is, when someone expects no freedom, the elimination of something that might potentially be possessed frequently results in a derogation of that item. As yet there have been no thoroughgoing explanations for this sour-grapes effect, but it is important to note that derogation is an extremely noticeable effect when alternatives are eliminated, especially in the absence of prior freedom.

This study makes our theoretical point clearly: reactance effects are to be observed only to the extent that someone initially expects freedom, and it is also instructive that an expectation of freedom can be established so readily by an easy laboratory manipulation.

Importance of Freedom   A freedom is important to the degree that it might lead to the satisfaction of needs that are central to the person's life. The freedom to select among types of food or shelter is more important than the freedom to choose a brand of facial tissue, and the freedom to decide for oneself about the advisability of birth control is more important than the freedom to arrive at one's own opinion about the quality of oats in the northern Yukon. A freedom is also more important if the person has the requisite capabilities to use the freedom wisely. The reason is that the correct use of a freedom is more likely to lead to satisfaction of needs than the incorrect use of freedom is. For example, someone who has never played tennis would place little importance on the freedom to use either a wooden or metal racquet, but the tennis pro may see the composition of the racquet as an all-meaningful issue.

This point about ability to use freedom has been documented in Wicklund and Brehm's (1968) experiment, discussed above as an example. The subjects in the example were the "highly competent" subjects, in that they had been told beforehand that they were indeed highly capable of making the decision required in the situation. An additional set of subjects were led to feel rather incompetent to make the forthcoming choice; accordingly, for them, the freedom should not have been as important. As would be expected, reactance effects occurred only for the "highly competent" subjects, and in contrast, the reaction of "low-competent" subjects to the high- (and low-) pressure communication was generally compliance.

It should be emphasized that the competence analysis is highly specific: we are talking only about the competence to make a specific, delimited decision, not about some more general competence or intelligence.

RESEARCH EXAMPLES

Reactance theory, given its unusually easy operationalization, has been extended through research to a number of applied contexts. Many of these applications have implications for opinion change, interpersonal attraction, and the behavior of the purchaser. We will present just a sample of these here.

Censorship

Very little about the psychological impact of censorship has ever been studied, yet (at least in the United States) most people tacitly agree that censorship is unconstitutional and somehow objectionable. Reactance theory can be a tool for analyzing the effect of censorship on people's attitudes about the subject matter censored. One illustrative study (Wicklund & Brehm, reported in Wicklund, 1974) was performed in a junior high school. Students were led to expect an assembly, at which a Mr. Feiffer was to give a speech advocating a reduction in the voting age. Students were excited about the prospect of this particular assembly, and for the most part they were highly favorable to the position Mr. Feiffer was to take. On the morning of the scheduled assembly an announcement was made to the students, explaining that the assembly was canceled. In one condition the expressed reason was Mr. Feiffer's illness, and in the "censorship" condition the speech was said to have been canceled because a school-board official was opposed to the position to be taken in the speech. The "censorship" condition carried a good deal of perceived intent to influence and should therefore have created more reactance than the "speaker sick" condition. The results supported this reasoning quite clearly: on a measure of opinion change toward or away from the speaker's position, most of the subjects exposed to the censorship manipulation shifted toward the speaker's position, whereas only a minority of subjects in the other condition showed such a shift.

High Pressure Selling

When a shopper enters a store and is interested in contemplating the alternatives carefully before buying, it is easy for a salesperson to introduce a strong element of reactance. For example, if the customer picks up a blouse and hears from behind her "That was made for you," there is a definite pressure to purchase that very item. The result, quite obviously, should be a tendency to reject that item and look further. This exact process was explored in a laboratory experiment by Wicklund, Slattum, and Solomon (1970).

Female college students were asked to examine six pairs of sunglasses, with the expectation that they would choose one of the pairs at the end of the examination period. The chosen pair was to be worn by the subject and modeled before a camera, but the subject also had the option of buying the chosen pair. Before the subject's perusal of the glasses, the experimenter made one of two remarks: In one condition, she indicated that she was highly interested in the subject's purchasing a pair of sunglasses, since she was working on a commission basis and stood to gain a profit from each subject who made a purchase. In the other condition she expressed disinterest in whether the subject made a purchase.

Then the subject was asked to open each sunglasses box, try on the sunglasses one by one, and assign a rating to each one. As the subject put on the glasses and looked into the mirror, the experimenter commented "Those are great" or, for other sunglasses, "Those were made for you." Similar remarks were made in each of the six instances, so that in every case the subject's freedom *not* to select the sunglasses in question was threatened. However, the threat value of the experimenter's remarks was much greater in the "commission" condition, since in that case the remark carried the implication that the subject should purchase the pair after modeling it.

How is freedom to be restored in this situation? Subjects gave ratings of the glasses as they examined them, and it would be expected that the relatively great reactance generated in the "commission" condition would be reflected in subjects' dislike for all the sunglasses. This is exactly what happened. Subjects rated the sunglasses lower when the "Those were made for you" remarks carried the implication that the subject should make a purchase.

When an Attractive Group Threatens Freedom

We have noted that reactance in an interpersonal situation is a function of how much pressure a person feels to abide by the wishes of others. If a freedom exists and is highly important, it can be threatened when others make efforts to change the person's free behavior. One source of such pressure is the attractiveness of the others. The more attractive those others are, the more pressure toward compliance is felt, and consequently, the more reactance they will generate in the person.

Brehm and Mann (1975) placed subjects in a group-decision situation. There was only one subject; the other members were accomplices of the experimenter, and the situation was arranged so that the subject would feel strong and repeated pressure from the group to change his opinion. In some cases the situation was arranged so that subjects would place a high value on making a correct independent judgment about the issue, so that the importance of their freedom to decide for themselves should have been extremely important. The degree of felt pressure to change was manipulated by varying the group's attractiveness, and it was argued that the relatively attractive group would generate a stronger pressure toward change than the less attractive group. The extent of reactance emanating from this differential pressure was assessed by measuring the change in the subject's opinion about the issue being discussed. It turned out that the reasoning of Brehm and Mann was correct: subjects shifted their opinions *away* from the group opinion to the extent that the group was attractive.

It should be noted that these results would ordinarily be seen as highly surprising. A commonly expected result, and one consistent with social comparison theory (Chapter 11), would be more *positive* social influence when the group is attractive. In fact, such a result did occur under other conditions, in which freedom of choice was of low importance. However, when importance was maximized (in the conditions described above), the impact of reactance outweighed the social comparison effect that would usually be expected.

Playing Hard to Get

The experiment by Brehm et al. on long-play records has some interesting implications for interpersonal attraction. If a person feels free to choose among several possible mates, but one of them is difficult to contact, the consequent threat to freedom should produce an increment in attractiveness. Wicklund and Ogden (as reported in Wicklund, 1974) examined this possibility by placing female subjects in either a choice or a no-choice condition, such that some subjects expected to choose one of five men, and others expected to be assigned one of the men. They were also led to expect a short get-acquainted period with one of five available college men. Shortly after subjects had given some initial attractiveness ratings of the men, but well before any choice, it was discovered that one of the men was late and thus possibly would not be available for the session. After the introduction of that threat to freedom, a second attractiveness measure was taken. It produced results quite parallel to those of the record study: in the choice condition, the threatened choice alternative (college male) tended to become more attractive, whereas that same alternative male was derogated in the no-choice condition.

SPECIAL TOPICS

Prior Exercise of Freedom

One of the potentially more interesting issues surrounding reactance theory is "Where does the expectation of freedom come from?" In the original statement of the theory it was suggested that repeated experiences with acting freely would result in coming to expect freedom in the future, and this means that reactance should be especially evident among people who have had more experience with the relevant freedoms.

For instance, suppose someone has always felt that the Republican candidate for president is the only realistic choice. This person's parents and grandparents were Midwestern Republicans, and so are the person's relatives and friends. In some objective sense the freedom to vote Democrat exists for this person, but it is evident that the specific behavioral freedom of pulling the Democrat lever has never been exercised. A contrasting case would be someone who typically has voted for the person rather than the party and who has voted Democrat and Republican on at least two or three occasions each.

Now comes the crucial question: if either one of these persons were approached by a neighbor the day before the presidential election and directed to "vote Republican or else!" who would show more reactance? (By now it should be evident that the reactance response will be to shift toward favoring the Democrat.) From the original theoretical formulation one might think that the second person, who has had experience in exercising the freedom to vote Democrat, would have a stronger expectation regarding that freedom and would therefore react more strongly against an attempted infringement on that same freedom.

Two experiments by Snyder and Wicklund (1976) were carried out in almost parallel fashion to our example, revealing a surprising answer to our question. It was the *first* person in our example who manifested the reactance. If subjects had never upheld the position that was threatened—that is, if they had never exercised the freedom to do the opposite of the communicator's recommendation *before* the communication—they reacted quite strongly against the communication. Perhaps this is even more surprising when one realizes that the communicator in this instance is arguing for a position with which the subject already agrees, and in order to show reactance, the person must shift toward a position that would presumably be unnatural or uncomfortable.

How is this phenomenon to be explained? It might be argued that the person who has already tried out both options has a certain security. Such a person should know that the alternative freedoms can be tried out again and again, more or less at will, simply because of the security of past experience. People who have always been one-party or one-side-of-the-issue, in contrast, may be insecure about their independence when an untried side of the issue is explicitly forbidden. The teenager who feels objectively the freedom to smoke but who has never tried it should act out rebelliously when a parent forbids smoking. Or a woman who has never had an affair might be especially sensitive, reactance-wise, when her insecure husband forbids her to have any kind of contact with other men. Thus, in general, it might be thought that those who react most strongly against forceful communication efforts are those who expect a freedom but who have never tried out the freedom at issue.

The Psychology of Giving Up

Chapter 18, on helplessness theory, treats a facet of human behavior that seems directly contrary to reactance. The central thesis of that chapter is this: when confronted with sufficient barriers to behaving or to goal attainment, the organism resigns itself to a condition of passivity and no longer tries to combat the frustrating or inhibiting conditions.

The purpose of a theoretical statement by Wortman and Brehm (1975) is to integrate these two perspectives and, in the process, to say something about the fall of freedom. Their argument, which will receive more elaboration in Chapter 18, is roughly as follows: If people expect to be able to progress freely toward some end—such as earning a day's salary, entering a classroom building, or solving a cognitive task—and there is either a threatened or actual block to their progress, reactance will ensue. The results will take the forms we have already described. However, there will be a point at which the obstacles become so frequent, insuperable, or repeated that one finally gives up and fails to show further reactance. In fact, at that point motivation in general should decline.

What this means theoretically is highly important in the present context. Freedoms are not terribly general, nor is a given freedom a freedom forever. Just as the expectation of freedom can develop in the first place by having experience with behaving freely in some domain, that same freedom can vanish through repeated experience with being unable to exercise the freedom that was once expected.

SUMMARY

Reactance theory is a characterization of the human proclivity to protect freedoms that are threatened before decisions. The theory is surprisingly easy to implement and requires only some assurance that the person being studied expects to be free in whatever domain is being studied. In the case of interpersonal influence, reactance is produced to the degree that felt pressure to change is generated. The result of this reactance-arousing pressure is often "boomerang" attitude change. In the case of impersonal threats (as when a consumer product may become unavailable), reactance is generated to the degree that the threat approaches an actual elimination of the choice. Thus reactance is stronger when the item does not show up than when someone merely hints that it may not arrive.

The course of reactance is affected by three central variables: strength of threat, expectation of freedom, and importance of freedom. With the combined use of these variables it is possible to generate a variety of interesting predictions about the efforts of humans to safeguard their freedoms—both overt behavioral freedoms and freedoms regarding attitudes and emotions.

SUGGESTED READING

Brehm, J. W. *A theory of psychological reactance.* New York: Academic Press, 1966.

Brehm, J. W. *Responses to loss of freedom: A theory of psychological reactance.* Morristown, N. J.: General Learning Press, 1972.

Clee, M. A., & Wicklund, R. A. Consumer behavior and psychological reactance. *Journal of* Consumer Research, 1980, *6*, 389–405.

Wicklund, R. A. *Freedom and reactance.* Hillsdale, N. J.: Erlbaum, 1974.

CHAPTER 18

THE PROCESS OF THEORETICAL DEVELOPMENT: LEARNED HELPLESSNESS

THUS far the reader's task has been easy. The theories presented here have been introduced as if they were correct from their inception and were never or seldom contradicted and as if the potential areas of application for these theories were known exactly. As it happens, we have purposely chosen theoretical statements that have already been thoroughly tested and refined. The current statements of these theories are often the end result of years of diligent work by investigators who have smoothed over the rough spots in the theories, added crucial variables for predictive precision, and defined more exactly just how far the notions can be applied. But these statements about crucial variables and predictive precision must sound a bit abstract. The purpose of this chapter is to shed light on the course of development of a theory—the theory of learned helplessness—and to show the twists and turns theorists take in working toward a theory that has both predictive power and generality. In the course of discussing this theory we will try to show what can happen to an explanatory principle, as well as the phenomenon it tries to explain, as investigators confront the theory with probing research and critical questions.

A CLASSIC EXPERIMENT IN LEARNED HELPLESSNESS

Every theory seems to carry special procedures, or instances of its application, that people can point to as characterizing the whole process under study. Bandura's theory of social learning is often exemplified through the classic study of children who imitated an adult beating up a Bobo doll, and cognitive dissonance theory is often represented by the procedure of offering people money to act in opposition to their fundamental beliefs. Although it can be misleading to cling onto such typifying examples, as we shall see below, our discussion of learned helplessness can be simplified by describing an experiment that follows directly from the helplessness concept, a study reported by Hiroto and Seligman (1975).

Undergraduate men and women were given 45 separate bursts of high-intensity noise (90 decibels). Some of these subjects were told that they could perform some behavior that would terminate this aversive noise on each of the 45 occasions. Subjects in this condition rapidly discovered that by pressing a button four times, they could immediately terminate the blasts. Another condition was highly comparable to this one, with one exception. Subjects soon found that the button was ineffective. They had originally expected some link between button pressing and noise termination, but their expectations about that causal link were quickly eliminated. Finally, Hiroto and Seligman created a third condition, in which subjects never expected to be able to terminate the noise. They found themselves listening passively to the loud noise, in line with original expectations.

After these encounters with the 90-decibel sounds, subjects were asked to attempt to solve a series of 20 anagrams. For instance, the subject would be given the letters "ERLKC" to rearrange into an acceptable English word ("CLERK"). Among other measures, their speed of solving these anagrams was calculated, producing the following results.

Subjects who had control over termination of the noise performed quite well on the anagrams, taking an average of around 20 seconds to solve each one. Similarly, the group that never expected any control—and was exposed to the entire series of 45 bursts—also performed well, taking about 25 seconds per anagram. The similarity of results in these two conditions suggests that the mere exposure to noise per se does not necessarily impede speed in coping with complex intellectual tasks. The exciting results were found in the group that originally expected the button to work but then found it to be ineffective. These subjects took over 40 seconds to solve each of the anagrams. It would appear that discovering a loss of personal control over aversive stimulation impairs later cognitive functioning.

This is the basic phenomenon: First someone encounters a situation in which there is no longer a good connection between behaviors tried out and the result. An accompaniment of this lack of control is often a "giving up" response, which can include loss of motivation as well as decrements in apparent ability to deal with further problems. This is the phenomenon called "learned helplessness," which was first investigated by Seligman and his coworkers (Overmier & Seligman, 1967; Seligman, 1975).

But why should the effect be called "helplessness"? *Helplessness* is a term that designates a general lowered state of functioning stemming out of experiences with uncontrollability. The helpless organism is to some degree unable to improve its own condition. It turns out that anagram-solving performance is not the only effect studied. Quality of motor performance has also been shown to suffer among people who lose control, and in the world of animals, dogs that receive inescapable shock are subsequently inept at learning how to escape shock, even when the opportunity arises. *Helplessness* then comes to mean a multiplicity of related events: giving up quickly (Glass & Singer, 1972), learning slowly, and more generally being less able to improve one's own situation.

LEARNED HELPLESSNESS THEORY: THE FIRST STATEMENT

The starting point for learned helplessness is the creating of conditions in which the organism, whether human or not, cannot affect its outcomes by responding. Another way of stating this is to say that responses and outcomes are independent. Dogs, cats, rats, and fish that are given inescapable shock (Maier & Seligman, 1976) can be characterized as not being able to do anything about their outcomes. No matter what efforts they put forth, the shock will come anyway. The subjects of Hiroto and Seligman (1975) who could not terminate the noise were in a psychologically comparable dilemma. In a still different context, people who are given unsolvable tasks (Klein, Fencil-Morse, & Seligman, 1976) are also in the position of having no outcome control. No matter how they approach the task, they will fail.

Seligman (1975) indicates that such situations result in a learned psychological condition that has three components:

1. The *cognitive* component of learned helplessness is the expectancy that there is no longer a connection between behavior and outcome. Hence, if people are asked about their extent of control, as in the experiment by Hiroto and Seligman, they should report a low degree of control. Or if they are put in a new situation in which there is in fact a relation between their behavior and their outcome, they will have more difficulty in learning this connection. For instance, children with a helpless expectancy would have more difficulty learning that they receive a gold star whenever they work on arithmetic problems than children without a helpless expectancy. This pessimistic expectancy is an important characteristic of learned helplessness.

2. The *motivational* component is the most often studied outcome of helplessness-inducing procedures. By "motivational" is meant the person's (or animal's) response of giving up, not trying, and similar behavioral effects. The common-sense associations the reader will have to the word *helplessness* are the effects we mean by motivational deficits.

3. Finally comes the *emotional* component. Seligman's concern here is with the fear that presumably comes from helplessness training, followed by depression, the latter being the primary focus. It is Seligman's thesis that temporary states of depression are preceded by helplessness-inducing conditions (Klein et al., 1976) and that long-term reactive depression is often associated with major helplessness-inducing circumstances.

These are the three related psychological effects that make up the condition of learned helplessness. But what turns learned helplessness into such an intriguing phenomenon is that these deficits are not typically limited to the original situation in which responding was ineffective. Rather, the deficits may generalize to a wide variety of new situations. As we saw, failure to control noxious stimulation led to later difficulties in solving mental tasks. And similarly, failure to control some aspect of a motor activity has a subsequent impact on solving mental problems (Hiroto & Seligman, 1975). The subject will often show poor intellectual performance, lack of trying, or other maladaptive behavior in situations that seem very different from the situation in which control was taken away.

What determines the scope of this generalization? Seligman (1975) indicates two factors. One of these is the similarity between the helplessness-inducing situation and the subsequent situation: generalization is greater the more similar the two situations are. By Seligman's reasoning, a state of helplessness should transfer (generalize) less from Situation 1 to Situation 2 if, for example, two clearly different skills are involved. Imagine, for instance, that a psychologist reduces your sense of control over solving crossword puzzles by shouting "Stop!" and jerking each puzzle away as you near completion. Half an hour later you are at home helping your father harvest tomatoes. There would be little reason to think that the helplessness manipulation would carry over to the tomato harvesting, since both the situations and the skills are unrelated.

The second determinant of generalization is the relative amount of psychological distress involved in the two situations. Generalization is normally more pronounced when the helplessness-inducing event is more distressing than the test situation. A mother who discovers that all three of her children have run away from home is likely to be more distressed, and hence experience deficits in a broader range of situations, than a mother whose pet canary has escaped. Returning to the experiment by Hiroto and Seligman just cited, the idea also seems to fit: the 90-decibel noise blasts (helplessness induction) were very likely more traumatic than the anagram tasks required in the test phase. Thus the sequence was from high trauma to lower trauma, thereby maximizing the possible generalization.

In summary, it is hardly surprising when someone has repeated difficulty solving a problem and then shows a lowered expectancy for success at that kind of problem. Such an effect hardly calls for a theory. The crucial phenomenon for the theory is therefore *generalization* from the original task to later activities. When a person cannot work a crossword puzzle and then fumbles when placing the turntable arm onto the record, or when the stench and noise of pollution affect reading comprehension, we then turn toward the theory as a possible explanation of a set of intriguing effects.

A PROBLEM FOR THE THEORY: REACTANCE ENTERS THE PICTURE

In a study by Roth and Kubal (1975), subjects underwent a set of experiences very much akin to those in earlier helplessness experiments. In the first phase of the experiment they were asked to work on concept-formation problems and received noncontingent feedback (feedback unrelated to their success—a helplessness induction) either three times, one time, or not at all. They then moved on to the second phase of the experiment, in which they were asked to discover the sequence in which a series of playing cards appeared. The number of problems solved in this playing-card situation was the primary measure. The prediction from what has gone above is clear: the stronger the helplessness training, the poorer should be performance on the playing-card task.

The results should be a surprise for anyone adhering to the assumptions of learned helplessness theory. Subjects who encountered noncontingent feedback three times showed a decrement in later performance compared with the control group, but subjects who experienced just *one* instance of noncontingent feedback showed an *increment* in performance. They actually performed better than subjects who never encountered helplessness training at all. Note that this effect was especially pronounced when the task performance associated with Phase 1 was described as highly important. The results were not as dramatic when the task was not viewed as important, suggesting that helplessness effects have something to do with the degree of threat to self-esteem or to ego maintenance.

Roth and Kubal's finding is not an isolated event in the helplessness literature. In a study by Hanusa and Schulz (1977) subjects were placed in a situation causing them to fail. The experiment was arranged so that some subjects could attribute their failure to effort, which should have been a relatively weak helplessness manipulation because an attribution to effort simply means that one should try harder next time. Other subjects were led to blame their failure on their own abilities—a decidedly stronger helplessness induction. If one's abilities are at fault, there is very little that can be done. Lack of the requisite abilities would seem to be virtually a prerequisite for helplessness. Remarkably enough, the greatest performance decrements on subsequent tasks were shown by subjects who attributed their original failure to *effort*, contrary to what would be expected from the original learned helplessness notion.

Perhaps the reader's first reaction to Roth and Kubal's and Hanusa and Schulz's findings is that they are simply flukes—improbable occurrences that interfere with clear theorizing one time in a million. Or perhaps there is something unique about those procedures that is responsible for the unique effect, a novelty that makes them noncomparable with the mainstream of helplessness investigations. Although such ponderings might make sense if these were isolated findings, it turns out that they are not unique at all. For instance, we need only think back to the previous chapter, on reactance, to find comparable effects. To name just one, Brehm et al. (1966), in their classic long-play-record study, found that subjects reacted to the elimination of a third-ranked record by raising their evaluation of it. To eliminate someone's choice alternative is to reduce the contingency between behavior and outcome; it is a kind of helplessness-inducing manipulation. In accordance with learned-helplessness theory, the subjects of Brehm et al. might have been expected to give up, to abandon interest in the third-ranked record. But they showed the opposite reaction, just as subjects have in other situations in which a behavior was blocked or partly blocked. Comparable effects have also been shown in other reactance research where the measures are more behavioral. All of this is to say that we now have to contend with a seeming contradiction: do reductions in control generate giving up, as Seligman would have it, or is the effect *increased* motivation to pursue what is difficult or impossible—in line with reactance theory?

One of the most sensible ways of coping with this kind of problem is to appeal to additional variables, known as "moderating" variables, which tell us the circumstances under which either of the processes might be found. We have already seen examples of these in several chapters. To name just two: (1) In the social facilitation chapter we saw that increments in drive produced both increases and decreases in responding. The moderating variable there was the relative dominance of the response. Dominant responses benefited from drive; subordinate responses suffered from drive. (2) In the cognitive dissonance chapter we saw that the amount of payment received for performing behaviors contrary to one's attitudes resulted in two opposing effects: sometimes attitudes would shift more in the direction of the behavior with high payment, and sometimes a greater shift would be found with low payment. The moderating variable here was choice: the degree of choice associated with performing the behavior determined which of these two effects would be found.

Wortman and Brehm (1975) have taken an analogous tack. They argue that learned helplessness theory and reactance theory share a common variable and that this variable can be used as a moderator variable to indicate when each theory is appropriate. The critical variable is the amount of helplessness training that the person has received. When a person expects to be able to control a set of outcomes, whether the receipt of a long-play record, success at a discrimination task, or termination of a noxious noise, reactance is generated when that control is challenged. The motivation to restore freedom should then result in an increased effort to obtain the record, solve the discrimination task, or eliminate the noxious noise. All this will occur with the first few challenges to freedom. However, there will come a point at which the person finally feels no more control. If the person's control is eliminated repeatedly, the reactance response will eventually cease, and the person will simply define the situation as one that cannot be directly controlled. At this point learned helplessness enters the picture, and response decrements are the end result.

Wortman and Brehm also propose that the importance of the person's endeavor is a second crucial moderating variable. Unimportant tasks that are not personally involving will not generate much reactance, nor will they result in helplessness. And it is instructive to note that the results of Roth and Kubal's experiment were obtained only when the Phase 1 task was characterized as highly personally involving. When the task was unimportant, the effects were not at all the same.

By bringing reactance theory into juxtaposition with learned helplessness theory, Wortman and Brehm have broadened the original area of inquiry. The "classic" helplessness phenomena were demonstrations that certain classes of very strong, repeated noncontingent experiences can result in response decrements. But these operationalizations of *noncontingency* did not exhaust the possibilities in the least. What about simple frustrations? What about decision alternatives that are eliminated? What about *threats* of noncontrol, rather than actual elimination of control? The class of situations not studied in the "classic" helplessness literature is probably the class of *weak inductions*, especially manipulations in which control is reduced only minimally or on only one occasion. This is a very important set of situations, both because such situations are common in everyday experience and because they have received considerable attention by researchers. And as it happens, it looks as though these were the situations in which "helplessness" inductions produced just the opposite of helplessness. If Wortman and Brehm are correct, it is only the stronger inductions of loss of control that should lead to learned helplessness as characterized by Seligman.

What, then, are the consequences of Wortman and Brehm's model? The obvious consequence is to broaden the researcher's perspective on the impact of altering someone's control. Their two-stage model points to great classes of settings that were never considered in the helplessness literature, perhaps because certain paradigms were settled upon early in the study of learned helplessness. This means that adopting Wortman and Brehm's model entails much more than confronting subjects with noxious stimulation or difficult tasks. Their model implies the study of reduction in control or *threat* of control reduction over a broad spectrum of situations.

ANOTHER PROBLEM FOR THE THEORY: EGOTISM

In Chapter 14, on achievement motivation, we noted a remarkable phenomenon associated with people who are highly anxious about failure:
they do not seem upset by tasks on which the chances of success are slim,
and more concretely, they choose such tasks when given a chance and are
also more persistent on these tasks.

Although our focus in that chapter was on stable differences in concern about failure, similar results should be obtained for people who are
threatened with failure experimentally. An illustration of this point is
found in a recent experiment by Frankel and Snyder (1978). Subjects
were asked to solve discrimination problems, which turned out to be either unsolvable (helplessness training) or else solvable. During the second
phase all subjects were asked to solve a series of anagrams (for example,
KMAE = MAKE, BNNAAA = BANANA). Although each subject worked
on the identical set of anagrams, this task was *described* to some subjects
as moderately difficult and to others as highly difficult.

Now to amplify the reasoning: Subjects who first encountered the
impossible discrimination task should have feared failure. Experiencing
failure is likely to induce failure anxiety, and by the arguments in the
achievement motivation chapter, such people should prefer either extremely easy or extremely difficult tasks. Since Frankel and Snyder offered no easy task in the second phase, the subjects who failed should
have been more motivated when the anagram task was described as extremely difficult, and, to be sure, they actually performed better at it than
when it was described as moderately difficult.

This result, just like the effects for high-failure-anxious people described in Chapter 14, is contrary to the initial statement of helplessness
theory. If anything, the combination of failure in Phase 1 and expectation
of failure in Phase 2 should have maximized helplessness effects and consequent giving up.

From Frankel and Snyder's viewpoint, helplessness effects in general are the outcome of failure-anxious subjects trying to avoid a further
instance of having to attribute failure to poor ability. Failure at a discrimination task presumably engenders failure anxiety. If the subsequent task,
whether anagrams or any other intellectual task, is viewed as moderately
difficult and solvable, there is a definite threat to the ego. If subjects try
hard and also fail at this, they have to conclude that their abilities are
seriously in question. However, if a person minimizes invested effort on

the second task—which means not persisting and not trying—failure probably cannot be attributed to ability. Instead, one can simply tell oneself that it was due to insufficient effort. Or, if the task is very difficult, failure has few implications for the subjects' ability level, since nearly everyone would be expected to fail. Therefore the effort-minimizing strategy is no longer necessary.

All of this is to say that Frankel and Snyder are reinterpreting helplessness effects as resulting from people's attempts to protect their egos. Rather than invest full effort in the Phase 2 task, which probably appears to be moderately difficult in the typical helplessness study, subjects who have failed in the earlier task prefer to hold back, allowing failure to be attributed to inadequate effort. This allows them to leave the situation with some feeling of ability intact.

What are the consequences of Frankel and Snyder's model? The reader should first note that this is a model about ego protection, in contrast to the original learned-helplessness theory. It assumes that people in "helplessness" situations experience ego threat and that they undertake a variety of mental calculations to avoid attributing failure to poor ability. This means that helplessness in animals, an early forté of helplessness researchers, cannot be studied in an ego-defense context.

Second, questions of generalization now arise. Seligman's original model allowed very broad generalization, and in fact Hiroto and Seligman (1975) even referred to the result of the experience of helplessness as the induction of a "trait." According to this position, uncontrollable outcomes such as electric shock, noise, or other noxious stimuli may lead to decrements in intellectual performance, motor performance, and a variety of other behaviors.

But questions arise when we talk about generalization in the context of Frankel and Snyder's ego-defensive model. One issue is the perceived level of difficulty of the test task. Only if the task were perceived as being moderately difficult would helplessness effects be expected, since tasks perceived as either very difficult or easy are not ego-threatening. More important, there are now stipulations about the nature of the initial helplessness-inducing task, for it must be ego-threatening before subjects will enter into the ego-preserving strategies proposed by Frankel and Snyder. When two intellectual problems are used (one for the helplessness-inducing phase and one for the test phase), the problem does not loom large. That is, if someone's ability to solve discrimination problems is threatened, the ego threat entailed should easily generalize to other cognitive tasks, such as anagrams. But what would uncontrollable noise have to do with later intellectual performance? The whole issue here hinges on whether ordinary aversive stimuli can have an ego-threatening or ability-questioning character. This remains an open issue for research.

At present, Frankel and Snyder's approach to "learned helplessness" phenomena calls for boundaries to be drawn. One is a limitation to humans and a second is a limitation to test tasks that are perceived to be of moderate difficulty. A third limitation is the necessity of being careful in making predictions in cases in which noncontingencies are created without directly involving subjects' abilities. A final boundary is constituted by the limitation of this approach to performance decrements. As we saw in the context of Wortman and Brehm's model, losing control can have a facilitative effect when the helplessness induction is weak, and, to be sure, Frankel and Snyder's analysis is not directed toward such possible facilitative effects of loss of control.

But there is another side to this issue of boundaries of the phenomenon. This model also opens up a whole new class of independent variables to be studied. The collected literature on learned helplessness shows a nearly exclusive use of failure or noxious stimulation as antecedents of lowered expectation for control. But within Frankel and Snyder's framework these kinds of stimuli are not necessary requirements for inducing helplessness, for the more general implication of their idea is that any ego-threatening situation suffices to bring about the effects. For instance, someone might complete a set of complex intellectual problems, with perfect contingency between behavior and outcome, but then discover that his performance was only in the 40th percentile. Such a person might very well be expected to show reduced responding on a subsequent and comparable task, for the reasons outlined by Frankel and Snyder. In short, by not trying on the second task, the person can avoid imputing potentially poor performance on that task to deficient ability. We find this implication of Frankel and Snyder's model extremely important, for it substantially broadens the class of situations leading to decrements in performance.

A further note: If one works within Frankel and Snyder's model, it is not exactly appropriate to refer to the phenomenon under study as "learned helplessness." If their explanation is correct, then there is nothing "helpless" about the person exhibiting performance decrements. To the contrary, such decrements simply reflect a calculated effort to rescue a threatened ego. Thus, to follow this model's implications is to stop studying "learned helplessness" per se: it is to study *some* of the phenomena originally included within the learned-helplessness model and to leave behind other of the phenomena attributable to that model. And most important, using the ego-threat model moves the field of study into new areas. All situations that threaten one's sense of integrity regarding abilities now become the target for investigation, and these include many of the phenomena not originally included within the classic learned-helplessness literature.

ONE FINAL DEVELOPMENT: LEARNED HELPLESSNESS AS AN ATTRIBUTIONAL PHENOMENON

If the reader is already familiar with the ideas basic to Weiner's attributional model of achievement motivation (Chapter 15), this last development in thinking about helplessness should be easy to assimilate. This recent revision, attributable to Abramson, Seligman, and Teasdale (1978), adopts the language of Weiner's model almost entirely and adds a bit more. The "bit more," necessary in order to account for the broad generalization effects, we will come to later. For a beginning it is important to understand why Abramson et al. (1978) proposed a revision in the original theory.

Internal versus External Helplessness

Abramson et al. find the original helplessness theory inadequate because it fails to distinguish between helplessness effects based on internal causes and those with outside causality. By now, given our several attribution chapters, this distinction should be familiar, and when applied to the helplessness context it looks like this: One route to bring forth helplessness is to confront someone with unsolvable problems but to characterize them as solvable. When no solution is forthcoming, it is likely that the attribution will be internal—to low ability. Abramson et al. call the helplessness that stems from this kind of attribution "personal" helplessness. Helplessness that comes from the outside, such as that stemming from repeated jackhammer blasts outside the classroom, is called "universal" helplessness. If the reader wants to avoid the difficulty of learning new terms, it is unnecessary to commit "personal" and "universal" to memory: *internal* and *external attribution* capture the idea adequately.

It might also be noted that the original theory generally predicted rather well, even though no explicit distinction was drawn between internal and external causality. One reason for making the distinction here is that we can differentiate two basic helplessness-inducing paradigms, one in which internal causality seems to dominate (failure experiences) and one in which external causality plays the greater role (noxious stimulation). The reason for this differentiation is that external and internal sources of helplessness may have quite distinguishable effects.

Generalization

Recall that the original theory (Seligman, 1975) suggested two determinants of generalization. One was the similarity between the helplessness-inducing setting and the test setting, and the second was whether the psychological distress associated with the helplessness induction was greater than the psychological distress associated with the test situation. Although each of these factors offers some testable implications, Abramson et al. now give attribution theory the task of describing generalization, and, to be sure, attribution theory is very specific in its analysis of generalization. For instance, if someone is rendered helpless through flunking all the coordination tests given to prospective automobile drivers, this person should then conclude that he has terrible motor coordination and therefore would expect to fail future tests of motor coordination. However, there would be little basis for assuming generalization to other types of tasks, such as a crossword puzzle, because the original attribution was to motor coordination, not to intellectual skill.

Weiner's Model Brought to Helplessness

The fourfold classification of attributions made in achievement settings is equally applicable to helplessness settings. (The reader may want to turn to Table 15–1, p. 209.) Abramson et al. propose that the lack of contingency between one's behavior and outcomes may be attributed to any of the four possible causes: inability, lack of effort, task difficulty, or bad luck. The particular attribution that is made is an important determinant of later performance deficits, as illustrated in the following example.

Imagine that someone is trapped in an elevator at night. All kinds of escape tactics are tried out, including pushing all the buttons, dialing the numbers listed next to the emergency telephone, screaming, and opening the trap door in the ceiling, but none of these results in being released. Finally the next morning the janitor discovers that someone is trapped in the elevator and arranges to have the authorities pry the doors open.

This sounds like a classic instance of helplessness training. By the time all these efforts are tried, the person should feel a genuine absence of contingency between all reasonable instrumental behaviors and the desired outcome. By the original theory, the person should now give up, show subsequent motivational deficits in further situations necessitating escape, suffer reduced cognitive functioning, and perhaps manifest depression. But things are not this simple for the new attributional model of Abramson et al. (1978).

First, we must concern ourselves with the kind of attribution the person is making for this perceived noncontingency. In this instance, let us assume that the attribution is external. The trapped person had the ability to push the buttons, to scream loudly enough to be heard throughout the building, and even to dismantle parts of the elevator in an effort to get free. Therefore the attribution is external—to the malfunctioning of the elevator and/or to the reality that no one is around to respond to the victim's pleas. The second issue in Table 15–1 is whether the attribution is stable or not—that is, whether the attribution consists in citing "bad luck" or "task difficulty" as the cause. In this instance we might want to say "bad luck," in that elevators are normally easy to operate. The attribution, then, is to something temporary—the person's bad luck in encountering a temporarily malfunctioning elevator.

What does this mean for behavior deficits in subsequent situations? From Weiner's model, this accidental elevator experience should have no implications for future performance: a single case of bad luck (an attribution to an unstable factor) holds no implications for one's future outcomes.

But let us change the example slightly. Suppose that the person knows that using the emergency telephone can get him out but that the crucial phone numbers are not posted systematically in the elevators. Further, suppose that he blames himself for not having remembered the phone numbers from an earlier occasion. In this case the attribution is internal, and it is to the stable trait of memory capacity or perhaps of learning quickly. In Weiner's terms, the attribution is to lack of ability, and there should therefore be implications for subsequent memory tasks. If the person takes part in a verbal learning experiment just after being released from the elevator, there could very well be a deficit. If the attribution for lack of contingency between behaviors and outcomes was to lack of memory ability, further situations calling for the same ability should be the ones in which performance will suffer.

It is apparent that the revised theory is highly specific. Following Weiner's reasoning closely, we can gain quite an exact idea of when and when not to expect deficits as a result of helplessness training. But note something important: What has happened to the original phenomena that the world found so exciting? That is, how does this attributional model explain the fact that noxious stimulation has an impact on later dealings with complex cognitive tasks?

Global versus Specific Attributions

The answer comes from Abramson et al. (1978) in the form of a variable that they add to the 2 × 2 scheme of Weiner. The variable refers to the generality of the person's attribution. In our previous examples we talked about attributions that were highly specific; for example, memory failure resulted in an attribution that had implications only for future memory tasks. However, in some instances people are inclined to make attributions of much broader scope. The person trapped in the elevator might have attributed the failure to get loose not just to bad memory, but perhaps to more general traits, such as low intelligence or a lack of important cognitive abilities. These overgeneralized attributions are called "global," which turns out to be a highly useful term. It is useful because it allows us to say that two events that are seemingly unrelated— such as failure to remember a phone number and subsequent typing performance—can have a mutual impact as long as the attribution for forgetting the phone numbers is a global one. And what determines whether the attribution is global? This Abramson et al. (1978) have not yet specified.

More needs to be said about the addition of the global-specific dimension to Weiner's fourfold table. Were we to confine ourselves to Weiner's table, we would conclude that the stable-unstable dimension is the factor that relates to generalization. Suppose that a golfer prepares to take a mighty swing at the ball and sneezes just as he cuts at the ball, and his iron chops deeply into the grass. Obviously the potential for generalization is quite limited, since a sneeze is not a stable part of a person's behavior. But imagine that a professional observes the same golfer play 18 holes, scoring 195, and points out a crucial flaw in the golfer's swing—this flaw owing to a war injury. In this case, the golfer can make a stable attribution to lack of potential and not expect much improvement.

What about the generalization of the deficit to other situations? Performance difficulties would be expected only in highly similar situations in which the war injury is perceived as relevant. For example, the golfer might expect that certain difficult croquet shots would also be affected. Thus, from Weiner's stability dimension the generalization issue seems quite clear.

At this point the reader might ask "If Weiner's stability dimension tells us so much about generalization, why do we bring the globality factor into our analyses?" Our golfer who makes a global attribution would go beyond the usual principles of attribution theory and would lower his expectations for performance in a variety of tasks that should be irrelevant to the war injury (kicking a football, typing, solving anagrams). But why would we think that the golfer would arrive at these expectations? Mainly because such phenomena have already been demonstrated in the laboratory (for example, by Hiroto & Seligman, 1975). Since normal attributional rules are insufficient to account for these phenomena, it is necessary to add another factor in order to account for them. This factor is "globality," whose determinants are (1) beyond the rules of attribution theory and (2) not stated in the Abramson et al. reformulation.

In summary, here are the bases of the revised theory. People in helplessness training attribute the noncontingencies to one of the four cells in Weiner's model. From these attributions we can say something very precise about the abilities or situations that will be affected subsequently by helplessness training, as in the elevator example. However, Weiner's system is too conservative to handle the more interesting helplessness effects, such as the opening study by Hiroto and Seligman, and so the "globality" concept becomes altogether crucial.

What New Comes Out of the Revised Model?

For one, Abramson et al. (1978) indicate that changes in self-esteem are an important consequence of attributions to ability. But aside from that, the new implications of the model exist only when we do without the globality dimension. If predictions can be made straight from Weiner's fourfold table, it is evident that the specificity of predictions is much improved over the original model. But is this specificity desired? As soon as we become interested in effects that entail a greater degree of generalization, the globality ingredient becomes necessary.

Do Attributions Really Mediate Helplessness Effects?

In the chapter on an attributional analysis of achievement motivation (Chapter 15), it was noted that attributions do not necessarily have clear causal connections to subsequent behaviors. As Weiner's analysis has been adopted in the revision by Abramson et al. of learned helplessness theory, an identical problem surfaces here. In the absence of evidence, it would be nice to think that an attribution to one's ability or to effort has a direct impact on the selection of subsequent behavior, but such a connection is rarely observable (Wortman & Dintzer, 1978). Accordingly, what basis is there for arguing that expectations for control stem from attributions, when in fact those attributions may not have any impact on behavior?

Further, one can raise the larger question of whether people invariably respond to helplessness-inducing situations by making attributions for their behavior. Hanusa and Schutz (1977) report a distinct absence of spontaneously mentioned attributions for failure among subjects in a helplessness paradigm, and the absence of attributions has also been documented by Diener and Dweck (1978). In the latter research two distinct kinds of subjects were run through a helplessness-inducing paradigm. One group, called "mastery-oriented," tended not to manifest helplessness symptoms when encountering uncontrollable situations. This group, remarkably enough, responded to failure by increasing the sophistication of their search for a solution to the cognitive problems and showed a profound lack of attributions of any kind for their previous failures. Another group of subjects, not mastery-oriented, showed the more characteristic response of blaming themselves for failure. In short, there seems serious reason to question whether attributions have anything to do with what we call helplessness effects.

SOME CONCLUSIONS ABOUT THE EVOLUTION OF A THEORY

In the course of describing the variety of approaches to helplessness and related phenomena, three questions have been implicit in our discussion. Here we will make these questions more explicit and summarize the evolution of helplessness theory at the same time.

1. *What happens when a theory encounters disconfirming evidence?* From our discussion we can find two answers to this question: Wortman and Brehm's (1975) solution is to introduce a separate psychological principle to account for those occasions on which reductions in control *increase* subsequent responding. With a low number of helplessness-training trials or a low-intensity helplessness training, reactance is likely to result. Then, after repeated or more intense experience with uncon-

trollable outcomes, the "giving up" phase ensues, and at this point the psychological processes discussed by Seligman enter. What determines which of these two processes dominates? According to Wortman and Brehm, a crucial factor is the amount of helplessness training. (And more generally, when contradictory evidence is dealt with in this way—by adopting a second psychological principle—it is usually possible to know when that second principle enters the picture on the basis of some particular variable.) A second solution to dealing with contradictory evidence comes from Frankel and Snyder (1978). Their approach resolves contradictions in findings not by invoking an extra variable, but instead by focusing on the nature of the dependent variable. They argue that a deficit in performance will occur to the degree that the test task is perceived as being moderately difficult but that no performance deficit will be found when the task is nearly impossible. Just one psychological process—ego threat—is postulated to account for these effects.

There may in general be a number of less theoretically satisfying ways to deal with contradictory evidence, such as finding fault with the methodology of experiments that produce unexpected results, but the two solutions provided above have proved to be the most useful steps in refining social psychological theories.

2. *Why are changes ever needed in a theory?* The first answer comes from the preceding discussion. Obviously, if a notion is repeatedly disconfirmed, it becomes important to understand the psychological basis of the disconfirmations, and this should lead to proposal of a new mechanism or at least modification of the preexisting one. The second answer is more general and probably more commonly in use: theories are altered (or replaced) when someone thinks of a new explanation for whatever phenomenon is being studied. A good case in point is Frankel and Snyder's account of helplessness effects. Using their notion, one sets aside the original psychological underpinnings of helplessness effects and views the "helpless" person as defending a threatened ego. Similarly, the attributional model of learned helplessness by Abramson et al. (1978) introduces a major modification in the psychological processes basic to helplessness. By this model, helpless people are those who have made certain kinds of attributions. But now comes the more important question: how do these theoretical modifications affect what is studied?

3. *How does the interpretation determine the domain?* This is the central issue. With the introduction of a new explanatory concept, whether reactance, ego threat, or attribution, the area of study shifts or enlarges in scope. Each new framework leads us in a variety of directions that never would have been implied by the original helplessness theory. For instance,

Wortman and Brehm's model does not limit itself to expectation of non-contingency, but more generally deals with threat to control. Similarly, with Frankel and Snyder's model, expectation of noncontingency is just one possible route to ego threat. Their scheme is a highly general one and makes predictions for all varieties of ego threat, including those that have to do with perception of noncontingency.

Not only does the domain for study move in different directions with these new interpretations, but the label for what we are studying changes at the same time. It makes no sense to refer to Wortman and Brehm's model as one of "learned helplessness," for many of the effects they describe represent improvements in performance. And it would seem much more reasonable to speak of Frankel and Snyder's theory as a theory of "ego defense," as the decrements in performance implied by their ideas are totally in the service of the threatened ego and do not reflect the "giving up" picture of the organism painted by Seligman's earlier approach. Finally, Seligman's own revision (Abramson et al.) introduces a decidedly attributional element into helplessness. In fact, given the adoption of Weiner's reasoning, it is hardly fair to characterize people as "helpless" within this attributional framework. Rather, the decremental responding in future situations is in many cases the outcome of logical thinking, in that it is based in calculations about one's own abilities or about the degree of insuperability of the environment. Thus the theory moves in the direction of answering the question "When do rational people lower their performance level?" and away from the simpler learned-expectancy process that was originally stipulated.

Where Do We Go from Here?

At this point readers should not throw up their hands in confusion, concluding that a simple phenomenon like helplessness seems to have too many explanations. Instead, one should think back to our original remarks in Chapter 1. The purpose of writing this book has been to offer a head start to those who want to figure out a problem on their own. Every problem can be approached in numerous ways, and if one's problem of interest is "Why do humans give up?," there are now at least three ways to approach the problem. Not all these approaches will lead to the same result, but at the same time, it is necessary to have these multiple approaches, given that multiple psychological processes can be identified in "helplessness" situations. The lesson is simple: it is a good idea to select a phenomenon of interest and to pursue an explanation that seems intuitively appealing, until that explanation is inadequate in scope or no longer applicable.

SUGGESTED READING

Abramson, L. Y., Seligman, M. E. P., & Teasdale, J. D. Learned helplessness in humans: Critique and reformulation. *Journal of Abnormal Psychology*, 1978, *87*, 49–74.

Glass, D. C., & Singer, J. E. *Urban stress: Experiments on noise and social stressors.* New York: Academic Press, 1972.

Maier, S. F., & Seligman, M. E. P. Learned helplessness: Theory and evidence. *Journal of Experimental Psychology: General*, 1976, *105*, 3–46.

Roth, S. A revised model of learned helplessness in humans. *Journal of Personality*, 1980, *48*, 103–133.

Seligman, M. E. P. *Helplessness: On depression, development, and death.* San Francisco: W. H. Freeman, 1975.

Wortman, C. B., & Brehm, J. W. Responses to uncontrollable outcomes: An integration of reactance theory and the learned helplessness model. In L. Berkowitz (Ed.), *Advances in experimental social psychology* (Vol. 8). New York: Academic Press, 1975.

Wortman, C. B., & Dintzer, L. Is an attributional analysis of the learned helplessness phenomenon viable? A critique of the Abramson-Seligman-Teasdale reformulation. *Journal of Abnormal Psychology*, 1978, *87*, 75–90.

APPENDIX

SOCIAL PSYCHOLOGICAL METHODS

THE chapters of this book discuss major current social psychological theories. Each of these theories will ultimately be evaluated on its ability to account for the results of existing research, to suggest ideas that can be tested in future research, and to predict correctly the outcome of that research. The purpose of this final chapter is to describe several research approaches that attempt to answer questions raised by theoretical statements and to draw out some of the methodological fine points in experiments summarized in the chapters. Designing research in social psychology is an art; each method has its own advantages and disadvantages.

HYPOTHESES AND VARIABLES

Research that attempts to investigate ideas raised by a theory is called hypothesis-testing research. On the basis of the theory, the researcher forms a hypothesis, which is a scientific statement of a relation between two or more variables. The reader has seen illustrations of hypotheses throughout the book. We will select one here to show how the hypothesis is carried from its formulation through the appropriate methodology.

The central idea in our chapter on social comparison was that humans have a need to evaluate their opinions and abilities and that this is done through comparison with others. Schachter (1959) suggested an interesting extension of this idea, proposing that people may also have a need to evaluate their emotional states. For instance, if a person suddenly feels exuberant for no apparent reason, there should be a desire to evaluate this feeling—to find out what it means, where it came from, and whether it is appropriate. Similarly, when placed in a threatening situation, people often develop feelings of fear, and by Schachter's reasoning there should then be a need to evaluate these feelings through comparison with others.

This reasoning led Schachter to propose an interesting hypothesis: people who feel fearful in the face of apparent danger will not want to be alone, but will seek out others in order to evaluate the appropriateness of their fear. More concretely, Schachter hypothesized that the need for affiliation would become stronger as the level of fear increased. Note that the hypothesis has two components, termed the independent variable and the dependent variable. The independent variable is the antecedent variable—degree of fear in this case. The researcher is interested in knowing the effects of this variable. The dependent variable is the consequent variable—need for affiliation. This is the variable that the hypothesis predicts will be affected by changes in the independent variable.

The experimental procedure used to investigate this hypothesis is a famous one in social psychology. The subjects were greeted by a certain Dr. Gregor Zilstein, who introduced himself as a member of the Medical School's Departments of Neurology and Psychiatry. Dr. Z. was wearing horn-rimmed glasses, was dressed in a laboratory coat, and allowed his stethoscope to dribble from his pocket.*

---

*Curiously, the details of this experiment constitute one of the best known folktales in social psychology. For example, a substitution of "hang from his pocket" or "drip from his pocket" for the original "dribble from his pocket" would immediately be spotted as fraudulent by anyone with a minimal sense of what is correct in social psychology.

Now comes the manipulation of the independent variable, level of fear. In the high-fear condition, the highly credible Dr. Z. pointed to a sophisticated-looking shock machine and explained to the subjects that they would be attached to the machine and would receive a series of very painful electric shocks while a number of physiological measures were taken. Since threat of electric shock is a compelling means of instigating fear, this procedure should have had the desired effect of creating a high level of fear. In contrast, other subjects, in the low-fear condition, were told that the shocks were of such low intensity that they would barely be able to feel them, and, of course, these shocks would be totally painless. The purpose of these instructions was to create a relatively low level of fear in this second group of subjects. It is also important to note that subjects were assigned randomly to one of the two conditions.

Next comes the measurement of the dependent variable—the outcome of the fear manipulation, which in this case was subjects' need to affiliate. To create a suitable context for this measure, subjects were told that there would be a 10-minute delay before the equipment was set up. Zilstein went to some effort to explain that the subject could, if she wished, wait alone in a room. Alternatively, she could wait together with some of the other subjects present. About five to eight subjects were present at each session, and so each of these had to be asked whether she would like to wait with the others who were present. In order to record subjects' preferences in a systematic way, the experimenter gave them a sheet on which they could check one of the following:

_____I prefer being alone.
_____I prefer being with others.
_____I really don't care.

In summary, the independent variable here was the fear level—high versus low—and the dependent variable was subjects' relative preference for waiting alone or with others.

This process of specifying the independent and dependent variables may be carried one step further. Both the independent and dependent variables may be identified at the conceptual (theoretical) and the operational levels. In our example of fear leading to affiliation, fear is the conceptual independent, or antecedent, variable. Note that fear is an abstract concept that must be implemented in some manner. The specific method used to implement this concept is the operational independent variable. In the present case the operational independent variable is defined in terms of the danger (threat of shock) implied by Dr. Zilstein's opening remarks.

Besides the procedure Schachter used to vary fear, one could imagine other operational definitions of this independent variable. For instance, some subjects might be shown an especially frightening horror movie, while others would see a Walt Disney film. Or some military recruits could be informed that they would be coming under heavy rifle fire during the next phase of their training, while others would expect only to march under conditions of dense fog. Finally, another alternative, which would require no experimental manipulation, would be to find subjects who are already highly anxious or afraid and designate them as the high-fear group. One would then hypothesize that these subjects would show more affiliation than people who are not so anxious.

In parallel fashion, the conceptual dependent variable (need to affiliate) may also be operationally defined in several ways. One of these was the elegant method chosen by Schachter, just described. Another would have been more on the level of overt behavior. For instance, Zilstein could have sent the group of six or so subjects into a laboratory complex of numerous small cubicles and then observed the resulting social structure. At one extreme, each of the six subjects might have taken a separate cubicle, and at the other extreme all six could have crowded into one room. Or finally, subjects could have been sent into a large room and the experimenter could have noted how far apart they sat. If subjects huddled together into one mass, this would likely represent high affiliation, whereas if they spaced themselves out carefully, there would be no reason to impute a high need for affiliation.

In Figure A-1 the relations among variables are diagramed. The upper portion of the figure depicts the hypothesis. On the left is the conceptual independent variable, and on the right is the conceptual dependent variable. It is important to note that the conceptual variables are abstract, in the sense of not being tied to any particular tangible events. The lower half of the figure depicts the operational variables. Keep in mind that "threat of shock" is just one of the many possible ways to operationalize the conceptual variable "fear." And on the dependent-variable side, the subject's check mark on the affiliation questionnaire is just one of numerous possible methods by which we can operationalize the conceptual variable "need to affiliate."

An additional type of variable in research is the *nuisance variable*, which interferes with investigation of the hypothesis. Nuisance variables are of two types: individual differences and confoundings.

Why might individual differences be a problem? Suppose that in the experiment just described, instead of being randomly assigned to conditions, subjects were assigned to conditions on some other basis, such as whether they arrived for their appointment early or late. Or suppose that, just by accident, it turned out that most of the subjects in the high-fear

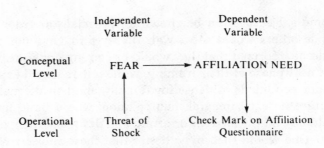

Figure A-1.   Conceptual and operational variables.

condition were first-born among their siblings, whereas subjects in the low-fear condition tended to be the youngest children in their families. A clever critic might then explain the results by noting that first-born people are generally more affiliative when they are afraid. Indeed, Schachter (1959) and Sampson (1965) have reported evidence for this proposition in several contexts. Thus nonrandom assignment in general opens up the possibility that the conditions differ in all kinds of ways with respect to preexisting individual differences. It would be no surprise if nonrandomness also led to differences between conditions in height, age, wealth, or even race of subjects. And to the extent that one of these individual differences leads to a potential alternative explanation, the investigator loses the capacity to conclude something about the theory.

Experimental *confoundings* are also sources of alternative explanations but have to do with imperfect experimental procedures rather than individual differences existing preexperimentally. Suppose that Dr. Zilstein had inadvertently, but systematically, referred to the subjects as a *group* when giving the high-fear instructions. He might have said "The *six of you* will undergo a series of physiological measures, and *all* of you should know that the accompanying electric shocks will really hurt." In contrast, suppose he always referred to the subjects as "individuals" in the low-fear condition. By delivering the instructions in this way he might unknowingly have created a group feeling in the high-fear condition, which would be a good explanation for these subjects' subsequent desire to affiliate. Of course one could still try to account for the results by citing fear, but the important point is that the confounding—Zilstein's group-oriented delivery in the high-fear condition only—would provide another perfectly good explanation. (We should hasten to add that there is in fact no reason to think that there was such a confounding in Schachter's experiment.)

The solution to the issue of experimental confoundings is clear. The researcher needs to arrange the experiment so that nothing differs between experimental conditions except the conceptual independent variable that is central to the experiment.

CONTROLLED EXPERIMENTS AND CORRELATIONAL STUDIES

Two general methods are used in social psychology to investigate hypotheses. These are controlled experiments and correlational studies.

Controlled Experiments

In a controlled experiment, each subject must have an equal chance of being assigned to any of the treatment conditions. As an example, consider the procedure often used in the investigations of attraction described in Chapter 3. Recall that many of these experiments investigated the hypothesis that the more similar two persons are, the more they will like each other. Similarity to the other was varied by giving subjects differential information about their agreement with another, where agreement had to do with various attitude issues. The dependent measure was liking for that other person. Now, suppose the experimenter wants to create three levels of the independent variable. Subjects are assigned to one of three conditions, such that they find the other agrees with them on 10%, 50%, or 90% of the attitude issues. One way of providing each subject with an equal chance of being in any of the treatment conditions would be to put three identical slips of paper labeled 10%, 50%, and 90% into a hat and, after a thorough mixing, draw out one of the slips. The subject would then be assigned to the treatment condition corresponding to that slip. The use of this or some similar random assignment procedure assures us that each subject has an equal chance of being assigned to any of the treatment conditions. This procedure is illustrated in the top half of Figure A-2. An alternative way for the experimenter to satisfy this definition of randomness is to assign every subject to *each* of the treatment conditions, as illustrated in the lower half of Figure A-2. This would mean that each subject is exposed to three different stimulus persons who vary in similarity of their attitudes to those of the subject. Note that it is impor-

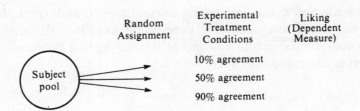

(a) A between-subjects experiment. Each subject is randomly assigned to one experimental treatment condition. Each subject sees only one stimulus person.

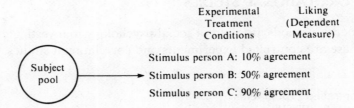

(b) A within-subjects experiment. Each subject participates in all experimental treatment conditions. Each subject sees all the stimulus persons.

Figure A-2.   Between and within designs.

tant for each subject to be exposed to the three stimulus persons in random order, in case the subjects' early experiences in the experiment have any effect on their later responses.

Correlational Studies

Correlational studies typically involve measuring a sample of people on two variables and then seeing how those variables are related. Note that the terms *independent variable* and *dependent variable* should not be used in this context. These terms imply a causal relation between variables, which, as we will see below, is not a legitimate interpretation of the results of a correlational study.

A characteristic example of the procedures of a correlational study and the type of conclusion that may be reached is provided by Eron (1963). He investigated the hypothesis that viewing violent TV programs is associated with high levels of aggression, using a big sample of young children as subjects. For each child he measured two variables: the level of violence in the child's favorite TV programs and the amount of aggression displayed in the school situation. He found that children who liked very violent TV programs tended to be aggressive, while children who liked nonviolent programs were much less aggressive.

The result obtained by Eron is described as a positive relationship: high values of variable 1 (TV violence) go with high values of variable 2 (aggression in school), and low values of variable 1 go with low values of variable 2. There are also negative, or inverse, relationships. In this case low values of variable 1 go with high values of variable 2, and high values of variable 1 go with low values of variable 2. For the TV violence-aggression relationship to be negative, viewing violent TV programs would be related to low levels of aggression in school, while viewing nonviolent TV programs would be related to high levels of aggression in school.

One can see the general approach taken in correlational studies. A sample of subjects is measured on two (or more) variables, and then the relationship (positive or negative) between those variables is calculated. Further, the investigator often tries to interpret the relationship in the sense of imputing causality to one of the variables (for example, concluding that TV violence causes juvenile delinquency). However, this can virtually never be done, as TV is not an independent variable in the sense described above. It is only the researcher's guess that TV, rather than other possible causes, has brought about aggressive behavior. The extent of these other possibilities is rather great, as we will now see.

The Advantages of Experimentation

Experiments have two distinct advantages over nonexperimental techniques. First, experiments immediately rule out individual-difference nuisance variables as a plausible explanation of the results. To clarify this point, reconsider the similarity-liking example and imagine that subjects had been assigned to treatment groups by the experimenter's drawing slips of paper as described above. With this procedure the experimenter can assume that the three treatment groups, on the average, are equal on all individual difference nuisance variables. One can expect that each of the treatment conditions will contain about the same number of males, blue-eyed people, geniuses, or neurotics. What this means is that in an experiment the researcher always knows what caused the results: it is clearly the operational independent variable (the manipulation), since the groups differ only in regard to their differential treatment by the experimenter.

In contrast, correlational studies are by nature ambiguous with regard to cause-and-effect relations. In the instance of a positive correlation between TV watching and children's aggression, it would be an interesting theoretical point if we could conclude that TV violence were the cause (Berkowitz, 1970; Parke, Berkowitz, Leyens, West, & Sebastian, 1977). But we cannot do this with any certainty on the basis of simple correlational results. For one, it might be that the children's aggression brings them to be interested in violent TV programs, and then our theoretical conclusion would be quite different than if the causal relation were from TV watching to aggression.

The problems do not stop with an analysis of the two primary variables under study. It may well be that some third variable is the causal factor behind each of the others. For instance, a child's parents might exhibit all kinds of aggression, carrying out furniture fights in front of the child and responding to every frustration with shouting and screaming. Further, the parents may really like aggressive TV programs, meaning that the TV set is always tuned to violent programs. Finally, children may be simply imitating their parents' aggressive behavior, so that they come across as highly aggressive when assessed by the psychologist. The conclusion in this case should be as follows: children from an aggressive home would be exposed to violent TV frequently and would also be high in aggressive behavior (owing to imitating the parents' behavior), but TV would have played no direct role in development of the child's aggressiveness. By this reasoning it would have made no difference if the family had been without television, and TV watching should therefore not be singled out as the instigator of aggressive behavior.

Another illustration of the third-variable problem is found in Croxton and Cowden (1955), who document the strong inverse relation between the price of corn and the severity of hay-fever cases. That is, the higher the price of corn, the less severe the hay-fever cases will be that year. Does this mean that low corn prices cause severe hay fever? Perhaps low corn prices cause people to eat more hay-fever-generating corn. Alternatively, could it be that hay fever influences the price of corn? In this instance it makes more sense to look for a third variable that is probably responsible for each of the others. In this case one could blame favorable weather, which brings about hay-fever attacks through high pollen counts and which also affects corn prices through the overproduction of corn. Such third variables are often difficult to identify in naturalistic settings because the researcher is generally unaware of the myriad of variables related to the central variables of interest.

INTERPRETING EXPERIMENTAL OUTCOMES

Whenever an experiment is conducted, a variety of outcomes is possible. The results of the experiment may support the hypothesis, support the hypothesis only under a restricted set of conditions, or provide no support at all. We will examine two of the more common experimental outcomes: (1) no difference between experimental treatment conditions and (2) differences between conditions consistent with hypotheses.

No Difference between Conditions

Suppose that Schachter had run his experiment without finding any differences in affiliation tendency as a function of fear. What would this outcome mean? Looking at Figure A-1, one can see that three links—represented by arrows—must be present for a relationship between the operational independent variable and the operational dependent variable to exist. (1) The operational independent variable (the manipulation) must lead to differences in the conceptual independent variable, (2) the operational dependent variable must accurately measure changes in the conceptual dependent variable, and (3) the hypothesis must be correct. If one or more of these links cannot be made, then no difference will be found between the treatment groups in the experiment. We will examine each of these links in turn.

Problems with the Independent Variable   The operational independent variable, or manipulation, must lead to differences in the conceptual independent variable. There may be a number of reasons why this would not come about in an experiment. Suppose, for example, that Schachter's subjects who heard the low-fear instructions became extremely fearful as soon as they heard the word *shock*. Had that happened, the high-fear instructions would have had little additional impact, as fear level would have already peaked. Or in the similarity-liking paradigm, it might have been that subjects were distracted just as they were supposed to read about the similarity or dissimilarity of the other. They would not have processed the information, and the conceptual variable of similarity would not have been manipulated.

Alternatively, the manipulation might have been too weak. Suppose, in the similarity-attraction paradigm, that the three others had been described as agreeing with the subject on 48%, 50%, and 52% of the attitudes, thereby creating three operational levels of agreement. These three levels of agreement might not be detectibly different to the subject, and hence the manipulation would obviously have been too weak.

Information about the researcher's success in establishing the link between the manipulation and the conceptual independent variable can be obtained by using a check on the manipulation. A manipulation check attempts to assess whether the desired changes in the conceptual independent variable were successfully created. In the similarity-attraction example, the experimenter might ask the subjects "How similar is the other person to you?" If subjects in the three conditions reported the same degree of similarity, this would suggest that the link between manipulation and conceptual independent variable had not been established. This failure of linkage would make it unlikely that differences would be obtained on the operational dependent variable as a function of the manipulation.

In his fear-affiliation experiment, Schachter took the possibility of a manipulation failure into account and took a check on the manipulation of fear immediately after the instructions from Dr. Zilstein. Subjects responded to the question "How do you feel about being shocked?" by answering on a five-point scale with extreme points labeled "I dislike the idea very much" to "I enjoy the idea very much." Needless to say, he found a dramatic difference between conditions.

Problems with the Dependent Variable   The operational dependent variable must accurately measure changes in the conceptual dependent variable. In some areas of psychology standardized methods of measuring conceptual dependent variables have been developed. For example, IQ tests are widely accepted as measures of general intelligence. However, in social psychology most methods of measurement have not been developed and standardized to a high degree. Consequently, social psychological measures should always be evaluated on two basic criteria: reliability and validity.

Reliability is the dependability of the measure; it is the extent to which the measure consistently produces the same results when applied under the same conditions.

Suppose that someone interested in Schachter's hypothesis wanted to test the derivation that subjects who are afraid will talk more to someone with whom they are waiting. One method of assessing amount of talking would be to have a single observer listen two times to a tape recording of a number of subjects speaking and count the words each time. The reliability of the count could be assessed by comparing the number of words obtained on the two occasions. In case the reader thinks it is silly to worry about the problem of consistency, it turns out that it is not a simple matter to count words in a conversation. Should the observer who hears "I dunno" from one speaker and "I do not know" from a second speaker count these utterances as containing two, three, or four words? Further problems develop when the count runs into the thousands and when the observer is prone to become bored or fatigued. If an observer listened to the same tape twice, scoring a word count of 783 the first time and 599 the second time, one would be inclined to say that the scoring was unreliable.

Another method of checking reliability would be to have two observers independently count the words and then to compare the records of these observers. Using either of these methods, if the two observational records are in close agreement, the measure is considered reliable. The less reliable the measure, the harder it is to produce differences on that measure between the experimental treatment conditions.

Validity refers to the effectiveness of the operational dependent variable in measuring the concept it is supposed to measure. That is, validity deals with whether the measure assesses the conceptual dependent variable. Validity is a complex issue, but two of the criteria for a valid measure may be outlined. First, if a well-established measure of the concept exists, any new measure should show a high level of agreement with the established measure. The standard measure in the similarity-attraction paradigm is an established questionnaire method of measuring liking. If someone wanted to be original, it might be suggested that the amount of eye contact initiated with the other person would also reflect liking. However, the eye contact measure would be judged as valid only to the degree that it corresponded to the questionnaire measure. Subjects who show a fondness for someone on the established questionnaire measure should also initiate more eye contact.

Second, one might call a measure valid if it successfully reflects the kinds of effects predicted by the theory. The theories and research selected for this book generally deal with measures shown repeatedly to have validity, and for this reason it is not easy for us to find an example of an invalid measure here.

Nonetheless, there are instances of less-than-valid measures in research we have not mentioned. A common paradigm in psychology for the study of aggression entails the subject's being able to deliver electric shocks to a victim (Berkowitz, 1962; Buss, 1961). As a function of frustration, provocation, or some other independent variable, researchers predict more aggression, defined in terms of greater shocking, in one condition than in another. But what does "greater shocking" mean—the speed of pressing the shock button, the force behind the button push, the length of time the button is held down, or the shock intensity delivered to the victim? We might think that any one of these would work as an empirical definition of the conceptual variable "aggression." But as it turns out, intensity of the shock delivered is the only measure that has worked with regularity over a wide range of experiments. That is, it is the only measure that seems to reflect the theoretical processes. The hypotheses cannot be confirmed with the other measures, nor do the other measures correlate consistently with shock intensity. One cannot really say that there are any compelling reasons for this fact, but the conclusion is simple: out of four presumably reasonable indicators of aggression, only one seems to be valid.

Problems with the Hypothesis   The final possibility is that the hypothesis may be false. This would mean that there is no causal link between the conceptual independent and conceptual dependent variables. But before a hypothesis is rejected, the researcher should question whether different levels of the conceptual independent variable were created and whether a reliable and valid measure of the conceptual dependent variable was used. Because of these questions researchers will often conduct several experiments, using different manipulations and dependent measures, before they lose confidence in a hypothesis.

Summary   The failure to obtain differences between experimental treatment conditions leads the researcher to examine the three links of the causal chain. Did the manipulation have the intended effect on the conceptual independent variable? Was the dependent variable reliable and valid? And finally, is the hypothesis correct?

Differences between the Conditions Consistent with the Hypothesis

The second outcome is that differences consistent with the hypothesis are found between the experimental treatment conditions. This is, of course, the desired outcome; it leads us to have increased confidence that our hypothesis is correct. At the same time, the researcher needs to consider other possible explanations of the results. We will discuss each of these possibilities in turn.

The first interpretation of a successful experimental outcome is that the researcher has successfully established the three links between the manipulation and dependent measure. The manipulation was successful in creating the intended differences in the conceptual independent variable, the hypothesis is correct, and the dependent measure was a reliable and valid measure of the conceptual dependent variable. If a check on the manipulation has been included, it can provide further support for this interpretation if it shows that the desired levels of the conceptual independent variable have been created.

However, many experiments are open to a second interpretation, that the manipulation had unintended effects that led to changes in a second conceptual independent variable. This problem, noted earlier, is termed "confounding." As an illustration of how this problem can be resolved, consider the following example.

Assume that each subject in a similarity-attraction experiment is exposed to three other persons: A, who agrees with the subject on 90% of the attitudes, B, who agrees on 50%, and C, who agrees on 10%. Also assume that by some accident in the experimental procedure A is the most physically attractive, B is intermediate in attractiveness, and C is least attractive. If the results conform to the hypothesis, there are two possible explanations of the results. (1) The greater the similarity of the subject to the other, the more the subject will like the other. (2) The higher the other's level of physical attractiveness, the more the subject will like the other.

How can the researcher decide which of the two explanations is correct? Within a single experiment some information can be obtained by examining checks on the manipulation and checks for confounding. Checks for confounding attempt to assess whether changes have occurred as a result of the manipulation in conceptual independent variables besides the one of interest. In the present example, a check for confounding would ask subjects "How physically attractive are persons A, B, and C?" Subjects' answers to this question would provide information about the relative level of perceived attractiveness of the three others.

How is this kind of information used to try to decide between the two possible explanations? If the manipulation check shows the desired pattern of differences while the check for confounding does not show differences as a function of the experimental treatment conditions, this suggests that the hypothesis under investigation is correct.

The information provided by manipulation checks and checks for confounding should be viewed cautiously. Sometimes subjects are unable to provide useful information about the conceptual independent variable because it is outside their awareness. One illustration of this problem comes from Slovic (1969), who reports that the factors stockbrokers reported using in their decisions were not the same as the factors they actually used, as determined from an analysis of their actual judgments. If an experimenter relied on these subjects' reports on the relative importance of each of the factors to rule out alternative hypotheses, the end result might be highly misleading.

Another difficulty in using these checks is that asking the subjects about the conceptual independent variable may cause them to focus on the variable and thus change its level. Suppose that nasty insults are used to anger subjects, and we then ask them how angry they are. If subjects realize they are angry and try to calm down and act in a more restrained manner, we have changed the level of the conceptual independent variable and have probably affected the outcome of the experiment. This is not meant to imply that manipulation checks necessarily must precede the dependent measure (as in Schachter's fear-affiliation experiment), but often one stands to gain a more accurate picture of the psychological processes created by collecting the manipulation check just after the independent variable is manipulated. In any case, one can easily see that there are several ambiguities associated with manipulation checks, and for this reason checks are best viewed as simply providing supplemental information, rather than crucial information on which the entire success of an experiment hinges.

There is a better method the researcher can use to distinguish between alternative interpretations of results. One can conduct a second experiment testing the same hypothesis but using a different manipulation of the conceptual independent variable. This is called a *conceptual replication*. A manipulation of the conceptual independent variable is devised that rules out the alternative explanation of the first experiment. Recall the previous example, in which both the similarity and physical attractiveness of the others provided potential accounts of the results. Instead of using three different stimulus persons, the researcher could have just one person play the role of the other. Depending on which conditions were being run, this person could be described as agreeing with the subject on 10%, 50%, or 90% of the attitudes. Using only one person would eliminate any possibility that subjects would perceive differences in the physical attractiveness of the other. If the same results were obtained as previously, the results of the conceptual replication would provide strong support for the similarity-liking hypothesis.

In summary, when there are alternative interpretations of the results of an experiment, two procedures may be used to help the researcher determine which is the correct interpretation. First, within a single experiment, the researcher may examine the checks on the manipulation and checks for confounding. Such checks will perhaps indicate which interpretation is more plausible. Second, the researcher may conduct a conceptual replication of the original experiment to eliminate the alternative explanation. This latter method provides especially good evidence concerning the viability of the researcher's original hypothesis.

EXPERIMENTER BIAS AND SUBJECT MOTIVATIONS

In evaluating research in social psychology, two types of confoundings are frequently discussed. These are experimenter bias and subject motivations. Experimenter bias is unintentional influence of the outcome of the experiment by the experimenter. Subject motivations are subjects' desires to alter their responses in some manner because of the unique nature of the experimental situation. These problems derive from the fact that in psychology both the experimenter and the subject are human beings who are capable of transmitting and receiving subtle cues from each other. Subjects can alter their responses in accordance with these cues, which are an unwanted part of the experimental manipulation.

Experimenter Bias

The problem of experimenter bias was first demonstrated by Rosenthal (1963, 1966). In an early investigation (Rosenthal & Fode, 1963), experimenters were given a set of pictures of people's faces. Some of the experimenters were given the expectation that subjects would rate the people as successful; other experimenters were given the expectation that subjects would rate the people as failures. Unknown to the experimenters, the pictures had previously been rated as neutral (neither successful nor unsuccessful) by a large group of undergraduates. Each of the experimenters then ran several subjects and recorded each subject's ratings of the degree of success being experienced by the person in the picture. The results showed that the subjects of the experimenters who expected ratings of success indeed rated the people as more successful than the subjects of the experimenters who expected ratings of failure. Thus, the experimenters communicated their expectations to the subjects in some manner affecting the results of the experiment.

Lest this seem like a magical process, it is likely that the experimenter's expectation was communicated through nonverbal channels (for example, facial expressions, posture) or paraverbal ones (for example, pauses in speech, tone of voice). The experimenter may have smiled unintentionally each time the subject gave a response consistent with the expectation and frowned each time the subject gave a response inconsistent with the expectation. These nonverbal cues could effectively, though unintentionally, communicate the experimenter's expectation to the subject.

How serious a problem is experimenter bias in social psychological research? This is a difficult question to answer, since research that has demonstrated experimenter bias effects has typically used procedures that are not entirely representative of those used in social psychological research. Much of the research in this area has used experimenters with little prior training in conducting experiments. In addition, each experimenter in the experimenter bias research generally runs only one treatment condition of the experiment, whereas in most social psychological research each experimenter runs all treatment conditions. Because these differences would probably tend to maximize the chances of showing an effect of experimenter bias, it is likely that experimenter bias research overestimates the extent of this problem in well-conducted experiments in social psychology.

Moreover, a number of control procedures have been devised that eliminate the problem of experimenter bias. For example, the experimenter can sometimes be kept blind to the hypothesis. If experimenters are unaware of the hypothesis, the most damage they can do is to communicate their suspicions about the nature of the hypothesis to subjects. Or the instructions can be automated so that experimenters do not have the opportunity to communicate their expectations to subjects; tape-recorded and written instructions are examples of this procedure. Finally, experimenters can be kept blind to the subject's treatment condition: the manipulation can be embedded in written instructions, or a second experimenter can manipulate the independent variable while the first experimenter is not present. Then the experimenters would not know in what direction to influence the subject even if they wanted to, since it would be difficult to discern the subject's treatment condition. The use of one or more of these control procedures effectively eliminates any chance that experimenter bias will influence the results of the experiment.

Subject Motivations

The problem of subject motivations has many similarities to that of experimenter bias. A major distinction between the two is in the source of the unintentional cues that the subjects use to guide their behavior: in experimenter bias the experimenter transmits expectancies to the subject, whereas in subject motivations the cues are more general aspects of the research situation. Indeed, subject motivations are just as much of a problem in correlational studies as they are in controlled experiments.

Three types of subject motivations have been of special interest to social psychologists. (1) One of these is called *evaluation apprehension* (Rosenberg, 1965), arising from the belief of subjects that they are being evaluated by the psychologist-experimenter in some manner. Consequently, subjects attempt to alter their responses in a socially desirable manner that will give the experimenter a favorable impression. If subjects in an aggression experiment believed that the experimenter was evaluating them, they might behave less aggressively in order to look good to the experimenter. (2) Another problem is *demand characteristics* (Orne, 1962), in which the subject discerns the hypothesis that the experimenter is attempting to test. The subject then tries to act in such a way as to confirm the experimenter's hypothesis. Returning to the case of similarity-liking research (Chapter 3), if demand characteristics were a problem, subjects would report that they liked the highly similar other best, not because of any real attraction to this person, but because they wanted to please the experimenter by confirming the hypothesis. (3) Third comes the problem of *negativism*, which again entails the subject's acting on a hypothesis that is imputed to the experimenter. In this case, however, the subject tries to disconfirm the hypothesis because of supposed negative feelings toward the experimenter or toward the research. In an experiment comparing the relative effectiveness of a well-written, highly believable communication and a poorly written communication filled with half-truths, negative subjects would be likely to follow the perplexing strategy of showing more attitude change when the communication is shoddy. Note, however, that since negativism implies that the hypothesis will be disconfirmed, it ceases to be a problem if results that confirm the hypothesis are obtained.

How serious is the problem of subject motivations? Some critics (for example, Silverman, 1976) have argued that the problem is widespread in social psychological research. But there are also reasons for thinking that subject motivations are not an integral part of every piece of research in social psychology. In order for these motivations to arise, there are two prerequisites: First, the motivation to act in some certain way must be aroused. With evaluation apprehension, for instance, subjects must become concerned about the experimenter's evaluation and decide to present themselves in a positive manner. Second, subjects must perceive cues in the setting to be used as guides in altering their behavior to be consistent with the aroused motive. These cues also must differ across the treatment conditions for subject motivation to provide an alternative explanation of the results. Thus, for evaluation apprehension to provide an explanation for the results of an experiment, the cues specifying the socially desirable response in the situation must differ between the experimental treatment conditions. Finally, for subject motivations to be problematic, subjects must have control over the dependent measure—that is, they must be able to alter their responses consciously. Because of the many requirements that must be met before subject motivations can affect research findings, they are probably not a serious problem in well-designed social psychological research.

The problem of subject motivations stems from subjects' awareness that they are being studied and their discernment of the nature of the research and/or the experimenter's hypothesis. Therefore, the procedures that have been developed to cope with subject-motivations problems all attempt to interfere with one of these sources of subject motivations. One procedure is to conduct the experiment in such a manner that subjects are unaware that they are being studied. For example, field experiments often can be conducted without subjects' knowledge that they are participants. To cite one case, West, Whitney, and Schnedler (1975) varied the characteristics of a motorist needing assistance and recorded the time that elapsed before a person stopped to help. It is unlikely that the motorists observing the ostensibly stranded driver were aware that they were subjects in a social psychological experiment. Another procedure is to minimize the subject's knowledge of the nature of the research. Through the use of these methods, the chance that the subject will discern the true nature of the research or the hypothesis can be minimized. Finally, as previously noted, the experimenter can use dependent measures of which the subject is unaware. One might take periodic, unpublicized readings of subjects' electrical meters to assess the effectiveness of a communication advocating conservation of electricity. A related method is to use measures over which the subject has little, if any, control, such as heart rate or other physiological measures.

Our discussion is not meant to imply that the research reported in this book as exemplary material is free of bias, subject motivations, or confounds. With the tools just discussed in hand, the reader is invited to scrutinize this research, and in some cases it will become apparent that safeguards were not totally adequate. More important is the realization that these tools were not widely known 10–20 years before this writing and that the dates associated with the research will sometimes be a hint about the susceptibility of the research to alternative explanations or other inadequacies.

A NOTE ON THE ETHICS OF RESEARCH

Many of the procedures we have discussed raise ethical issues about the treatment of subjects in social psychological research. Unfortunately, some of the procedures that best rule out the problem of subject motivations and ensure the validity of experimental results are also those that raise the most serious questions about the rights and welfare of the subject.

Interest in ethical issues is not confined to social psychology; most professional organizations whose members conduct research with humans (for example, the American Medical Association, the American Sociological Association) have established ethical guidelines for the conduct of research. The American Psychological Association is no exception and has developed guidelines that apply to any psychological investigation. The actual research guidelines focus on such issues as keeping subjects anonymous; informing subjects, before the experiment, about what will happen; and not inflicting physical or psychological abuse on subjects.* Further, as of this writing, the greater part of research conducted in the United States is subject to additional examination by university, hospital, or other institutionally based review boards.

Social psychologists have been concerned about a number of these ethical issues. When subjects do not know that they are participants in the research, the problem of invasion of privacy arises. Subjects may engage in behaviors that they would prefer not be observed and recorded. A subject who sits together with another, supposedly waiting for an experiment

---

*The concern with establishing ethical codes for psychological research is not limited to North American psychologists. Among the various ethical codes to be found around the world are the following kinds of stipulations: (1) *Quality of research.* To take one instance, the code for the Federal Republic of Germany indicates that one should try to design research so as to minimize possible misleading interpretations of the results. (2) *Watching one's colleagues or students.* The code for Great Britain makes clear that it is the

to begin, would probably prefer not to have a discreet tape recording made of him telling racist jokes. To minimize this problem, social psychologists often attempt to get the informed consent of subjects before their participation in the research. Subjects' responses also should be recorded in such a way as to ensure confidentiality. Finally, when informed consent is not possible, the behaviors chosen for observation are generally public behaviors that could be viewed by anyone.

Another issue in many laboratory experiments is that subjects are misinformed about the nature of the experiment in order to eliminate subject motivations that interfere with the results. To alleviate this problem, researchers should employ only mild deceptions. In addition, at the completion of the experiment, each subject should be debriefed—fully informed about any misinformation presented in the experiment and the necessity for its use in the research. Every attempt should be made to restore subjects to their original psychological state and to restore equality to the experimenter-subject relationship.

Finally, in some experiments subjects are exposed to stressful manipulations that might possibly have long-term negative consequences for some subjects. Once again, experimenters should employ the least stressful manipulation that provides an adequate test of the hypothesis. There are probably research questions that cannot be investigated experimentally because the procedures required would pose too great a risk. But when stressful conditions are employed, the experimenter must at least attempt to return the subjects to their original psychological state—this being accomplished through debriefing. The more stressful the procedures, the longer and more elaborate should be the debriefing. Finally, experimenters who use stressful procedures are expected to provide long-term follow-ups to detect and correct any harmful consequences of the experiment. Such follow-ups have thus far failed to detect any negative consequences of participation in social psychological research (Holmes, 1976).

Ethical questions are always difficult for social psychologists, since one must balance the rights of subjects against the need for important and exacting research. At the same time, it must be remembered that

investigator's responsibility to ensure that research conducted by associates conforms to ethical regulations. (3) *Subject's or respondent's power over the researcher's data supply.* Holland gives subjects the explicit right to request that their data be deleted from the researcher's data file. According to this guide a subject could give responses with the knowledge that the responses will be filed away anonymously on a computer data bank and then return a year later to insist that these responses be taken off the data bank. (4) *Investigator's responsibility to report the results of the study to subjects.* The code for Sweden requires that investigators inform the subject of the outcome of the research, insofar as this is feasible.

ceasing research activity or conducting faulty and incomplete research as solutions to the problems cited above also raise ethical issues. If psychologists respond to ethical requirements by performing inadequate research, which brings ambiguous conclusions, then the time sacrificed by subjects is in vain. The best solution is to balance the requirements of a sound design with respect for the integrity of the subject.

SUGGESTED READING

Carlsmith, J. M., Ellsworth, P. C., & Aronson, E. *Methods of research in social psychology*. Reading, Mass.: Addison-Wesley, 1976.

Diener, E. & Crandall, R. *Ethics in social and behavioral research*. Chicago: University of Chicago Press, 1978.

Kruglanski, A. W. The human subject in the psychology experiment: Fact and artifact. In L. Berkowitz (Ed.), *Advances in experimental social psychology*, Vol. 8. New York: Academic Press, 1975.

Rosenthal, R. & Rosnov, R. L. *Artifact in behavioral research*. New York: Academic Press, 1969.

Selltiz, C. Wrightsman, L. S. & Cook, S. W. *Research methods in social relations*. New York: Holt, Rinehart, & Winston, 1976.

REFERENCES

Abelson, R. P. Modes of resolution of belief dilemmas. *Journal of Conflict Resolution*, 1959, *3*, 343–352.

Abelson, R. P., Aronson, E., McGuire, W. J., Newcomb, T. M., Rosenberg, M. J., & Tannenbaum, P. H. (Eds.), *Theories of cognitive consistency: A sourcebook.* Chicago: Rand McNally, 1968.

Abelson, R. P., & Rosenberg, M. J. Symbolic psycho-logic: A model of attitudinal cognition. *Behavioral Science*, 1958, *3*, 1–13.

Abramson, L. Y., Seligman, M. E. P., & Teasdale, J. D. Learned helplessness in humans: Critique and reformulation. *Journal of Abnormal Psychology*, 1978, *87*, 49–74.

Adams, J. S. Toward an understanding of inequity. *Journal of Abnormal and Social Psychology*, 1963, *67*, 422–436.

Adams, J. S. Inequity in social exchange. In L. Berkowitz (Ed.), *Advances in experimental social psychology* (Vol. 2). New York: Academic Press, 1965.

Adams, J. S., & Freedman, S. Equity theory revisited: Comments and annotated bibliography. In L. Berkowitz & E. Walster (Eds.), *Advances in experimental social psychology* (Vol. 9). New York: Academic Press, 1976.

Adams, J. S., & Rosenbaum, W. B. The relationship of worker productivity to cognitive dissonance about wage inequities. *Journal of Applied Psychology*, 1962, *46*, 161–164.

Allen, V. L. Effect of extraneous cognitive activity on dissonance reduction. *Psychological Reports*, 1965, *16*, 1145–1151.

Amabile, T. M., DeJong, W., & Lepper, M. R. Effects of externally imposed deadlines on subsequent intrinsic motivation. *Journal of Personality and Social Psychology*, 1976, *34*, 92–98.

Amsel, A. The role of frustrative nonreward in noncontinuous reward situations. *Psychological Bulletin*, 1958, *55*, 102–119.

Archer, R. L., Hormuth, S. E., & Berg, J. H. Self-disclosure and self-awareness. Paper presented at annual meeting of the American Psychological Association, New York, 1979.

Aronson, E. The theory of cognitive dissonance: A current perspective. In L. Berkowitz (Ed.), *Advances in experimental social psychology* (Vol. 4). New York: Academic Press, 1969.

Aronson, E., & Cope, V. My enemy's enemy is my friend. *Journal of Personality and Social Psychology*, 1968, *8*, 8–12.

Aronson, E., & Linder, D. Gain and loss of esteem as determinants of interpersonal attractiveness. *Journal of Experimental Social Psychology*, 1965, *1*, 156–171.

Ashour, A. S. The contingency model of leadership effectiveness: An evaluation. *Organizational Behavior and Human Performance*, 1973, *9*, 339–355.

Atkinson, J. W. Motivational determinants of risk-taking behavior. *Psychological Review*, 1957, *64*, 359–372.

Atkinson, J. W. *An introduction to motivation.* New York: Van Nostrand, 1964.

Atkinson, J. W. Motivation for achievement. In T. Blass (Ed.), *Personality variables in social behavior*. Hillsdale, N. J.: Erlbaum, 1977.

Atkinson, J. W., & Cartwright, D. Some neglected variables in contemporary conceptions of decision and performance. *Psychological Reports*, 1964, *14*, 575–590.

Atkinson, J. W., & Feather, N. T. (Eds.). *A theory of achievement motivation*. New York: Wiley, 1966.

Atkinson, J. W., & Litwin, G. H. Achievement motive and test anxiety conceived of as motive to approach success and to avoid failure. *Journal of Abnormal and Social Psychology*, 1960, *60*, 52–63.

Austin, W., & Walster, E. Reactions to confirmations and disconfirmations of expectancies of equity and inequity. *Journal of Personality and Social Psychology*, 1974, *30*, 208–216.

Averill, J. R., & Opton, E. M. Psychophysiological assessment: Rationale and problems. In P. McReynolds (Ed.), *Advances in psychological assessment* (Vol. 1). Palo Alto, Calif.: Science and Behavior Books, 1968.

Ax, A. F. The physiological differentiation between fear and anger in humans. *Psychosomatic Medicine*, 1953, *15*, 433–442.

Baker, K. Experimental analysis of third-party justice behavior. *Journal of Personality and Social Psychology*, 1974, *30*, 307–316.

Bandler, R. J., Madaras, G. R., & Bem, D. J. Self-observation as a source of pain perception. *Journal of Personality and Social Psychology*, 1968, *9*, 205–209.

Bandura, A. Influence of models' reinforcement contingencies on the acquisition of imitative responses. *Journal of Personality and Social Psychology*, 1965, *1*, 589–595. (a)

Bandura, A. Vicarious processes: A case of no-trial learning. In L. Berkowitz (Ed.), *Advances in experimental social psychology* (Vol. 2). New York: Academic Press, 1965. (b)

Bandura, A. *Social learning theory*. Morristown, N. J.: General Learning Press, 1971.

Bandura, A. *Social learning theory*. Englewood Cliffs, N. J.: Prentice-Hall, 1977.

Bandura, A., Grusec, J. E., & Menlove, F. L. Observational learning as a function of symbolization and incentive set. *Child Development*, 1966, *37*, 499–506.

Bandura, A., Grusec, J. E., & Menlove, F. L. Some social determinants of self-monitoring reinforcement systems. *Journal of Personality and Social Psychology*, 1967, *5*, 449–455.

Bandura, A., & Huston, A. C. Identification as a process of incidental learning. *Journal of Abnormal and Social Psychology*, 1961, *63*, 311–318.

Bandura, A., & Jeffery, R. W. Role of symbolic coding and rehearsal processes in observational learning. *Journal of Personality and Social Psychology*, 1973, *26*, 122–130.

Bandura, A., Jeffery, R. & Bachicha, D. L. Analysis of memory codes and cumulative rehearsal in observational learning. *Journal of Research in Personality*, 1974, *7*, 295–305.

Bandura, A., & Kupers, C. J. The transmission of patterns of self-reinforcement through modeling. *Journal of Abnormal and Social Psychology*, 1964, *69*, 1–9.

Barefoot, J. C., & Straub, R. B. Opportunity for information search and the effect of false heart-rate feedback. *Journal of Personality and Social Psychology*, 1971, *17*, 154–157.

Bar-Tal, D., & Frieze, I. H. Causal attributions and information seeking to explain success and failure. *Journal of Research in Personality*, 1976, *10*, 256–265.

Bem, D. J. An experimental analysis of self-persuasion. *Journal of Experimental Social Psychology*, 1965, *1*, 199–218.

Bem, D. J. Self-perception: An alternative interpretation of cognitive dissonance phenomena. *Psychological Review*, 1967, *74*, 183–200.

Bem, D. J. Attitudes as self-descriptions: Another look at the attitude-behavior link. In A. G. Greenwald, T. C. Brock, & T. M. Ostrom (Eds.), *Psychological foundations of attitudes*. New York: Academic Press, 1968.

Bem, D. J. Self-perception theory. In L. Berkowitz (Ed.), *Advances in experimental social psychology* (Vol. 6). New York: Academic Press, 1972.

Bem, D. J. Self-perception theory. In L. Berkowitz (Ed.), *Cognitive theories in social psychology*. New York: Academic Press, 1978.

Berkowitz, L. *Aggression: A social psychological analysis*. New York: McGraw-Hill, 1962.

Berkowitz, L. The contagion of violence: An S-R mediational analysis of some effects of observed aggression. In W. J. Arnold & M. M. Page (Eds.), *Nebraska Symposium on Motivation* (Vol. 18). Lincoln: University of Nebraska Press, 1970.

Berscheid, E., & Walster, E. When does a harmdoer compensate a victim? *Journal of Personality and Social Psychology*, 1967, *6*, 435–441.

Bradley, G. W. Self-serving biases in the attribution process: A reexamination of the fact or fiction question. *Journal of Personality and Social Psychology*, 1978, *36*, 56–71.

Brehm, J. W. Postdecision changes in the desirability of alternatives. *Journal of Abnormal and Social Psychology*, 1956, *52*, 384–389.

Brehm, J. W. Motivational effects of cognitive dissonance. In M. R. Jones (Ed.), *Nebraska Symposium on Motivation*. Lincoln: University of Nebraska Press, 1962.

Brehm, J. W. *A theory of psychological reactance*. New York: Academic Press, 1966.

Brehm, J. W. *Responses to loss of freedom: A theory of psychological reactance*. Morristown, N. J.: General Learning Press, 1972.

Brehm, J. W., & Cohen, A. R. *Explorations in cognitive dissonance*. New York: Wiley, 1962.

Brehm, J. W., & Mann, M. Effect of importance of freedom and attraction to group members on influence produced by group pressure. *Journal of Personality and Social Psychology*, 1975, *31*, 816–824.

Brehm, J. W., Stires, L. K., Sensenig, J., & Shaban, J. The attractiveness of an eliminated choice alternative. *Journal of Experimental Social Psychology*, 1966, *2*, 301–313.

Brehm, J. W., & Wicklund, R. A. Regret and dissonance reduction as a function of postdecision salience of dissonant information. *Journal of Personality and Social Psychology*, 1970, *14*, 1–7.

Brock, T. C. Cognitive restructuring and attitude change. *Journal of Abnormal and Social Psychology*, 1962, *64*, 264–271.

Brock, T. C., & Buss, A. H. Dissonance, aggression, and evaluation of pain. *Journal of Abnormal and Social Psychology*, 1962, *65*, 197–202.

Brown, R. *Social psychology*. New York: Free Press, 1965.

Buss, A. H. *The psychology of aggression*. New York: Wiley, 1961.

Byrne, D. Response to attitude similarity-dissimilarity as a function of affiliation need. *Journal of Personality*, 1962, *30*, 164–177.

Byrne, D. *The attraction paradigm*. New York: Academic Press, 1971.

Byrne, D., Baskett, G. D., & Hodges, L. Behavioral indicators of interpersonal attraction. *Journal of Applied Social Psychology*, 1971, *1*, 137–149.

Byrne, D., & Clore, G. L. A reinforcement model of evaluative responses. *Personality*, 1970, *1*, 103–128.

Byrne, D., Ervin, C. R., & Lamberth, J. Continuity between the experimental study of attraction and real-life computer dating. *Journal of Personality and Social Psychology*, 1970, *16*, 157–165.

Byrne, D., & Clore, G. L. A reinforcement model of evaluative responses. *Personality: An International Journal*, 1970, *1*, 103–128.

Campbell, J. P., Dunnette, M. D., Lawler, E. E., III, & Weick, K. E. *Managerial behavior, performance, and effectiveness*. New York: McGraw-Hill, 1970.

Cantor, J. R., Zillmann, D., & Bryant, J. Enhancement of experienced sexual arousal in response to erotic stimuli through misattribution of unrelated residual excitation. *Journal of Personality and Social Psychology*, 1975, *32*, 69–75.

Carlsmith, J. M., Ebbesen, E. B., Lepper, M. R., Zanna, M. P., Joncas, A. J., & Abelson, R. P. Dissonance reduction following forced attention to the dissonance. *Proceedings of the 77th Annual Convention of the American Psychological Association*, 1969, *4*, 321–322.

Carver, C. S. Physical aggression as a function of objective self-awareness and attitudes toward punishment. *Journal of Experimental Social Psychology*, 1975, *11*, 510–519.

Chapin, M., & Dyck, D. B. Persistence in children's reading behavior as a function of N length and attribution retraining. *Journal of Abnormal Psychology*, 1976, *85*, 511–515.

Chemers, M. M., & Rice, R. W. A theoretical and empirical examination of Fiedler's contingency model of leadership effectiveness. In J. G. Hunt & L. L. Larson (Eds.), *Contingency approaches to leadership*. Carbondale: Southern Illinois University Press, 1974.

Chemers, M. M., Rice, R. W., Sundstrom, E., & Butler, W. Leader esteem for the least preferred coworker score, training, and effectiveness: An experimental examination. *Journal of Personality and Social Psychology*, 1975, *31*, 401–409.

Chemers, M. M., & Skrzypek, G. J. An experimental test of the Contingency Model of leadership effectiveness. *Journal of Personality and Social Psychology*, 1972, *24*, 172–177.

Clore, G. L. Interpersonal attraction: An overview. In J. W. Thibaut, J. T. Spence, &

R. C. Carson (Eds.), *Contemporary topics in social psychology*. Morristown, N. J.: General Learning Press, 1976.

Clore, G. L., & Byrne, D. A reinforcement-affect model of attraction. In T. L. Huston (Ed.), *Foundations of interpersonal attraction*. New York: Academic Press, 1974.

Clore, G. L., & Gormly, J. B. Knowing, feeling, and liking: A psychophysical study of attraction. *Journal of Research in Personality*, 1974, *8*, 218–230.

Cohen, A. R. An experiment on small rewards for discrepant compliance and attitude change. In J. W. Brehm & A. R. Cohen, *Explorations in cognitive dissonance*. New York: Wiley, 1962.

Cottrell, N. B. Social facilitation. In C. G. McClintock (Ed.), *Experimental social psychology*. New York: Holt, Rinehart & Winston, 1972.

Cottrell, N. B., Wack, D. L., Sekerak, G. J., & Rittle, R. H. Social facilitation of dominant responses by the presence of an audience and the mere presence of others. *Journal of Personality and Social Psychology*, 1968, *9*, 245–250.

Covington, M. V., & Omelich, C. L. Are causal attributions causal? A path analysis of the cognitive model of achievement motivation. *Journal of Personality and Social Psychology*, 1979, *37*, 1487–1504.

Croxton, F. E., & Cowden, D. J. *Applied general statistics* (2nd ed.). Englewood Cliffs, N. J.: Prentice-Hall, 1955.

Csoka, L. S., & Fiedler, F. E. The effect of military training: A test of the contingency model. *Organizational Behavior and Human Performance*, 1972, *8*, 395–407.

Deaux, K. *The behavior of women and men*. Monterey, Calif.: Brooks/Cole, 1976.

de Charms, R., & Davé, P. N. Hope of success, fear of failure, subjective probability, and risk-taking behavior. *Journal of Personality and Social Psychology*, 1965, *1*, 558–568.

Deci, E. L. Effects of externally mediated rewards on intrinsic motivation. *Journal of Personality and Social Psychology*, 1971, *18*, 105–115.

Derlaga, V. J., & Chaikin, A. L. *Sharing intimacy: What we reveal to others and why*. Englewood Cliffs, N. J.: Prentice-Hall, 1975.

Diener, C. I., & Dweck, C. S. An analysis of learned helplessness: Continuous changes in performance, strategy, and achievement cognitions following failure. *Journal of Personality and Social Psychology*, 1978, *36*, 451–462.

Diener, E., & Wallbom, M. Effects of self-awareness on antinormative behavior. *Journal of Research in Personality*, 1976, *10*, 107–111.

Dienstbier, R. A., & Munter, P. O. Cheating as a function of the labeling of natural arousal. *Journal of Personality and Social Psychology*, 1971, *17*, 208–213.

Drachman, D., & Worchel, S. Misattribution of arousal as a means of dissonance reduction. *Sociometry*, 1976, *39*, 53–59.

Duval, S. Conformity on a visual task as a function of personal novelty on attitudinal dimensions and being reminded of the object status of self. *Journal of Experimental Social Psychology*, 1976, *12*, 87–98.

Duval, S., & Wicklund, R. A. *A theory of objective self awareness*. New York: Academic Press, 1972.

Elig, T. W., & Frieze, I. H. A multi-dimensional scheme for coding and interpreting perceived causality for success and failure events: The Coding Scheme of Perceived Causality (CSPC). JSAS: *Catalog of Selected Documents in Psychology*, 1975, *5*, 313.

Entwistle, D. R. To dispel fantasies about fantasy-based measures of achievement motivation. *Psychological Bulletin*, 1972, *77*, 377–391.

Eron, L. D. Relationship of TV viewing habits and aggressive behavior in children. *Journal of Abnormal and Social Psychology*, 1963, *67*, 193–196.

Escalona, S. K. The effect of success and failure upon the level of aspiration and behavior in manic-depressive psychoses. University of Iowa *Studies in Child Welfare*, 1940, *16*, 199–302.

Fazio, R. H., Zanna, M. P., & Cooper, J. Dissonance and self-perception: An integrative view of each theory's proper domain of application. *Journal of Experimental Social Psychology*, 1977, *13*, 464–479.

Feather, N. T. The study of persistence. *Psychological Bulletin*, 1962, 77, 377–391.

Feather, N. T. A structural balance approach to the analysis of communication effects. In L. Berkowitz (Ed.), *Advances in experimental social psychology* (Vol. 3). New York: Academic Press, 1967.

Festinger, L. A theoretical interpretation of shifts in level of aspiration. *Psychological Review*, 1942, *49*, 235–250.

Festinger, L. A theory of social comparison processes. *Human Relations*, 1954, 7, 117–140.

Festinger, L. *A theory of cognitive dissonance*. Stanford, Calif.: Stanford University Press, 1957.

Festinger, L. *Conflict, decision, and dissonance*. Stanford, Calif: Stanford University Press, 1964.

Festinger, L., & Carlsmith, J. M. Cognitive consequences of forced compliance. *Journal of Abnormal and Social Psychology*, 1959, *58*, 203–210.

Festinger, L., Gerard, H. B., Hymovitch, B., Kelley, H. H., & Raven, B. The influence process in the presence of extreme deviates. *Human Relations*, 1952, *5*, 327–346.

Fiedler, F. E. A note on leadership theory: The effect of social barriers between leaders and followers. *Sociometry*, 1957, *20*, 87–93.

Fiedler, F. E. A contingency model of leadership effectiveness. In L. Berkowitz (Ed.), *Advances in experimental social psychology* (Vol. 1). New York: Academic Press, 1964.

Fiedler, F. E. The effect of leadership and cultural heterogeneity on group performance: A test of the contingency model. *Journal of Experimental Social Psychology*, 1966, *2*, 237–264.

Fiedler, F. E. *A theory of leadership effectiveness*. New York: McGraw-Hill, 1967.

Fiedler, F. E. Recent developments in research on the contingency model. In L. Berkowitz (Ed.), *Cognitive theories in social psychology*. New York: Academic Press, 1978. (a)

Fiedler, F. E. The contingency model and the dynamics of the leadership process. In L. Berkowitz (Ed.), *Advances in experimental social psychology* (Vol. 11). New York: Academic Press, 1978. (b)

Fiedler, F. E., & Chemers, M. M. *Leadership and effective management.* Glenview, Ill.: Scott, Foresman, 1974.

Fiedler, F. E., Chemers, M. M., & Mahar, L. *Improving leadership effectiveness: The Leader Match concept.* New York: Wiley, 1976.

Fiedler, F. E., & Mahar, L. The effectiveness of contingency model training: A review of the validation of Leader Match. *Personnel Psychology,* in press.

Foa, U. G., Mitchell, T. R., & Fiedler, F. E. Differentiation matching. *Behavioral Science,* 1971, *16,* 130–142.

Frankel, A., & Snyder, M. L. Poor performance following unsolvable problems: Learned helplessness or egotism? *Journal of Personality and Social Psychology,* 1978, *36,* 1415–1423.

Frey, D. (Ed.). *Kognitive Theorien der Sozialpsychologie.* Bern: Huber, 1978.

Frey, D., Wicklund, R. A., & Scheier, M. F. *Die Theorie der objektiven Selbstaufmerksamkeit.* In D. Frey (Ed.), *Kognitive Theorien der Sozialpsychologie.* Bern: Huber, 1978.

Frieze, I. H. Causal attributions and information seeking to explain success and failure. *Journal of Research in Personality,* 1976, *10,* 293–305.

Frieze, I. H., & Weiner, B. Cue utilization and attributional judgments for success and failure. *Journal of Personality,* 1971, *39,* 591–606.

Fromkin, H. L., & Snyder, C. R. *The psychology of uniqueness.* New York: Plenum, 1980.

Fulbright, J. W. *The arrogance of power.* New York: Vintage, 1966.

Gelfand, D. M. The influence of self-esteem on rate of verbal conditioning and social matching behavior. *Journal of Abnormal and Social Psychology,* 1962, *65,* 259–265.

Gergen, K. J. *The psychology of behavior exchange.* Reading, Mass.: Addison-Wesley, 1969.

Gerst, M. S. Symbolic coding processes in observational learning. *Journal of Personality and Social Psychology,* 1971, *19,* 7–17.

Gibbon, J., Baldock, M. D., Locurto, C., Gold, L., & Terrace, H. S. Trial and intertrial duration in autoshaping. *Journal of Experimental Psychology: Animal Behavior Processes,* 1977, *3,* 264–284.

Gibbons, F. X. Sexual standards and reactions to pornography: Enhancing behavioral consistency through self-focused attention. *Journal of Personality and Social Psychology,* 1978, *36,* 976–987.

Glass, D. C. Changes in liking as a means of reducing cognitive discrepancies between self-esteem and aggression. *Journal of Personality,* 1964, *32,* 531–549.

Glass, D. C., & Singer, J. E. *Urban stress: Experiments on noise and social stressors.* New York: Academic Press, 1972.

Goethals, G. R., & Darley, J. M. Social comparison theory: An attributional approach. In J. M. Suls & R. L. Miller (Eds.), *Social comparison processes.* New York: Wiley, 1977.

Goldman, C. An examination of social facilitation. Unpublished manuscript, University of Michigan, 1967.

Goldsen, R. K., Rosenberg, M., Williams, R. M., & Suchman, E. A. *What college students think*. New York: Van Nostrand, 1960.

Goldstein, D., Fink, D., & Mettee, D. R. Cognition of arousal and actual arousal as determinants of emotion. *Journal of Personality and Social Psychology*, 1972, *21*, 41–51.

Golightly, C., & Byrne, D. Attitude statements as positive and negative reinforcements. *Science*, 1964, *146*, 798–799.

Götz-Marchand, B., Götz, J., & Irle, M. Preference of dissonance reduction modes as a function of their order, familiarity, and reversibility. *European Journal of Social Psychology*, 1974, *4*, 201–228.

Gouaux, C. Induced affective states and interpersonal attraction. *Journal of Personality and Social Psychology*, 1971, *20*, 37–43.

Grabitz, H.-J., & Gniech, G. *Die kognitiv-physiologische Theorie der Emotion von Schachter*. In D. Frey (Ed.), *Kognitive Theorien der Sozialpsychologie*. Bern: Huber, 1978.

Graen, G., Alvarez,K., Orris, J. B., & Martella, J. A. Contingency model of leadership effectiveness: Antecedent and evidential results. *Psychological Bulletin*, 1970, *74*, 285–296.

Green, D. Dissonance and self-perception analyses of "forced compliance": When two theories make competing predictions. *Journal of Personality and Social Psychology*, 1974, *29*, 819–828.

Greenberg, J., & Leventhal, G. S. Equity and the use of overreward to motivate performance. *Journal of Personality and Social Psychology*, 1976, *34*, 179–190.

Griffitt, W. Attitude similarity and attraction. In T. L. Huston (Ed.), *Foundations of interpersonal attraction*. New York: Academic Press, 1974.

Griffitt, W., & Guay, P. "Object" evaluation and conditioned affect. *Journal of Experimental Research in Personality*, 1969, *4*, 1–8.

Griffitt, W., & Veitch, R. Preacquaintance attitude similarity and attraction revisited: Ten days in a fall-out shelter. *Sociometry*, 1974, *37*, 163–173.

Gutman, G. M., & Knox, R. E. Balance, agreement, and attraction in pleasantness, tension, and consistency ratings of hypothetical social situations. *Journal of Personality and Social Psychology*, 1972, *24*, 351–357.

Haisch, J., & Frey, D. *Die Theorie sozialer Vergleichsprozesse*. In D. Frey (Ed.), *Kognitive Theorien der Sozialpsychologie*. Bern: Huber, 1978.

Hakmiller, K. Threat as a determinant of downward comparison. *Journal of Experimental Social Psychology*, 1966, Supplement 1, 32–39.

Hamilton, J. O. Motivation and risk taking behavior: A test of Atkinson's theory. *Journal of Personality and Social Psychology*, 1974, *29*, 856–874.

Hanson, L. R., & Blechman, E. The labeling process during sexual intercourse. Unpublished manuscript, University of California at Los Angeles, 1970.

Hanusa, B. H., & Schulz, R. Attributional mediators of learned helplessness. *Journal of Personality and Social Psychology*, 1977, *35*, 602–611.

Harvey, J. H., Ickes, W. J., & Kidd, R. F. (Eds.). *New directions in attribution research* (Vol. 1). Hillsdale, N. J.: Erlbaum, 1976.

Harvey, J. H., Ickes, W. J., & Kidd, R. F. (Eds.). *New directions in attribution research* (Vol. 2). Hillsdale, N. J.: Erlbaum, 1978.

Heckhausen, H. *Hoffnung und Furcht in der Leistungsmotivation.* Meisenheim (Glan), Federal Republic of Germany: Hain, 1963.

Heckhausen, H. Achievement motive research: Current problems and some contributions towards a general theory of motivation. In W. J. Arnold (Ed.), *Nebraska Symposium on Motivation* (Vol. 16). Lincoln: University of Nebraska Press, 1968.

Heckhausen, H. *Fortschritte der Leistungsmotivationsforschung.* In H. Thomae (Ed.), *Handbuch der Psychologie* (2nd ed.). Göttingen, Federal Republic of Germany: Hogrefe, in press.

Heider, F. Social perception and phenomenal causality. *Psychological Review,* 1944, *51,* 358–374.

Heider, F. Attitudes and cognitive organization. *Journal of Psychology,* 1946, *21,* 107–112.

Heider, F. *The psychology of interpersonal relations.* New York: Wiley, 1958.

Henchy, T., & Glass, D. C. Evaluation apprehension and the social facilitation of dominant and subordinate responses. *Journal of Personality and Social Psychology,* 1968, *10,* 446–454.

Hewitt, J. Liking and the proportion of favorable evaluations. *Journal of Personality and Social Psychology,* 1972, *22,* 231–235.

Hiroto, D. S., & Seligman, M. E. P. Generality of learned helplessness in man. *Journal of Personality and Social Psychology,* 1975, *31,* 311–327.

Hirschman, R. Cross-modal effects of anticipatory bogus heart rate feedback in a negative emotional context. *Journal of Personality and Social Psychology,* 1975, *31,* 13–19.

Holmes, D. S. Debriefing after psychological experiments: II. Effectiveness of postexperimental desensitizing. *American Psychologist,* 1976, *31,* 868–875.

Homans, G. C. *Social behavior: Its elementary forms.* New York: Harcourt, Brace, 1961.

Horner, M. Sex differences in achievement motivation and performance in competitive and non-competitive situations. Unpublished doctoral dissertation, University of Michigan, 1968.

Hull, C. L. *Principles of behavior.* New York: Appleton, 1943.

Humphreys, L. G. The effect of random alternation of reinforcement on the acquisition and extinction of conditioned eyelid reactions. *Journal of Experimental Psychology,* 1939, *25,* 141–158.

Hunt, J. G. Fiedler's leadership contingency model: An empirical test in three organizations. *Organizational Behavior and Human Performance,* 1967, *2,* 209–308.

Irle, M., & Möntmann, V. (Eds.). *Theorie der kognitiven Dissonanz* (by L. Festinger, originally published 1957). Bern: Huber, 1978.

Jones, E. E. The rocky road from acts to dispositions. *American Psychologist,* 1979, *34,* 107–117.

Jones, E. E., & Davis, K. E. A theory of correspondent inferences: From acts to dispositions. In L. Berkowitz (Ed.), *Advances in experimental social psychology* (Vol. 2). New York: Academic Press, 1965.

Jones, E. E., Davis, K. E., & Gergen, K. J. Role playing variations and their informational value for person perception. *Journal of Abnormal and Social Psychology*, 1961, *63*, 302–310.

Jones, E. E., & de Charms, R. Changes in social perception as a function of the personal relevance of behavior. *Sociometry*, 1957, *20*, 75–85.

Jones, E. E., & Gerard, H. B. *Foundations of social psychology*. New York: Wiley, 1967.

Jones, E. E., & Harris, V. A. The attribution of attitudes. *Journal of Experimental Social Psychology*, 1967, *3*, 1–24.

Jones, E. E., & Nisbett, R. E. *The actor and the observer: Divergent perceptions of the causes of behavior.* Morristown, N. J.: General Learning Press, 1971.

Jones, S. C., & Regan, D. T. Ability evaluation through social comparison. *Journal of Experimental Social Psychology*, 1974, *10*, 142–157.

Karabenick, S. A. Fear of success, achievement and affiliation dispositions, and the performance of men and women under individual and competitive conditions. *Journal of Personality*, 1977, *45*, 117–149.

Kelley, H. H. Attribution theory in social psychology. In D. Levine (Ed.), *Nebraska Symposium on Motivation* (Vol. 15). Lincoln: University of Nebraska Press, 1967.

Kelley, H. H. *Attribution in social interaction.* Morristown, N. J. General Learning Press, 1971.

Kelley, H. H. The processes of causal attribution. *American Psychologist*, 1973, *28*, 107–128.

Kelley, H. H. Action and perception: An attribution analysis of social interaction. Katz-Newcomb Lecture, University of Michigan, 1975.

Kiesler, C. A., & Corbin, L. Commitment, attraction, and conformity. *Journal of Personality and Social Psychology*, 1965, *2*, 890–895.

Kiesler, C. A., Nisbett, R. E., & Zanna, M. P. On inferring one's beliefs from one's behavior. *Journal of Personality and Social Psychology*, 1969, *11*, 321–327.

Kiesler, C. A., & Pallak, M. S. Arousal properties of dissonance manipulations. *Psychological Bulletin*, 1976, *83*, 1014–1025.

Klein, D. C., Fencil-Morse, E., & Seligman, M. E. P. Learned helplessness, depression, and the attribution of failure. *Journal of Personality and Social Psychology*, 1976, *33*, 508–516.

Klinger, E. Fantasy *n* Achievement as a motivational construct. *Psychological Bulletin*, 1966, *66*, 291–308.

Koffka, K. *Principles of Gestalt psychology*. New York: Harcourt, Brace and World, 1935.

Köhler, W. *Dynamics in psychology*. New York: Liveright, 1940.

Kukla, A. Attributional determinants of achievement-related behavior. *Journal of Personality and Social Psychology*, 1972, *21*, 166–174.

Landy, D., & Aronson, E. The influence of the character of the criminal and his victim on the decisions of simulated jurors. *Journal of Experimental Social Psychology*, 1969, *5*, 141–152.

Latané, B. Studies in social comparison—introduction and overview. *Journal of Experimental Social Psychology*, 1966, Supplement 1, 1–5.

Lawler, E. E., Koplin, C. A., Young, T. F., & Fadem, J. A. Inequity reduction over time in an induced overpayment situation. *Organizational Behavior and Human Performance*, 1968, *3*, 253–268.

Le Bon, G. *The crowd.* New York: Viking, 1960. (Originally published, 1896.)

Lerner, M. J., Miller, D. T., & Holmes, J. G. Deserving and the emergence of forms of justice. In L. Berkowitz & E. Walster (Eds.), *Advances in experimental social psychology* (Vol. 9). New York: Academic Press, 1976.

Lerner, M. J., & Simmons, C. H. Observer's reaction to the "innocent victim": Compassion or rejection? *Journal of Personality and Social Psychology*, 1966, *4*, 203–210.

Leventhal, G. S. Fairness in social relationships. In J. Thibaut, J. T. Spence, & R. C. Carson (Eds.), *Contemporary topics in social psychology*. Morristown, N. J.: General Learning Press, 1976.

Liebling, B. A., Seiler, M., & Shaver, P. Self-awareness and cigarette-smoking behavior. *Journal of Experimental Social Psychology*, 1974, *10*, 325–332.

Linder, D. E., Cooper, J., & Jones, E. E. Decision freedom as a determinant of the role of incentive magnitude in attitude change. *Journal of Personality and Social Psychology*, 1967, *6*, 245–254.

Mahone, C. H. Fear of failure and unrealistic vocational aspiration. *Journal of Abnormal and Social Psychology*, 1960, *60*, 253–261.

Maier, S. F., & Seligman, M. E. P. Learned helplessness: Theory and evidence. *Journal of Experimental Psychology: General*, 1976, *105*, 3–46.

Mandler, G. *Mind and emotion.* New York: Wiley, 1975.

Mandler, G., & Kremen, I. Automatic feedback: A correlational study. *Journal of Personality*, 1958, *26*, 388–399.

Mandler, G., & Sarason, S. B. A study of anxiety and learning. *Journal of Abnormal and Social Psychology*, 1952, *47*, 166–173.

Manis, M., & Dovalina, I. Base-rates *can* affect individual prediction. Unpublished manuscript, University of Michigan, 1979.

Mann, R. D. A review of the relationships between personality and performance in small groups. *Psychological Bulletin*, 1959, *56*, 241–270.

Matlin, M. W., & Zajonc, R. B. Social facilitation of word associations. *Journal of Personality and Social Psychology*, 1968, *10*, 455–460.

McArthur, L. A. The how and what of why: Some determinants and consequences of causal attribution. *Journal of Personality and Social Psychology*, 1972, *22*, 171–193.

McArthur, L. Z. The lesser influence of consensus than distinctiveness information on causal attributions: A test of the person-thing hypothesis. *Journal of Personality and Social Psychology*, 1976, *33*, 733–742.

McClelland, D. C. *The achieving society.* New York: Van Nostrand, 1961.

McClelland, D. C., Atkinson, J. W., Clark, R. A., & Lowell, E. L. *The achievement motive.* New York: Appleton-Century-Crofts, 1953.

McClelland, D. C., Clark, R. A., Roby, T. B., & Atkinson, J. W. The projective expression of needs: IV. The effect of the need for achievement on thematic apperception. *Journal of Experimental Psychology*, 1949, *39*, 242–255.

McCormick, T. F. An investigation of standards of correctness by inducing conformity and consistency pressures within the framework of objective self-awareness. Unpublished doctoral dissertation, University of Texas at Austin, 1979.

McGrath, J. E., & Julian, J. W. Interaction processes and task outcome in experimentally created negotiation groups. *Journal of Psychological Studies*, 1963, *14*, 117–138.

Mehrabian, A. A questionnaire measure of individual differences in achieving tendency. *Educational and Psychological Measurement*, 1978, *38*, 475–478.

Mettee, D. R., & Aronson, E. Affective reactions to appraisal from others. In T. L. Huston (Ed.), *Foundations of interpersonal attraction*. New York: Academic Press, 1974.

Meumann, E. Haus-und Schularbeit: Experimente an Kindern der Volkschule. Die Deutsche Schule, 1904, *8*, 278–303; 337–359; 416–431.

Michela, J. L., & Peplau, L. A. Applying attributional models of achievement to social settings. Paper presented at the convention of the Western Psychological Association, Seattle, 1977.

Miller, D. T., & Ross, M. Self-serving biases in the attribution of causality: Fact or fiction? *Psychological Bulletin*, 1975, *82*, 213–225.

Miller, N. E. Theory and experiment relating psychoanalytic displacement to stimulus-response generalization. *Journal of Abnormal and Social Psychology*, 1948, *43*, 155–178.

Mischel, W. *Personality and assessment*. New York: Wiley, 1968.

Mischel, W., & Liebert, R. M. Effects of discrepancies between observed and imposed reward criteria on their acquisition and transmission. *Journal of Personality and Social Psychology*, 1966, *3*, 45–53.

Moulton, R. W. Effects of success and failure on level of aspiration as related to achievement motives. *Journal of Personality and Social Psychology*, 1965, *1*, 399–406.

Murray, H. A. *Thematic Apperception Test manual*. Cambridge, Mass.: Harvard University Press, 1943.

Murstein, B. I. Critique of models of dyadic attraction. In B. I. Murstein (Ed.), *Theories of attraction and love*. New York: Springer, 1971.

Newcomb, T. M., Koenig, K. E., Flacks, R., & Warwick, D. P. *Persistence and change: Bennington College and its students after 25 years*. New York: Wiley, 1967.

Newtson, D. Dispositional inference from effects of actions: Effects chosen and effects foregone. *Journal of Experimental Social Psychology*, 1974, *10*, 480–496.

Nisbett, R. E., & Schachter, S. The cognitive manipulation of pain. *Journal of Experimental Social Psychology*, 1966, *2*, 227–236.

Nisbett, R. E., & Wilson, T. D. Telling more than we can know: Verbal reports on mental processes. *Psychological Review*, 1977, *84*, 231–259.

O'Connor, P., Atkinson, J. W., & Horner, M. Motivational implications of ability grouping in schools. In J. W. Atkinson & N. T. Feather (Eds.), *A theory of achievement motivation*. New York: Wiley, 1966.

Orne, M. T. On the social psychology of the psychological experiment: With particular reference to demand characteristics and their implications. *American Psychologist*, 1962, *17*, 776–783.

Orvis, B. R., Cunningham, J. D., & Kelley, H. H. A closer examination of causal inference: The roles of consensus, distinctiveness, and consistency information. *Journal of Personality and Social Psychology*, 1975, *32*, 605–616.

Overmier, J. B., & Seligman, M. E. P. Effects of inescapable shock upon subsequent escape and avoidance learning. *Journal of Comparative and Physiological Psychology*, 1967, *63*, 28–33.

Pallak, M. S., Brock, T. C., & Kiesler, C. A. Dissonance arousal and task performance in an incidental verbal learning paradigm. *Journal of Personality and Social Psychology*, 1967, *7*, 11–20.

Parke, R. D., Berkowitz, L., Leyens, J. P., West, S. G., & Sebastian, R. J. Some effects of violent and nonviolent movies on the behavior of juvenile delinquents. In L. Berkowitz (Ed.), *Advances in experimental social psychology* (Vol. 10). New York: Academic Press, 1977.

Patchen, M. *The choice of wage comparisons*. Englewood Cliffs, N. J.: Prentice-Hall, 1961.

Paulus, P. B. (Ed.). *Psychology of group influence*. Hillsdale, N. J.: Erlbaum, 1980.

Paulus, P. B., & Murdoch, P. Anticipated evaluation and audience presence in the enhancement of dominant responses. *Journal of Experimental Social Psychology*, 1971, *7*, 280–291.

Pessin, J. The comparative effects of social and mechanical stimulation on memorizing. *American Journal of Psychology*, 1933, *45*, 263–270.

Pittman, T. S. Attribution of arousal as a mediator in dissonance reduction. *Journal of Experimental Social Psychology*, 1975, *11*, 53–63.

Plutchik, R., & Ax, A. F. A critique of "Determinants of emotional states" by Schachter and Singer (1962). *Psychophysiology*, 1967, *4*, 79–82.

Pryor, J. B., Gibbons, F. X., Wicklund, R. A., Fazio, R. H., & Hood, R. Self-focused attention and self report validity. *Journal of Personality*, 1977, *45*, 513–527.

Rabbie, J. M., Brehm, J. W., & Cohen, A. R. Verbalization and reactions to cognitive dissonance. *Journal of Personality*, 1959, *27*, 407–417.

Raynor, J. O. Future orientation in the study of achievement motivation. In J. W. Atkinson & J. O. Raynor (Eds.), *Motivation and achievement*. Washington, D.C.: Winston, 1974.

Reckman, R. F., & Goethals, G. R. Deviancy and group-orientation as determinants of group composition preferences. *Sociometry*, 1973, *36*, 419–423.

Rescorla, R. A., & Wagner, A. R. A theory of Pavlovian conditioning: Variations in the effectiveness of reinforcement and nonreinforcement. In A. H. Black & W. R. Prokasy (Eds.), *Classical conditioning II: Current research and theory*. New York: Appleton-Century-Crofts, 1972.

Rest, S. Schedules of reinforcement: An attributional analysis. In J. H. Harvey, W. J. Ickes, & R. F. Kidd (Eds.), *New directions in attribution research* (Vol 1). Hillsdale, N. J.: Erlbaum, 1976.

Rice, R. W. Construct validity of the least preferred co-worker score. *Psychological Bulletin*, 1978, *85*, 1199–1237. (a)

Rice, R. W. Psychometric properties of the esteem of least preferred coworker (LPC scale). *Academy of Management Review*, 1978, *3*, 106–118. (b)

Rice, R. W., & Chemers, M. M. Predicting the emergence of leaders using Fiedler's contingency model. *Journal of Applied Psychology*, 1973, *57*, 281–287.

Rosenberg, M. J. When dissonance fails: On eliminating evaluation apprehension from attitude measurement. *Journal of Personality and Social Psychology*, 1965, *1*, 28–42.

Rosenberg, M. J. The conditions and consequences of evaluation apprehension. In R. Rosenthal & R. L. Rosnow (Eds.), *Artifact in behavioral research*. New York: Academic Press, 1969.

Rosenkrans, M. A., & Hartup, W. W. Imitative influences of consistent and inconsistent response consequences to a model on aggressive behavior in children. *Journal of Personality and Social Psychology*, 1967, *7*, 429–434.

Rosenthal, R. On the social psychology of the psychological experiment: The experimenter's hypothesis as an unintended determinant of experimental results. *American Scientist*, 1963, *51*, 268–283.

Rosenthal, R. *Experimenter effects in behavioral research*. New York: Appleton-Century-Crofts, 1966.

Rosenthal, R., & Fode, K. L. Three experiments in experimenter bias. *Psychological Reports*, 1963, *12*, 491–511.

Ross, L. The intuitive psychologist and his shortcomings: Distortions in the attribution process. In L. Berkowitz (Ed.), *Advances in experimental social psychology* (Vol. 10). New York: Academic Press, 1977.

Ross, M., & Shulman, R. F. Increasing the salience of initial attitudes: Dissonance versus self-perception theory. *Journal of Personality and Social Psychology*, 1973, *28*, 138–144.

Roth, S. A revised model of learned helplessness in humans. *Journal of Personality*, 1980, *48*, 103–133.

Roth, S., & Kubal, L. Effects of noncontingent reinforcement on tasks of differing importance: Facilitation and learned helplessness. *Journal of Personality and Social Psychology*, 1975, *32*, 680–691.

Sampson, E. E. The study of ordinal position: Antecedents and outcomes. In B. Maher (Ed.), *Progress in experimental personality research* (Vol. 2). New York: Academic Press, 1965.

Savitsky, J. C., Rogers, R. W., Izard, C. E., & Liebert, R. M. The role of frustration and anger in the imitation of filmed aggression against a human victim. *Psychological Reports*, 1971, *29*, 807–810.

Schachter, S. Deviation, rejection, and communication. *Journal of Abnormal and Social Psychology*, 1951, *46*, 190–207.

Schachter, S. *The psychology of affiliation*. Stanford, Calif.: Stanford University Press, 1959.

Schachter, S. The interaction of cognitive and physiological determinants of emotional state. In L. Berkowitz (Ed.), *Advances in experimental social psychology* (Vol. 1). New York: Academic Press, 1964.

Schachter, S. *Emotion, obesity, and crime*. New York: Academic Press, 1971.

Schachter, S., & Singer, J. E. Cognitive, social, and physiological determinants of emotional state. *Psychological Review*, 1962, *69*, 379–399.

Scheier, M. F. Self-awareness, self-consciousness, and angry aggression. *Journal of Personality*, 1976, *44*, 627–644.

Scheier, M. F., Carver, C. S., & Gibbons, F. X. Self-focused attention and reactions to fear. *Journal of Research in Personality*, in press.

Schmitt, D. R., & Marwell, G. Withdrawal and reward reallocation as responses to inequity. *Journal of Experimental Social Psychology*, 1972, *8*, 207–221.

Sears, D. O. Political socialization. In F. I. Greenstein & N. W. Polsby (Eds.), *Handbook of political science* (Vol. 2). Reading, Mass.: Addison-Wesley, 1975.

Seligman, M. E. P. *Helplessness: On depression, development, and death.* San Francisco: W. H. Freeman, 1975.

Shaban, J., & Jecker, J. Risk preference in choosing an evaluator: An extension of Atkinson's achievement-motivation model. *Journal of Experimental Social Psychology*, 1968, *4*, 35–45.

Sigall, H., & Ostrove, N. Beautiful but dangerous: Effects of offender attractiveness and nature of the crime on juridic judgment. *Journal of Personality and Social Psychology*, 1975, *31*, 410–414.

Silverman, I. Ethical restraints to a valid experimental social psychology. In B. Latané (Chair), *Ethical issues in social psychological research: Some current thoughts.* Symposium presented at the annual meeting of the American Psychological Association, Washington, D. C., 1976.

Singer, J. E. Sympathetic activation, drugs, and fright. *Journal of Comparative and Physiological Psychology*, 1963, *56*, 612–615.

Skinner, B. F. *Verbal behavior.* New York: Appleton-Century-Crofts, 1957.

Slovik, P. Analyzing the expert judge: A descriptive study of stockbrokers' decision processes. *Journal of Applied Psychology*, 1969, *53*, 255–263.

Snyder, C. R., & Endelman, J. R. Effects of degree of interpersonal similarity on physical distance and self-reported attraction: A comparison of uniqueness and reinforcement theory predictions. *Journal of Personality*, 1979, *47*, 492–505.

Snyder, M. L., & Jones, E. E. Attitude attribution when behavior is constrained. *Journal of Experimental Social Psychology*, 1974, *10*, 585–600.

Snyder, M. L., Stephan, W. G., & Rosenfield, D. Attributional egotism. In J. H. Harvey, W. J. Ickes, & R. F. Kidd (Eds.), *New directions in attribution research* (Vol. 2). Hillsdale, N. J.: Erlbaum, 1978.

Snyder, M. L., & Wicklund, R. A. Prior exercise of freedom and reactance. *Journal of Experimental Social Psychology*, 1976, *12*, 120–130.

Sogin, S. R., & Pallak, M. S. Bad decisions, responsibility, and attitude change: Effects of volition, foreseeability, and locus of causality of negative consequences. *Journal of Personality and Social Psychology*, 1976, *33*, 300–306.

Sohn, D. Affect-generating powers of effort and ability self-attributions of success and failure. *Journal of Educational Psychology*, 1977, *69*, 500–505.

Spence, K. W. *Behavior theory and conditioning.* New Haven, Conn.: Yale University Press, 1956.

Spinoza, B. de. *Philosophy of B. de Spinoza* (R. H. M. Elwes, trans.). New York: Tudor, 1936. (Originally published, 1677.)

Staub, E. *Positive social behavior and morality* (Vol. 2). New York: Academic Press, 1979.

Stephenson, G. M., & White, J. H. An experimental study of some effects of injustice on children's moral behavior. *Journal of Experimental Social Psychology*, 1968, *4*, 460–469.

Stern, R. M., Botto, R. W., & Herrick, C. D. Behavioral and physiological effects of false heartrate feedback: A replication and extension. *Psychophysiology*, 1972, *9*, 21–29.

Stevens, L., & Jones, E. E. Defensive attribution and the Kelley cube. *Journal of Personality and Social Psychology*, 1976, *34*, 809–820.

Stogdill, R. M. Personal factors associated with leadership: A survey of the literature. *Journal of Psychology*, 1948, *25*, 35–71.

Stogdill, R. M. *Handbook of leadership*. New York: Free Press, 1974.

Storms, M. D. Videotape and the attribution process: Reversing actors' and observers' points of view. *Journal of Personality and Social Psychology*, 1973, *27*, 165–175.

Suls, J. M., & Miller, R. L. (Eds.). *Social comparison processes*. New York: Hemisphere, 1977.

Taylor, D. A., Altman, I., & Sorrentino, R. Interpersonal exchange as a function of rewards and costs and situational factors: Expectancy confirmation-disconfirmation. *Journal of Personality and Social Psychology*, 1969, *5*, 324–339.

Taylor, S. E., & Mettee, D. R. When similarity breeds contempt. *Journal of Personality and Social Psychology*, 1971, *20*, 75–81.

Triplett, N. The dynamogenic factors in pacemaking and competition. *American Journal of Psychology*, 1898, *9*, 507–533.

Valins, S. Cognitive effects of false heartrate feed-back. *Journal of Personality and Social Psychology*, 1966, *4*, 400–408.

Vallacher, R. R., & Solodky, M. Objective self-awareness, standards of evaluation, and moral behavior. *Journal of Experimental Social Psychology*, 1979, *15*, 254–262.

Valle, V. A., & Frieze, I. H. Stability of causal attributions as a mediator in changing expectations for success. *Journal of Personality and Social Psychology*, 1976, *33*, 579–587.

Veroff, J., Wilcox, S., & Atkinson, J. W. The achievement motive in high school and college age women. *Journal of Abnormal and Social Psychology*, 1953, *48*, 108–119.

Wallington, S. A. Consequences of transgression: Self-punishment and depression. *Journal of Personality and Social Psychology*, 1973, *28*, 1–7.

Walster, E., & Prestholdt, P. The effects of misjudging another: Overcompensation or dissonance reduction? *Journal of Experimental Social Psychology*, 1966, *2*, 85–97.

Walster, E., Walster, G. W., & Berscheid, E. (Eds.). *Equity: Theory and research*. Boston: Allyn & Bacon, 1978.

Waterman, C. K. The facilitating and interfering effects of cognitive dissonance on simple and complex paired associates learning tasks. *Journal of Experimental Social Psychology*, 1969, *5*, 31–42.

Weiner, B. *Theories of motivation: From mechanism to cognition*. Chicago: Markham, 1972.

Weiner, B. Achievement motivation as conceptualized by an attribution theorist. In B. Weiner (Ed.), *Achievement motivation and attribution theory*. Morristown, N. J.: General Learning Press, 1974.

Weiner, B. Achievement strivings. In H. London & J. Exner (Eds.), *Dimensions of personality*. New York: Wiley, 1978. (a)

Weiner, B. An attributionally-based theory of motivation and emotion: Focus, range, and issues. Unpublished manuscript, University of California at Los Angeles, 1978. (b)

Weiner, B., Frieze, I. H., Kukla, A., Reed, L., Rest, S., & Rosenbaum, R. M. Perceiving the causes of success and failure. In E. E. Jones, D. E. Kanouse, H. H. Kelley, R. E. Nisbett, S. Valins, & B. Weiner (Eds.), *Attribution: Perceiving the causes of behavior*. Morristown, N. J.: General Learning Press, 1972.

Weiner, B., Heckhausen, H., Meyer, W.-U., & Cook, R. E. Causal ascriptions and achievement behavior: A conceptual analysis of effort and reanalysis of locus of control. *Journal of Personality and Social Psychology*, 1972, *21*, 239–248.

Weiner, B., Nierenberg, R., & Goldstein, M. Social learning (locus of control) versus attributional (causal stability) interpretations of expectancy of success. *Journal of Personality*, 1976, *44*, 52–68.

Weiner, B., Russell, D., & Lehrman, D. Affective consequences of causal ascriptions. In J. H. Harvey, W. J. Ickes, & R. F. Kidd (Eds.), *New directions in attribution research* (Vol. 2). Hillsdale, N. J.: Erlbaum, 1978.

Weiner, B., & Sierad, J. Misattribution for failure and enhancement of achievement strivings. *Journal of Personality and Social Psychology*, 1975, *31*, 415–421.

Wells, G., & Harvey, J. H. Do people use consensus information in making causal attributions? *Journal of Personality and Social Psychology*, 1977, *35*, 279–293.

Wertheimer, M. Untersuchungen zur Lehre von der Gestalt: II. *Psychologische Forschung*, 1923, *4*, 301–350.

West, S. G., Whitney, G., & Schnedler, R. Helping a motorist in distress: The effects of race, sex, and neighborhood. *Journal of Personality and Social Psychology*, 1975, *31*, 691–698.

Wheeler, L., Shaver, K. G., Jones, R. A., Goethals, G. R., Cooper, J., Robinson, J. E., Gruder, C. L., & Butzine, K. W. Factors determining the choice of comparison other. *Journal of Experimental Social Psychology*, 1969, *5*, 219–232.

Wicker, A. W. Attitudes versus actions: The relationship of verbal and overt behavioral responses to attitude objects. *Journal of Social Issues*, 1969, *25*, 41–78.

Wicklund, R. A. *Freedom and reactance*. Hillsdale, N. J.: Erlbaum, 1974.

Wicklund, R. A. Objective self-awareness. In L. Berkowitz (Ed.), *Advances in experimental social psychology* (Vol. 8). New York: Academic Press, 1975.

Wicklund, R. A. The influence of self-awareness on human behavior. *American Scientist*, 1979, *67*, 187–193.

Wicklund, R. A., & Brehm, J. W. Attitude change as a function of felt competence and threat to attitudinal freedom. *Journal of Experimental Social Psychology*, 1968, *4*, 64–75.

Wicklund, R. A., & Brehm, J. W. *Perspectives on cognitive dissonance*. Hillsdale, N. J.: Erlbaum, 1976.

Wicklund, R. A., & Duval, S. Opinion change and performance facilitation as a result of objective self-awareness. *Journal of Experimental Social Psychology*, 1971, 7, 319–342.

Wicklund, R. A., & Frey, D. Self-awareness theory: When the self makes a difference. In D. M. Wegner & R. R. Vallacher (Eds.), *The self in social psychology*. New York: Oxford University Press, 1980.

Wicklund, R. A., Slattum, V., & Solomon, E. Effects of implied pressure toward commitment on ratings of choice alternatives. *Journal of Experimental Social Psychology*, 1970, 6, 449–457.

Wortman, C. B., & Brehm, J. W. Responses to uncontrollable outcomes: An integration of reactance theory and the learned helplessness model. In L. Berkowitz (Ed.), *Advances in experimental social psychology* (Vol. 8). New York: Academic Press, 1975.

Wortman, C. B., & Dintzer, L. Is an attributional analysis of the learned helplessness phenomenon viable? A critique of the Abramson-Seligman-Teasdale reformulation. *Journal of Abnormal Psychology*, 1978, 87, 75–90.

Wrightsman, L. S. Effects of waiting with others on changes in level of felt anxiety. *Journal of Abnormal and Social Psychology*, 1960, 61, 216–222.

Yerkes, R. M., & Dodson, J. D. The relation of strength of stimulus to rapidity of habit formation. *Journal of Comparative and Neurological Psychology*, 1908, 18, 459–482.

Zajonc, R. B. Social facilitation. *Science*, 1965, 149, 269–274.

Zajonc, R. B., Heingartner, A., & Herman, E. M. Social enhancement and impairment of performance in the cockroach. *Journal of Personality and Social Psychology*, 1969, 13, 83–92.

Zajonc, R. B., & Nieuwenhuyse, B. Relationship between word frequency and recognition: Perceptual process or response bias? *Journal of Experimental Psychology*, 1964, 67, 276–285.

Zajonc, R. B., & Sales, S. M. Social facilitation of dominant and subordinate responses. *Journal of Experimental Social Psychology*, 1966, 2, 160–168.

Zanna, M. P., & Cooper, J. Dissonance and the pill: An attribution approach to studying the arousal properties of dissonance. *Journal of Personality and Social Psychology*, 1974, 29, 703–709.

Zanna, M. P., Kiesler, C. A., & Pilkonis, P. A. Positive and negative attitudinal affect established by classical conditioning. *Journal of Personality and Social Psychology*, 1970, 14, 321–328.

Zillmann, D. Attribution and misattribution of excitatory reactions. In J. H. Harvey, W. J. Ickes, & R. F. Kidd (Eds.), *New directions in attribution research* (Vol. 2). Hillsdale, N. J.: Erlbaum, 1978.

Zimbardo, P. G. (Ed.). *The cognitive control of motivation*. Glenview, Ill.: Scott, Foresman, 1969.

Zuckerman, M. Attribution of success and failure revisited; or, The motivational bias is alive and well in attribution theory. *Journal of Personality*, 1979, 47, 245–287.

Zuckerman, M., & Wheeler, L. To dispel fantasies about the fantasy-based measure of fear of success. *Psychological Bulletin*, 1975, 82, 932–946.

NAME INDEX

Skrzypek, G. J., 231, 232, 236
Slattum, V., 252
Slovic, P., 292
Snyder, C. R., 34
Snyder, M. L., 124, 142, 143, 255, 266,
    267, 268, 275, 276
Sogin, S. R., 72
Sohn, D., 216
Solodky, M., 185
Solomon, E., 252
Sorrentino, R., 33
Spence, J. T., 37, 97
Spence, K. W., 12
Spinoza, B., 67
Staub, E., 51
Stephan, W. G., 142, 143
Stephenson, G. M., 92
Stern, R. M., 171
Stevens, L., 141
Stires, L. K., 246
Stogdill, R. M., 224, 233
Storms, M., 125
Straub, R. B., 172
Suchman, E., 176
Suls, J. M., 159
Sundstrom, E., 233

Tannenbaum, P. H., 67
Taylor, D. A., 33
Taylor, S. E., 36
Teasdale, J. D., 269, 277
Terrace, H. S., 31
Thibaut, J. W., 37, 97
Thomae, H., 206
Triplett, N., 18

Valins, S., 168, 171, 172, 209, 221
Vallacher, R. R., 185
Vallé, V. A., 215, 216
Veitch, R., 33, 36

Veroff, J., 204

Wack, D. L., 19
Wagner, A. R., 30
Wallbom, M., 176, 177, 181
Wallington, S. A., 92
Walster, E., 84, 85, 90, 91, 93, 97
Walster, W., 84, 97
Warwick, D. P., 114
Waterman, C. K., 72
Weick, K. E., 233
Weiner, B., 203, 208, 209, 210, 211, 212,
    213, 214, 215, 216, 217, 218, 219,
    220, 221, 269, 271, 272, 273
Wells, G., 141
Wertheimer, M., 55
West, S. G., 286, 296
Wheeler, L., 158, 205
White, J. H., 92
Whitney, G., 296
Wicker, A. W., 183
Wicklund, R. A., 69, 78, 79, 80, 111,
    115, 177, 179, 185, 187, 246, 251,
    252, 254, 255, 257
Wilcox, S., 204
Williams, R. M., 176
Wortman, C. B., 256, 265, 268, 274,
    276, 277
Wrightsman, L. S., 154

Yerkes, R. M., 203
Young, T. F., 88

Zajonc, R. B., 11, 12, 13, 14, 15, 16,
    17, 18, 19, 20, 21, 72
Zanna, M. P., 24, 25, 76, 78, 107, 109,
    112
Zillman, D., 166
Zimbardo, P. G., 76
Zuckerman, M., 143, 205

SUBJECT INDEX

Achievement motivation, 2–3, 5
    and approach motivation, 192–194
    and avoidance motivation, 194–195,
        201
    and expectancy of failure, 194–195
    and expectancy of success, 192–193,
        211–214, 217, 219, 221
    fear of failure, 194–206, 208, 210–
        211, 213–214, 219
        measurement of, 194
    fear of success, 205
    incentive value of
        avoiding failure, 194–195
        succeeding, 192–193, 219
    manipulation of, 204
    measurement of, 192, 203–204

    relationship to performance, 202–203
    sex differences in, 204–205
    theory of, 190–206
Achievement-oriented individuals,
    attributions of, 210–211, 213
Actor, definition of, 117
Actor-observer differences, 218–219
Adrenalin, 163–165, 166, 169–170, 172–
    173
Affect, 25, 29–31, 36, 178–179, 181
    generalization of, 30
Affective response, 212–217
Affiliation, 153–154, 214, 279–282, 287
Aggression, 43–44, 182, 284–285, 286,
    289–290, 295
Animal versus human research, 13,

Entities (in attribution) *(continued)*
134–136, 140, 142–143
attribution to, 130–131, 133, 135–138, 142–143
distictiveness among, 209–210
Equity:
and commitment, 90–92
and equality, 94
and need, 94
and self-worth, 88
theory of, 53, 81–97
Ethics:
codes for psychological research, 297–298
in research, 297–299
Evaluation:
aversiveness of, 178–181
apprehension, 295–296
need for, 145
Expectancy of success and behavior, 213–214, 219–221
Expectancy X value theory, 219
Experimental design:
between subjects, 284
within subjects, 284
Experimental manipulation, 280–281, 285, 287–288, 290–292
effects of weak, 287–288
Experimental outcomes, interpretation of, 287–293
Experimenter bias, 293–295
methods of controlling, 294
External justification; 74–75, 106, 111–113
Extinction, 30–31

Facilitation, 11–13
Failure-oriented individuals, attributions of, 210–211, 213
False consensus effect, 140
Forced compliance procedure, 74–75, 111
Free choice (in attribution), 138–139, 143
Free-choice procedure, 73, 111
Freedom, 244–257
elimination of, 248–249
importance of, 251
prior exercise of, 255–256
threats to, 245–246, 248

Gestalt psychology, 53–56
equality factor, 55–56
Prägnanz, law of, 56, 59, 69
proximity factor, 55–56
Great-person notion, 223–224
Group Atmosphere scale, 225, 234, 236

Habit, 9–14
Hard-to-get, 254
Heart rate feedback, bogus, 167–168, 171
Helplessness (see *Learned helplessness*)
High-pressure sales, 252–253
Hypothesis, 279–283, 287, 290–292, 295–296

Imitation, 9, 40–47, 286
Implicit affective response, 24–25, 28–30
Independent variable, 35, 279–284, 287–288, 290, 292
conceptual, 280–283, 287–288, 290–291
operational, 280–282, 287, 290
Individual differences:
in defining dominance, 15
least-preferred-coworker scale, 227–229, 231–232, 234, 237–241
as nuisance variables, 281–282, 285
projective test, 192, 203
Test Anxiety Questionnaire, 194
Thematic Apperception Test, 192, 194, 204
Inertial tendency, 201
Internal-external dimension, in attribution and achievement, 208–218
Internality dimension and affect, in attribution and achievement, 211–212, 215–216, 218
Interpersonal distance, 34
Interpersonal judgment scale, 26, 34
Intrinsic motivation, 108
Invasion of privacy, 297–298

Just world, 63

Leader-match, 234–235
Leader-member relations, 225–228, 230–231, 233–234, 236–237, 239
Leaders:
experience, 236
needs, 239
status, 236
style, 225, 227–228, 234, 237, 241
traits of, 224
Leadership, 5–6
theory of, 222–241
training, 233–235, 237, 241
Learned helplessness:
and attribution theory, 214, 269–274
and aversive stimulation, 259–260
and egotism, 266–269
original theory of, 260–262
and reactance theory, 256–257, 263–265
Learning theory, 8–51
Least-preferred-coworker (LPC) scale, 227–229, 231–232, 234, 237–241
interpretation of, 238
reliability of, 237–238
Leaving field, 86
Liking (see *Attraction, interpersonal*)
Luck, 142
Luck attribution, 208–212, 214–216

Manipulation check, 288, 291–293
Mental rehearsal, 9, 41, 50
Mere presence, 19–20
Modeling, 9, 40–47, 286
Motor reproduction, 41–42

Negativism, 295
Nonrandom assignment, 281–282